WHAT PEOPLE ARE SAYING ABOUT

THE WAKEFUL WORLD

In a mindful encounter between herself (her self) and the wider worlds of nature and scholarly debate, Emma Restall Orr contributes philosophically, provocatively and proactively to current debates about animism and panpsychism. She does far more than survey the scenery, she leads us on a journey towards re-integration within a self-aware cosmos full of engaging subjects. New science and ancient philosophy contribute to her careful and grounded consideration of the value of being a thoughtful animist today.
Graham Harvey, Reader in Religious Studies, The Open University Author of *Animism: Respecting the Living World.*

Emma Restall Orr has accomplished a most difficult task: combining academic-quality research with an accessible and compelling narrative. The concepts of animism, panpsychism, and mind in nature are all explored with great dexterity and insight. *The Wakeful World* offers a fascinating and powerful vision of animism for the present day — a vision that promises to reconnect us to the living Earth.
David Skrbina PhD, Author of *Panpsychism in the West.*

The Wakeful World sets out to map a philosophical grounding for contemporary animism, and as both an animist and philosopher, Restall Orr is well placed to draw such a map. The result is more than a provocative and thoughtful model of how philosophy can illuminate our understanding of animism: Restall Orr's animist perspective returns the favour, opening up new horizons for philosophy itself.
Adrian Harris PhD, Ecopsychologist
Environmental Network

i

This original and lively book brings back animism – a most useful range of ideas which reductivists have somewhat wildly abandoned during the last century – into focus once more just when it is badly needed to cure current confusions about mind and body. In clear, contemporary language Emma Restall Orr deploys a new vision of this distracted scene that will surely prove really helpful.

Dr Mary Midgley, Moral Philosopher

The Wakeful World

Animism, Mind and the Self
in Nature

The Wakeful World

Animism, Mind and the Self in Nature

Emma Restall Orr

MOON BOOKS

Winchester, UK
Washington, USA

First published by Moon Books, 2012

Moon Books is an imprint of John Hunt Publishing Ltd., Laurel House, Station Approach,
Alresford, Hants, SO24 9JH, UK
office1@jhpbooks.net
www.johnhuntpublishing.com
www.moon-books.net

For distributor details and how to order please visit the 'Ordering' section on our website.

Text copyright: Emma Restall Orr 2011

ISBN: 978 1 78099 407 9

A CIP catalogue record for this book is available from the British Library.

Design: Stuart Davies

Printed and bound by CPI Group (UK) Ltd, Croydon, CR0 4YY

We operate a distinctive and ethical publishing philosophy in all
areas of our business, from our global network of authors to
production and worldwide distribution.

CONTENTS

Dedication

This books is written in honour of my grandfathers
- Leslie and Geoffrey, their fathers, and their fathers before
them - and all who strive to find philosophical clarity in the
brutal chaos of ordinary reality.

Foreword

Before opening the gate and bidding the reader stride on into the wordscape of this book, it is worth offering a few notes of explanation, of introduction and of thanks.

Firstly, some readers may know my previous books. It is a policy I maintain *not* to reread my older writings to ensure a continuity of ideas. If what I present here in some way contradicts what I have written earlier, I can only hope that the newer work can be seen as a development, and not a sliding back into error. In the same way that it can be a delight to watch an actor grow older over decades, their seriousness of youth transforming into the gravitas of experience, I enjoy the opportunity of witnessing a writer's journey of discovery, whether in fiction or nonfiction: I trust my readers will not only allow me the same process of change and growth, but feel that my work as a whole is richer because of it.

As a metaphysics, this text is offered as a sort of prequel to my *Living With Honour: A Pagan Ethics*, published in 2007. In that book, I used the term *Pagan to describe a belief system based wholly upon nature. There are large parts of modern Paganism the focus of which is very much human nature, and the power of the mind to manipulate and influence; with these being so very far from my own spiritual and philosophical practice, it would not have been accurate to use the simple word Pagan. The animism described in this text could be said to be a main strand of *Paganism.

Throughout the book, particularly in the first half, I use a good many quotes from other thinkers. While I have usually referenced the quote within the text, I have not noted page numbers as might be found in a more academic style. Furthermore, I dislike the aesthetics of footnotes. I have, however, provided a comprehensive bibliography.

A note here on my use of gender may be appreciated by those sensitive to such things. Consciously I do not give a gender to the earth or to nature, nor do I call any deity male or female other than the Christian God or where otherwise it may be immediately relevant. However, when talking of the notional animist, I refer to *him*: this is simply because I am a *her*, and I like the way that bounces.

Finally, I would like to thank my beautiful and brilliantly intelligent husband, David, for his unfailing support, his editorial advice and his gentle patience throughout the nine months of this book's gestation and creation.

I thank too the handful of readers who graciously gave their time to read the text and comment before its submission, allowing me to make changes where otherwise I would have looked more foolish than I naturally do. I thank too Tori Green, for her exquisite photograph that gives colour and form to the cover of the book. Thank you.

First Words

An essential part of a philosopher's work is to root out assumptions, and tear them apart. For in seeking answers to those questions that sit on the very edge of language, on the edge of what is thought possible to understand, it is our assumptions that are often the greatest obstacle in our thinking. As beliefs we hold about the world, they are so fundamental that they are easily hidden. Whether or not their foundations are justifiable or tenable, they are hard to defend for they seem perfectly evident, unquestionable fact.

Five years ago, through the process of writing *Living With Honour: A Pagan Ethics*, my focus was on how our understanding of value affects our behaviour and relationships. My aim was to expound an ethics that, while based on animistic Paganism, did not resort to spiritual jargon. Using the divine as a backstop in any philosophical debate is as unhelpful as responding to a bright child's curiosity with the retort 'just because', and I was determined not to dilute rational argument with unreasoned belief. The goal should not have been hard to achieve; after all, there is no transcendent creator in animism, no god who set the clocks ticking and decides which ones to fix when they falter; nothing exists outside of nature. In other words, my philosophy does not require that I believe in something I cannot experience directly. There was no excuse. However, as I neared the end of the book, I became increasingly aware that I had made a declaration of faith. Needless to say it was the single most important idea of the book. The very foundation of my thesis was based upon an assumption.

In essence, the thesis states that nature's worth does not accrue from how useful it is proved to be to humankind. Nor is it sentiment, aesthetics or some other human judgement that confers value on nature. As a whole and in its every part, as every creature and every fragment, nature has *inherent value*. Albeit simplistically put, that is the basis of animism.

It is easy enough to argue the ethical implications of such a perspective, and in the book I did so with what I hoped was meticulous reasoning and care. Because those implications are so significant, effectively backing a deep green ethical conviction, some proponents feel no need to seek an argument beneath what is seen to be their self-evident foundation: of course nature has inherent value. Yet, even given the rationale of environmental sustainability, the argument's defence seems too close to the shrug of 'just because'. The assumption remains untouched. Recognising this to be the case, it was a natural decision for me to write this book. I was eager to face the question: what does give nature its inherent value?

As a metaphysics, the book strides right into the heart of the debate about mind and matter, about consciousness, the self and who we actually are. It is a conversation that has been going on within our heritage of Western thought for over two and half thousand years. Because animism perceives a wakefulness where other worldviews find none, a central part of my aim is to locate that perspective within the broader debate, asking whether its answers adequately respond to the key questions that have been discussed for so very long.

This is a book about nature, then, but it is not an epistemology; in other words, it isn't just about the way in which we perceive and understand the world in order that we might make good decisions and live ethically. As an ontology, it reaches to find *what nature is* regardless of how we perceive it, while also recognising that such perception is what makes us who and what we are.

This is where I begin.

In Chapter One, *The Enquiry*, I present the questions the book will be asking, and why I believe it is so crucial that such questions are asked, and answered. Working as a base for the book, outlining its purpose, the chapter describes the nourishment that fuels my words, for the questions aren't easy: I look at why they are so hard to express with acuity, let alone answer, exploring our assumptions, what we believe to be our sources of information and how we process that information in order to find understanding or knowledge. Because the terminology of such discussions is often so loose, allowing for so much misinterpretation, there is also some initial work on definitions.

One might imagine that from there I would head straight into an account of the animistic view, but I have chosen to take the path a good deal more slowly. A decade ago I was invited onto BBC Radio 4 to contribute to a moral debate. At the time, my ability to articulate my beliefs may have been fairly well honed for an audience of spiritual seekers, but before a panel of sceptics I found myself entirely naked. I was a barefoot primitive armed with a bow and arrow facing the cavalry, each man bearing a loaded gun. My naïvety, however, was not ignorance, it was the inability to process and respond to such a reasoned onslaught with quick enough precision where that reasoning was based upon a paradigm entirely different from my own. I could perceive the obstacle to clarity that needed to be removed, but could not describe it in a soundbite and answer the volleys of attack within the few minutes allotted me by the programme's producer. My speed of mind was slowed further by the shock of facing a row of pugnacious self-professed intellectuals, many of whom were employed by think tanks, who appeared not to have the capacity to consider a perspective outside the narrow parameters of their own Christian or secular metaphysics. Michael Gove was one of the panel; now Secretary of State for Education, his rigid blinkers enabled him to understand so few words of my language that his immediate interpretation of animism was alarmingly puerile.

The experience stayed with me, always reminding me just how strong fundamental assumptions can be, and how readily they undermine the ability to hear a perspective that cannot be placed easily within their doctrine. As a result, in my presentation of animism here I begin with the methodical building of a philosophical foundation. Chapter Two, *Spirit*, looks at how we experience the world as if through an apparent observer who, sitting in our heads, interacts with our body. This separate self has provoked and sustained notions of soul, of spirit and mind through the past millennia; the chapter reviews religious and philosophical convictions about dualism, finding its roots, touching on idealism. Acknowledging how spirit or mind may feel elusive compared to the apparently tangible, Chapter Three, *Matter*, goes on to consider the physical world, the nature of matter, and the philosophies of mechanism and materialism that have developed over the past four hundred years, philosophies from which was created the worldview now so vigorously promulgated in the West.

In Chapter Four, *Integration*, alternative views are explored. Here there are ideas that have rejected the polarisation accepted as evident within philosophical circles and general thinking, ideas that have a long if tattered history within Western thinking, and the first clear bricks of animism are added to the structure. By Chapter Five, *Moments*, it becomes possible to consider radically different perspectives: an integrated metaphysics of animism begins to emerge. In Chapter Six, *Interaction*, and Chapter Seven, *The Self*, the animist thesis is laid out in full, considering what it means for nature to be comprehensively minded. This allows the focus of the penultimate, Chapter Eight, *Consciousness*, to shift from metaphysics to what such a thesis means in practice: the experience of self, of conscious awareness, and the question of free will.

Chapter Nine I have entitled *The Point*, for in forming the book's conclusions, it considers whether such an enquiry is of any value, and if it is, what the implications of that might be.

Finally in these introductory words, it may be worth suggesting for whom I believe this book may be an interesting and relevant read.

The majority of books on the subject of consciousness are written by academics, using language thick with jargon that makes their ideas hard to decipher without the slow initiation of study. At the other extreme, some are written by New Age thinkers who, basing their ideas on personal visions, are writing for the lucrative self-help, self-realisation market, encouraging the notion that we can all create our own world. Adding to the collection are the many works written over the past few millennia, little tomes and great treatises that explore metaphysics from every philosophical and spiritual angle, books that are often hidden within academic libraries even though they are exquisitely insightful and easy to read.

Knowing I would find its limitations too restricting to inspire, and its innate politics too frustrating to endure, I myself chose not to follow the paths of academia. As a Druid, however, I have studied a good number of the key texts of Western philosophy, together with the sacred scriptures and poetry of religious traditions from around the world, and as a Druid I find the philosophies of the New Age often naïve and irritating. In consequence, my aim here is to maintain a style that is accessible to the nonacademic, while presenting a thesis that can hold its own in any company. Working with that balance, my perspective is both philosophical and spiritual, my language interweaving the empiricism of the sacred with the emotional nature of reason.

As a book on animism, this one takes a different tack from the norm as well. The majority of academic studies focus on non-Western cultures, peoples whose lifestyles are so different from our own that their metaphysical beliefs, embedded as they naturally are within their environment and heritage, can be hard to put into Western language without dilution or misinterpretation. I have read too many tracts on animistic societies where the writer is unaware just how erroneously he has presented a belief system because of his inability to see the extent of his own metaphysical assumptions and step outside of them. This book explores Western animism: not the animism of the Amazon rainforest or South East Asia, but animism as it exists within educated, twenty first century British culture.

Further expressing the practical focus of animism, instead of looking to the teachings of the East and elsewhere, the journey of this book is one that stays within my own ecosystem. Both philosophically and spiritually the roots of my thinking are found deep in my own heritage of Western thought and culture. As such, in many ways they reach further back than those of a *civilised* world, into our history and prehistory, finding an indigenous animism that looks to the wholeness of nature for its principal teachings, not just the fine lines of rational abstraction.

This book is offered, then, to any whose interest takes them to the study of the mind-body problem, those inspired to consider consciousness, self, nature and human nature, particularly if the standards of modern materialism or Christian dualism have failed to offer answers that really satisfy. Where the reader's interest is in animism, Pagan and other old religious traditions, my aim is to express a thesis to explain what may underlie those beliefs. For those unused to the language of philosophy, the slow build of ideas should facilitate understanding. Whoever reads this book, and for whatever reasons, however, my hope is that its ideas will challenge and provoke thought.

Finally, as an essentially anarchistic tradition, it would be inappropriate for me to declare my words to be valid for every animist, but I can offer my own understanding, and with an assurance that my views lie within the mainstream of Western animistic Paganism. Furthermore, in tune with its naturally anarchic tone, I would emphasise that my hope is not that the reader agrees with my every word: my aim is to contribute to the discussion, not just proposing answers but making it clear just why I think these issues are so important to consider. For perhaps it is only when we have fully addressed them and found our own answers that we can feel a confidence about our place within nature, the place of humankind in general, and from there begin to craft a sustainable future.

The first question, though, is why the subject is one that we *must* discuss.

Chapter One

The Enquiry

Let's begin with a dog.

It's an interesting example because, while it may be easy to dismiss the snarling, starving feral hound as a mindless bundle of instincts, there is also the risk of ascribing almost human intelligence to the pampered family pet. Recognising the need to see through such layers of bias or projection, there are serious questions to ask here. How about: what does the dog actually know? Is it making decisions or just reacting to its immediate environment, working solely on drives and compulsions? In other words, does it have free will? What does it feel when it finds food, or the reassurance of company, or when it is left alone? When it smells something familiar, how does it experience the memory? What would it feel if it were kicked, or hit by a car?

Three hundred years ago or so, inspired by the dawning of a new science, a dog was widely considered to be devoid of all thought and incapable of feeling pain. A biological explorer may have observed how it screamed if cut open while still alive, but this was not considered proof that the creature was suffering. Lacking human reason - or the ability to reason claimed by and for the educated white male - its noise was a mechanical response much like the reflex jerking of a knee lightly tapped with a hammer. Reason, given by God to humanity alone, was a part of our immortal soul; where no reason was evident, there was no soul, and therefore no need for protection from harm or hurt.

In his *Essays* of 1580, the French thinker Michel de Montaigne affirmed that 'animals employ the same method and the same reasoning as ourselves', but such a view was not reflective of the way in which our society was progressing. Writing some fifty years later, it was the perspective of thinkers such as René Descartes that became useful to an increasingly developed world. Descartes' goal was that of a dedicated philosopher, but his vision of nature as mechanistic supported the new wave of scientific exploration that in turn allowed for the growth in technology, industry and population. Without sentience, a dog - or a horse, an ox, pig, even an African slave - was valuable only so far as its existence was of use to humankind. Furthermore, how it might be used was not subject to the moral limitations in play when engaging with someone who can feel.

Note that I am using the neutral pronoun: it. I am not a dog lover, I have never owned a dog, nor would I wish to share my space with one if I had the choice. Does that influence my language, or am I simply avoiding the need to specify the dog's gender? The way we use words allows me to neuter the creature without it seeming strange; I couldn't do the same if I were referring to a human being. Indeed, if the dog in question were a specific individual, and cared for as such, it would be natural to use the appropriate gender, and in doing so he or she would immediately be drawn closer in our imagination.

A beekeeper may speak of his harem of working girls, but the bee that is carelessly crushed for being in the kitchen instead of the flowerbed is more likely to be given no gender at all. With a brain the size of a pinhead, containing less than a million neurons, bees still appear to have the ability to abstract information, learning about their environment and communicating something of their experience to other bees. Can we ask the same questions of a busy honeybee: what does she know, and does she remember? When her leg baskets are heavy with soft yellow pollen, her belly full of nectar, and her sisters dancing with exuberance the map to another feast, what does she *feel*? What does she know?

With no neurons at all, an apple tree is in a flow of constant interaction within its environment. How does it experience the changes in light, moisture or warmth to which it responds? When the children are climbing its branches does it feel the weight, or the pressure on its roots when one jumps to the grass, or the bees in its blossom or the cut of the pruning knife? Does it anticipate its fruiting or, having no memory, is it merely following the processes laid down by nature with no knowing at all? (As hermaphrodites, with male and female reproductive parts, our language doesn't allow me to play the gender game here.)

If such questions are not dismissed out of hand, our answers become even more interesting when considering an entity that might be referred to as lifeless. A pebble kicked across the track, a stone on a river bed softly worn away by the waters' movement over many centuries, a mountain quarried: each image provokes a different feeling within us as human readers, but how many of those key questions seem even remotely relevant? Given the pace of its existence from emergence to dissipation, what does rock know, what does rock feel, what is the experience of being and changing for rock?

Like so many in this philosophical field, the answers may seem obvious, but just a little light can reveal the base assumptions and suddenly the questions can feel just a little awkward. When considering a newborn human infant or a foetus two months earlier still in its gestational pool, or an adult in a coma or in the thick of a psychotic mania, the responses all too readily become entangled in beliefs, rigid and tremulous with fears and assertions. Does it know? Does it feel? To ask the same of a stretch of woodland, a wetland ecosystem, or even a virus, the language of these key questions may need to be slightly altered, but the essential meaning is the same: even where it doesn't directly or immediately affect us, how much consideration need we have for the other's wellbeing? Should we care?

In his book about the soul, *Summa Contra Gentiles*, Thomas Aquinas wrote that as rational human beings we are obliged to look after the irrational flora and fauna of our world: 'the very condition of the rational creature, in that it has dominion over its actions, requires that the care of providence should be bestowed on it for its own sake'. In other words, the intellect is what allows freedom; those without it are slaves, who should naturally be given into the care of those who are free. It could be argued that there is a profound sanity in the words, a vivid recognition of responsibility, relevant as much today as in his thirteenth century Italy. Yet his premise is the assumption that all of nature - except humanity - is mindless. Carefully interpreting his god's logic, he decrees that humanity must care for the earth, but not for its own sake: the natural world in its entirety was created specifically for our use.

The majority of his contemporaries would have agreed that humankind holds a special position on the earth, our God-given ability to reason according us the right to absolute rule. As a foundation stone of the Christian West, his assurance of free dominion over the rest of nature has given a moral authority to those who have nurtured the consumerist compulsion that has in turn brought us to the brink of this current environmental crisis. Staring over the abyss, many have begun to query not just whether we are competent stewards of the earth, but, from a Christian and a secular perspective, whether the basis of that stewardship has any validity.

When we pose the key questions, then, I would suggest what we are searching for is a line of demarcation. On one side there are individuals, creatures who *feel*, who remember, whose existence in some way we can perhaps imagine. Sensing common ground, we may experience an empathy, a connection, and extend an embrace of consideration and concern, squealing with recognition when we perceive that they are suffering, because they can suffer, and striving to protect them from any unnecessary harm. Across the line, on the other side, are *things*: creatures we do not or cannot or don't want to relate to, who we believe have no personal reality for they have no real awareness.

Sticky bundles of chemicals, they are natural mechanisms, replaceable objects, and as such we need have no qualms about using them to satisfy our own needs or desires.

Drawing a line implies a black and white distinction and I do so for good reason. It is not that I believe such a line can be drawn and held to with validity, but because the decision is one that is constantly being made. In the reality of our worlds, we are required to make such decisions, and when we do so they express the practical application of our beliefs and assumptions, our day to day ethics. An acre of plantation spruce, a grove of birch and oak, a child fidgeting in an aeroplane or our own child screaming in obliterating rage, a slug, a bee, a hoverfly or butterfly, a meandering river, an ancient track, a feral hound, a puppy, a piglet: should I allow it to be what it wants to be, or can I do with it what I want?

Finding an Answer

Questions about the essence of nature, of consciousness and knowledge, have been asked by philosophers for at least two and a half thousand years. In our Western heritage, such ideas reach back to the Greek Milesians of the sixth century BCE. Thales, living in what is now Anatolia on the Aegean coast of Turkey, is often hailed as the first within Western philosophy: his surviving ideas are the earliest to explore the essence of nature without using the language of mythology, the tales of gods and heroes. As Aristotle recounted a few hundred years later, Thales had suggested that 'water is the material cause of all things'. Remembering it was an era with no science of chemical elements, simply the aching desire to understand why the world works as it seems to do, it is wonderful to consider such ancient visions, to breathe them in and imagine their process of emergence. Perhaps there were others in his community with whom he could discuss such things, but perhaps he was alone, sitting on the warm stones, gazing out over the seas under a clear blue sky, striving for insight.

For many thinkers, myself included, it is this itching compulsion of curiosity that inspires the exploration; nature appears to operate in such mind-blowing and counterintuitive ways, so disingenuously at times, deceiving our senses and overturning the strictures of logic, that further investigation is irresistible. For some, throughout our history, that curiosity has been melded with politics and ambition, the demands of church, court or capital guiding or compromising the depth, breadth or publication of ideas. Declarations about the nature of the world have been made in order to glorify some god or other, a leader or hero, or indeed to assert or affirm the supremacy of mankind. Some thinkers have been inspired to write in order to critique the prevailing consensus, pouring scepticism into a society in defiance of its complacency, or to provoke opposition of an unjust authority.

Reviewing the profusion of writings from Thales right through to essays published by today's academics and blogging philosophers, the lack of agreement is explicit. Although some concur with this or that broad premise, there are no conclusions - or none that aren't quickly and comprehensively shredded by the next writer. Even where a few physicalists declare that they have, in the spirit of scientific confidence, crafted a thesis of consciousness that is just about to be proven by neurological research, a raft of philosophers will surround it and submerge it in counter argument. American professor of mind, Georges Rey, states it cogently: 'We have no adequate explanations of such basic activities as perception, thinking, reasoning, language, decision making, motor control, much less creativity, scientific insight, morally responsible action, or any of the various, quite special phenomena associated with conscious experience'. The reality is that the actual substance of nature and our experience of it are subjects still held within the arena of philosophy - because philosophers get involved in debates where there are no solutions.

Arguably, there can be no solution. John Scotus, a ninth century Irish thinker, declared that it was not possible for any sentient being to understand its own nature. Twelve hundred years later, Colin McGinn, a British philosopher known for his critical approach to any belief-based assertion, suggests that as human beings we are 'cognitively closed', unable to understand mind or matter simply because we haven't the innate capacity to do so. In other words, perhaps the way in which we gather information about our world, and ourselves, is fundamentally inadequate for the task.

So how do we source knowledge? When functioning with ease, the impossibility of knowing anything with any certainty slips our mind, and in particular perhaps the great deal that we take for granted moment by moment. Yet throughout our waking hours, and even as we sleep, we are ingesting and digesting information. It is not just our perceptive ability that needs to be effective in order that we survive and thrive: we must have confidence that we are processing that information in a way that is usefully accurate. Before we consider the problems of how we take in information, then, let's consider for a moment a part of that process of digestion.

As human beings we are very proud of our ability to think. Some spend more time doing it than others, navigating its paths with some satisfaction, while others seldom do it with awareness and have a tendency to stumble into traps and tangles of logic - but we all think. Consciously thinking, we have the ability to consider, weighing up ideas against each other, following routes of reasoning, coming to conclusions. Presenting our thoughts, to ourselves or to another, we might justify our perspective by outlining the logical foundations. In philosophy, this is understood as the basis of *rationalism*: we acquire knowledge by putting together what we have logically figured out must be the relevant facts.

To early Greek thinkers like Socrates, whose arguments were presented (or constructed) in the writings of Plato, this kind of deductive intellectual argument was what philosophy was all about. His train of thought in the *Republic* makes me howl with laughter: his logical machinations veer between wisdom and the wise cracks of an irritating smart aleck. He wasn't concerned with metaphysics, focusing instead on the importance of ethics, but his system was based wholly upon the authority of human reason. Indeed, the conviction that it is possible to achieve a purely reasoned understanding, having transcended the subjectively emotional and sensuous and found a universal objectivity, provided the rational stance with its determined position of validity. For a good part of the past few millennia this ability to reason was seen as the principal distinction between humanity and the nonhuman world: the irrational man was a beast who had lost his God-given reason.

In his *Meditations on First Philosophy*, Descartes wrote, 'It is quite evident that existence can no more be separated from the essence of God than the fact that its three angles equal two right angles can be separated from the idea of a triangle'. It is a beautiful little book, the simple clarity of his thought processes shining through the pages: the sentence I quote here is a sweet example of his meticulously rational thinking. He knew that physical science required hands-on exploration, but metaphysics, like mathematics, he asserted, *must* be based on reason, for here the only proofs available to the thinker are those of the perfectly reasoned explanation.

Published just after his death in 1677, thirty six years after Descartes was writing, Baruch Spinoza gave his *Ethics* the mathematical framework of Euclidian geometry, believing this to be the only way of presenting a consummately rational thesis. Accused of atheism, Spinoza's work now reads as a rich celebration of God, or his understanding of the divine creator as the very essence of reason. Writing in Latin he used the word *ratio*: not the logically restrictive notion that we might assume today, his was a natural reason, the rationale of intrinsic harmony that allows for the critical viability of nature. Beneath our human perception of the world, the 'order and connection of ideas is the same as the order and connection of things', he wrote in *Ethics*; in other words, nature is a fabric of connecting threads only revealed through divine reason. For Spinoza, seeking understanding through rational means was a spiritual quest both to understand and *experience* God.

In the history of Western philosophy, rationalism has been an important thread across continental Europe, but in Britain the tradition of *empiricism* arose early in our heritage: the belief that an idea can only become knowledge once it has been adequately tried and tested. Indeed, in *Albion*, Peter Ackroyd equated the history of our British islands' philosophy with the history of empiricism, 'from the writings of Duns Scotus in the thirteenth century to the local pragmatism of the twentieth century', inspiring and inspired by our innate and heuristic eccentricity.

If a thesis cannot be checked by experience, the empiricists declared, it cannot be justifiably proposed. Thinking and the use of the intellect are, of course, invaluable, but experience of the world is crucial in the acquiring of knowledge. For while analysis by reason provides a useful perspective, an observer remains detached, reaching only a superficial understanding. Reality as we sense it through our eyes and fingers, our breath and heart, feels entirely separate from the rational world: to use an old word, it lacks *sensibility*. Writing in the late nineteenth century, the American philosopher and psychologist, William James, put it beautifully: 'Thought deals thus solely with surfaces. It can name the thickness of reality, but it cannot fathom it'.

The tussle between rationalism and empiricism is intrinsic to philosophy. Even where a thinker considers himself to be presenting a balanced view, his critics will dismantle his arguments based upon his lack of sufficient reasoning, inconclusive experimentation, or even indict him of subjectivity. Throughout this book, I do the same: questioning the notion of objectivity, celebrating the sensuous tangibility of experience, I hope to present a thesis that is nonetheless also based on reasoning. They are important starting blocks to bear in mind, ever reminding us to question how an argument is justified. Kant was one of the first to flag up the problem *philosophically*.

In common with many philosophers of continental Europe, Immanuel Kant began as a rationalist. Living in eighteenth century Königsberg, then capital of Prussia, now a Russian exclave on the Baltic coast, Kant remains one of the most significant and influential writers when it comes to the investigation of the stuff of nature. A man exquisitely wrapped up in the deepest philosophical explorations, he seems to have gathered and distilled an extraordinary breadth of human understanding in a way that few others have ever achieved. Although far from unsuccessful in the first years of his career, in his late forties it was the work of Scottish historian and philosopher David Hume that stopped him in his tracks. Hume's consummate scepticism had unexpectedly woken him, he famously said, from his 'dogmatic slumber'.

British philosophy was widely available in German translation at the time, and Hume was an interesting character whose very grounded yet radical approach would have been quite different from much that Kant was reading. In *A Treatise of Human Nature*, Hume affirmed the difference between rational 'Relations of Ideas' and empirical 'Matters of Fact': the former could be proven by reason and analysis but the latter could not. However, he wondered whether some statements - notably cause and effect - had not been wrongly designated. After all, on what basis do we believe a certain action to be the cause of another action? To Hume, this was empirical not rational knowledge: an

observed causality, he expounded, was no more than a probability based upon experience. 'It is not, therefore, reason which is
the guide of life, but custom. That alone determines the mind in
all instances to suppose the future conformable to the past.
However easy this step may seem, reason would never, to all
eternity, be able to make it.' Cause and effect cannot be proven.

Kant was thrown into a period of deep thought. Recognising
the need to reconsider his metaphysics, for just over a decade he
published nothing. In 1781, after eleven years of relative
isolation, he presented his *Critique of Pure Reason*. Little read at
the time, and equally so now, it is nonetheless considered by
many to be one of the seminal works of Western philosophy. It is
not an easy read; he seems to write in order to clarify ideas for
himself rather than to communicate them to others, but bear with
me as I explain - for his ideas were extraordinarily insightful.
Kant dismantles the apparent complexity of nature revealing its
exquisite simplicity, and in a way that is perfectly in keeping with
the animistic perspective.

Simple rationalism, the *Critique* stated, was not enough to gain
knowledge about the world. What was needed was a weave of
clear logical thinking and evidence from experience. Yet the
traditionally accepted distinction between the rational (called the
a priori, or *what reason tells us*) and the empirical (the *a posteriori*,
or *what experience shows us)* was no longer sufficient. Seeking
more clarity, he added two further descriptives: the *analytic* and
the *synthetic*. The analytic is in many ways a confirmation of the
rational and the example he gave was very much of his time: 'all
bodies are extended', in other words, it is self-evident that matter
takes up space and always will. The synthetic, on the other hand,
is the intuited understanding that is accrued from experience. His
example was, 'all bodies are heavy': experience reveals to us that
matter has weight.

From there he was able to create his weave, presenting a third
way in which we process information. He called this the synthetic

a priori. It describes what we need to understand in order to make sense of our world.

Essentially, Kant is questioning how we can know anything about the world. A vast amount of unprocessed sensory information surrounds and saturates us, moment by moment. That we don't just drown in it is because we have a way of processing that data. But how do we process it? This was Kant's response: using the filters of a bank of related and relevant concepts already in place, we are able to transform raw sensory input into comprehensible and useful experience. He wrote, 'Thoughts without content are empty, intuitions without concepts are blind': if a wave of sensory input (what he means by *intuitions*) corresponds with an idea previously formed in our minds, we are able to process that data into experience and knowledge. Where we have no concepts that relate to the data, the raw data either entangles us in confusion or slips straight past us, as if unobserved.

So, while affirming that 'all our knowledge begins with experience', he declares that knowledge doesn't actually come from the world around us. It is a beautiful paradox, simply solved. For example, if an apple sits before us, it is only because we have had a previous experience of an apple, and therefore hold a concept of apple in our memory, that we see it as an apple, that we know it to be an apple. In this way, what we see is recognised and ordered only through our ability to reason, which in turn develops our skills of reasoning, enlarging our ability to seize useful perceptions from the flood of data intrinsic to the business of living. The learning begins in infancy and continues throughout our lives until we no longer feel the need or desire to learn.

The apple is a tangible example of how we understand our perception, but there are statements that sit more broadly as synthetic *a priori* knowledge. Here we return to Hume, for an example Kant gave is that 'every event must have a cause', believing he had found a way of satisfactorily explaining the problem presented him by Hume's scepticism. For even if we cannot prove the connection between a cause and its apparent effect, a conceptual understanding of the apparent connection allows us to function. Into the same category Kant placed many of the new scientific principles, such as Newton's laws of motion, together with pure mathematics. Furthermore, although Hume lived in a society that was fairly liberal, allowing him the scope to question freely, Kant's circumstance on the continent made it necessary for him to express and support belief in the Christian Church: delicately he placed the metaphysics of deity within this same category. Though God's existence was unprovable, the practice of belief was necessary, allowing us to understand order, balance, and regulation within the world.

Indeed, many statements based on the synthetic *a priori* are the most interesting in life. When it comes to these aspects of nature, we cannot experiment sufficiently, nor seek direct experience in a way that satisfies the empiricist, nor can we use simple reasoning to prove their universal factuality. This was Kant's directive then: to understand how our reasoning mind is forming concepts that allow coherent experience, recognising that our experience in turn forms further concepts, and so on. Most of the process is happening without conscious awareness. Yet, by being aware of the process, we have the opportunity to review our reasoning, to critique the conceptualisation we are using to perceive the world, and from there to recognise with brute honesty just where we are depending upon poor reasoning or assumptions, and thus where we are placing our declarations of faith.

And here is the denouement.

Instinctively we imagine that we gain knowledge about the world through our perception. However, as Kant says, 'objects must conform to our cognition': our understanding of what we see is formed *by* what understanding we already have in place.

Furthermore, as human beings, we have particular sensory apparatus through which we take in our surroundings. The scope of our knowledge is both limited and sculpted by that apparatus, making our experience of the world distinctly human.

As a consequence, the way we see the world is not actually the world *in itself*. What we see is our idea of it. The truth is, we have no notion of what the world is other than through the veils of our perception.

Such a statement sounds obvious - now. In Kant's day, it was an utterly radical assertion. He himself proclaimed it to be a Copernican revolution: 243 years earlier, in the northern Polish city of Frombork, the astronomer Nicolaus Copernicus had published *On the Revolutions of the Celestial Spheres*, placing the sun at the centre of the universe and setting the once still and focal earth out on its spinning orbit. Inspired by brilliant thinkers before him, including Pythagoras and the twelfth century Persian mathematician al-Aūsī, Copernicus wasn't willing to accept that God had created a system as clumsy and tenuous as that described by Aristotle and Ptolemy, the main sources of astronomical understanding in the mediaeval West. What he found was an aesthetically satisfying if wholly revisionist solution. Protecting himself from the wrath of Rome, he laid it out in language too thickly technical for the non-scientist to comprehend: it took the Church over seven decades to realise the implications of what he was saying. *Revolutions* was still on the *Index of Prohibited Books* when Kant was writing his *Critique*, the astronomer's heliocentricity having turned the view of the universe entirely upside down. Kant's own revelation about perception would do the same.

If the old Prussian hadn't said it, no doubt someone else would have done, but for me the fact that it is now obvious is a piece of Kantian wizardry. He removed humanity's certainty that what we are perceiving is what is actually before us: effectively, he made the universe disappear. Of course, he tried to replace it with a reassurance about the efficacy of our media of perception and comprehension, showing the value of a world formed by the percipient's mind, but the explosive effect of that foundational thesis was not diluted. Solid rock turned to thin air. We were no longer passive receivers of sensory information. The possibility of objective perception slipped away, falling wholly out of reach. Suddenly we became the active agents in how we experience and understand the world.

This sense-dependent and mind-dependent reality Kant called the phenomenal world. That which was so harshly thrown beyond our human perception he called the *noumenon*, the realm of nature *in itself*. If his God did exist, this is where such a god would be: beyond the scope of human experience, perception or knowledge.

Making Sense

In his book *Confessions*, British philosopher Bryan Magee recounts when, as a child, he first saw this unbridgeable gap between what exists around us and our perception of it. The realisation induced a terrifying isolation in him: 'nothing you can ever do can make you experience anything other than the deliverances of your own consciousness'. Kant wasn't the first or last to see the illusion of reality, but what he did was *systematise* the idea sufficiently to present it as both rationally impeccable and empirically valid. Nothing in philosophy or science has since proved him wrong.

Of course, it is natural to imagine that our eyes are merely windows, looking out at the world that is coloured and shaped and scented exactly as we perceive it to be. The empiricism of mechanistic science, still so endemic and philosophically dominant in our culture, pushes this instinctive conviction as close to the limit as it can, not only believing but evangelically asserting its perceptions to be objective and authoritative facts. Yet, when it comes to understanding perception, modern science does not help. For example, photons reflecting off objects hit the retina of the eyes, provoking an electrochemical response, the data of which is relayed along the optic nerves to the visual cortex of the brain. How the brain makes a coherent image of that data is still a complete mystery to today's scientists, let alone how memories of previously formed images are stored for new images to be compared and comprehended. With the crux of the process still entirely unaccounted for, the explanation so far presented must be lacking something fundamental. Or perhaps it could be wrong: a visual illusion crafted by a series of beliefs built one upon another.

The British philosopher and novelist Raymond Tallis, writing in the *New Scientist* (January 2010), commented on how the 'material world, far from being the noisy, colourful, smelly place we live in, is colourless, silent, full of odourless molecules, atoms, particles, whose nature and behaviour is best described mathematically'. As an atheist, such a vision may inspire his scientific bent, but for many it is startling, a world entirely drained of its aesthetics and meaning. Insightful as Tallis is, he is no more able to know accurately what nature is *in itself* than you or I. What he is so potently describing is an idea about the limit of our perceptive ability. Yet where do those limitations leave us? Do we abandon the valiant expeditions of ontology, leaving the search for nature's essence to the hyper-rationalists and empirical mechanists of today, rearranging numbers and computer-generated images of electrons in strip-lit offices?

If we cannot know nature as it is beyond our perception, can we ask any worthwhile questions about mind and matter, about consciousness? We quickly hit another problem, after all. Any and every observation, even if that is of our own mental states through meticulously focused introspection, is phenomeno-logical; in other words, even when inwardly reflecting upon our own thoughts and feelings, we are doing so using the tools of perception which filter and alter what we encounter just as they do when we look around us. We *apperceive* ourselves having perceptions (our perceptions are altered in the digestive process), instead of observing those perceptions directly.

As this book began, I laid out my intention of looking at why it is important to explore the nature of consciousness, the essence of mind and matter, for the foundation of any practical ethics is metaphysics. Our beliefs about what has the ability to think, to remember, to feel, to perceive, to experience, have implications that are all-pervasive, influencing decision-making and behaviour in every aspect of our lives: what is worthy of consideration, of empathy and care, of respectful communication? What has inherent value, on account of having faculties that give it individuality, a sense of self-determinism, the ability to suffer?

Integral to that investigation has been the analysis of how we process information about the world, gaining knowledge through reasoned thinking and through the evidence of experience. Our culture tends to polarise these two, and by doing so polarises the notion of objectivity and subjectivity, favouring the former by presenting it as nature's truth. In practice though, naturally, we use reason to understand our experience, not just by way of thinking but as ideas that help us to make sense of the world. Kant clarified this by explaining how previously crafted concepts allow for comprehensible experience. However, in doing so he dismantled the rational possibility that we might know nature objectively, or indeed - with any accuracy - if we might know it at all.

In early twentieth century Vienna a group of thinkers gathered to discuss the extent to which the strict rationalism of logical semantics and mathematics could be taken within the structure of empiricism. Called the logical positivists, they asserted their belief that, unless something could be scientifically proven, it was speculative, dependent on faith, and not worthy of exploration. Needless to say, within the parameters of the irrelevant was placed the entirety of metaphysics, and indeed a key aim was the removal of religion, at long last, from the realms of philosophy and science. Magee dismisses their stance as unphilosophical, for they were not looking to understand 'the nature of reality', nor the ethics that stem from that. I agree with Magee - their focus of enquiry was not the truly unsolvable problems that define the remit of philosophy - but it is important to acknowledge this natural desire to ignore anything about which we can't establish any security of certainty. The influence of logical positivism continues in some arenas of academia to this day.

Yet even if we have no certainty, on a day to day basis our experience of life is *real*. John Locke, writing in 1689, referred to the little we understand about nature as giving us only a 'twilight of probability'. He went on to emphasise that even that small amount of knowledge must be 'accommodated to be the use of life': in other words, we mustn't discard that understanding on the basis of its limitations or uncertainty, but must make the very most of what we do know. That may not be provable objective facts, but what we each perceive is *our* world, our own world, a world generated by the beliefs and understanding already in place that let us make sense of it, allowing us to function. That is what is *real*.

Real: it's a word I have used here a number of times, and consciously so. It is worth analysing. The oldest extent of its roots is Latin, *res*, meaning a thing, but if we are questioning whether or not we can ever know anything about *things*, such a definition is not enough. Its association with property and land goes back to its earliest documented use, and that guides my understanding of the word and the way that I use it, for it reminds me that the real is something we feel to be wholly graspable, palpable, tangible. What we believe to be real, we need to be fully grounded. The definition I propose then is this: what is real is that which we need to believe exists in order that we might function. Indeed, its embrace is the very structure of our lives: the land and the skies, the walls and floors of home, the desk I sit at and the keyboard that I tap as I write, the carrot and salad leaves of my lunch. This is my reality.

Equally, words based upon real need to be flagged up, such as *realise*: in the process of a realisation I am adding that thing into the framework of my reality. It is a definition that keeps our willingness to believe overt. If I am unable to believe a friend's betrayal, I dismiss it as unreal, refusing to bring the idea into my reality.

I am not talking about our psychological attitudes towards the world, our feelings *about* it. Something is *real*ised by very much deeper levels of belief, those that are beyond the reach of questioning, for they are intrinsic to our rudimentary functionality. Doubt is incomprehensible. In this way, my definition dovetails with Kant's thesis of knowing: the right concepts must be in place for raw sensory data to become intelligible perception, he says; if they are, then we have the possibility of reality.

A handful of other words, already used here a number of times, are terms that can be defined in various ways, especially within the context of the mind-body enquiry. As we come to the close of this first chapter, it is worth clarifying these, both in terms of their roots and use within our English language, but also outlining the specific meaning with which I use them in this text.

The handful I have chosen are: perception, experience, sentience and consciousness. Rather than considering the ways in which we think or digest information, these deal with how we ingest the world. Their general definitions are close: in the defining of one, dictionaries tend to use the others in explanation. Finding sharper distinctions between them is necessary, however, if the words are to be of any value here.

Of course, the problem with such a task is that we risk slipping into infinite regress, needing to define the words that are used in our definitions. Where I don't define a term, it can be assumed that I am using it in line with common usage and remain, at least within the immediate context, content with such a broad and blurred meaning. Furthermore, as these four are key terms in the debate, I offer here just the briefest pen sketches, swift and simple descriptives, knowing that through the course of the book each sketch will be extended and coloured, as I build the idea of what I mean by the mindedness of nature.

As a starting point, let us consider what it means to *perceive*.

The ancient root at the beginning of the word is **per-*, which speaks of the act of moving through or across, implying the traversing of new ground or the need for courage to do so. Such Proto Indo-European (PIE) snippets of language can almost be felt in the body. Dating back five or six thousand years, like our rhythms and our movements as we dance, and fight, and make love, like our genes and the tides of our emotions, these ancient syllables are like whispers of the distant past. Spoken aloud the sounds hum within us, very often communicating the same feelings and meanings that they did for our ancestors.

Considering the word as a whole, we find the Latin *percipere*, which can be translated as to gather: the verb *capere* means to take or to grasp, the *per* prefix providing a sense of pulling something across a divide. Although much used in philosophical discussion about consciousness, perceive is not a word commonly heard in day to day speech, perhaps because actually its connotation is quite fuzzy. Perception offers the idea of an observer, yet 'I can see the man is close' is quite different from 'I can perceive the man is close'. The observing *I* is still there but it isn't about vision.

This offers an important clue, a crucial tangent, for taking the word observer, the principal definition of its Latin root, *servare*, is not about seeing but about attending to something. When we perceive, we are attentive, paying attention, and gathering infor-mation in whatever manner is appropriate, according to our means within that moment and its context. It may be visual, or auditory, or tactile: we may be blind, bound, and deafened by some irrelevant sound and yet, attentive to the man's presence, intuit his proximity in a way that is somehow inexplicable. The word seems fuzzy then, while at the same time being powerful in an elementary or primitive way. Within this text, then, I use the word thus: to perceive is to gather information by simply being attentive.

The next word is *experience*.

The roots of this word move alongside the last, reaching deep into the same PIE *per-*, then finding its way into the Latin, where the *per-* grows into *peritus*, meaning tested, skilled or experienced, the prefix *ex* bringing an additional quality of extraction. In common usage, we talk of experience as implying lessons learned from practical contact. Thus, we would more normally use the word in the context of having had an experience of something. On the whole, my own use of the word is more specific only in its relationship to the other key terms: after moments of interaction, we are left with the effects of what we have perceived.

In the context of this book, however, the immediate act of experiencing is important as well. 'I can experience the man as being close' has implications about awareness. Here I would suggest that, where we talk of experiencing rather than perceiving the contents of a moment, it is the *effects* of the interaction that are being noted. Again, I return to Kant: the feedback cycle of experience, provoking the crafting of concepts, that in turn allow for more fully comprehended experience, and so on.

Sentience is the next term, defined in the *Oxford English Dictionary* (*OED*) as the ability to perceive or feel. The Latin derivation reveals its thickest root: at its simplest, *sentire* means to feel. Heading back towards Middle English, in the sixteenth century the word retains the same meaning, having arrived in English from Latin via the French. However, I also have a strong *sense* of the word in the Old English, where the root *sið* takes us more directly back to the PIE **sent-*. This offers definitions that speak of journeying, travelling, a path or way, adding to the depth and breadth of the word. Holding the word *sense* with an awareness of this ancient root inspires me in how I use it now, for it hums with the vibrancy of a current, the energy of a movement, experienced or anticipated.

In common usage, sense and feel are often seen as synonymous, but the distinction is interesting. The word *feel* comes to us through Old English and the Germanic tongues, rooting in the ancient PIE **pal-*. The meaning has barely changed to this day, the main thrust indicating feeling, yet the broader scope of the **pal-* root is about touch. Turning to consider the example used with the words above, seeking a definition of sentience for the purpose of this book, the sentence changes its tone again: 'I can sense the man as being close'. The implication is that we are perceiving his proximity because we *feel* it - but not through touch; this is not necessarily a tangible perception. However, crucially, it is a perception that is nonetheless experienced *bodily*.

Sentience, sense - and all their close semantic relations, including sensory, sensation, sensible, sensibility, nonsense and common sense - all contain this hum of very physical energy. The perception is not one that can be held in the ethereal realms of mental abstraction. Even when we are talking about something making sense, there is a sensation of the idea in question settling, grounded by the practicalities of reality.

The fourth term in this series is *consciousness*. It is a word that could be anticipated as fundamental to such a book as this. However, as a word that holds considerable power in our language and our society, I will handle it with care. Indeed, it will take me a good while to return to it over the course of this text. Consequently, to offer a comprehensive definition at this point would be entirely premature, but not to place an initial suggestion would also be lacking.

As a very basic starting point, the Latin root word is *scire*, which means to know. Accepting that it is simplistic but a beginning, I would suggest then that within the term consciousness there is an element of knowing. Returning to the same example: 'I am conscious of the man being close' encourages us to take in the whole sentence, for the man and his location are not just provocation for or experience of a perception or sensation; the man has become an entity in time and space. The observing *I* is no longer passive in receiving the information, but has used it to construct an idea, an understanding out of which to craft a response.

There are, of course, words vital to any discussion on the mind-body question that I have not yet defined. Indeed, I have spoken of how we take in and process information about the world, but not touched upon the dilemma that runs in perfect parallel to that: what is this *I* that perceives, feels and knows?

In the next chapter I shall be addressing this idea of the observer, exploring our understanding of the mind, and looking at the ideas of spirit and soul, acknowledging their place within our heritage and our world today.

Chapter Two

Spirit

As infants, it appears that we have no sense of the world as separate from ourselves. Entirely integrated with the immediate environment, although the warm fluidity of the womb is exchanged for a world of space and air, where there is comfort and nourishment during those first months the ease of this oneness is maintained: it is the haven of loving attention that is the ideal of maternal care. As the infant's perception grows, however, his experience of his world slowly extending, he strives to understand the intricacies of cry and response, of touch and feeling, and the sensation of undifferentiated oneness begins to fragment.

With eyes beginning to focus, the importance of visual input comes into play, curiosity arousing his interest as he watches the dancing of colour and movement. It is a fascinating time to watch a human being, often missed by mothers too busy to lie beside a child for long periods of gently shared exploration: keen to grab hold of the hand that is moving in front of his face, an infant will reach for that hand, at first quite unaware that it is his own hand he is reaching for, even using the hand itself to do the reaching. Grabbing his foot instead, he sucks on a toe, or wraps his fingers around another finger, sucking it tightly - and discovers that at times such an action doesn't produce the same sensation, for it is someone else's finger. Connecting what he sees with how he is feeling, months pass as he begins to realise that there are objects that are separate from himself.

When there is no light shaping the world into countless patterns and forms, the wholeness is retained a good deal longer. Where the infant's needs are immediately met - the baby sleeping in the mother's bed finds a breast in the darkness, sating his hunger while barely waking - his experience is not overwhelmed by the distraction of visual input. Where a craving is not met by the smallest murmur or movement though, he learns to cry out, shaking his world for a response, reaching out across the gap that has brought him into an unresponsive place of solitude.

I write as a mother and philosopher, not a behavioural scientist; other examples could be given, other interpretations. What gradually emerges in the child, I would suggest, is the sense of a distinction between the *I* and the Other: as the world around becomes more concretely formed, the sense of his own self begins to find its shape too. Of course, as Kant explained, that world is a phenomenological reality, slowly created by the lessons learned from each action and interaction. It is how nature *appears* to be to the human mind. But that is all we have, its detail provided by the all-important thinking *I*.

Further, for the tiny child, perhaps the most crucial aspect of his world is what happens when he interacts with it, and here the key issue is whether or not there will be a response to his cry. In the course of his exploration, he comes to learn that some things do respond to him and some simply don't. If he kicks up a fuss, the effects differ according to what he is addressing: the mother burbles words of love, the mobile whirls, the sister squeals, the toy squeaks. Some things, such as the table, don't appear to react at all, however hard he hits them. Others, like books or drinking cups, can be erratic: if he persists with his attention, the world sometimes changes, the cup fills with juice, the story comes to life with words read aloud, and at other times nothing happens at all.

Nature is filled with mystery. Just what it is that distinguishes something that is likely to respond from something that won't is not easy to formulate in those first months and years. To the infant, the difference between the cuddly toy and the cat is very hard to grasp, until his own clumsy grasping provokes the cat to scratch. When I was a child the old radiogram looked like any other piece of furniture, but now and then this particular wooden cabinet was filled with music and voices; with the array of devices that nowadays bleep and sing and talk, it seems inevitable that an infant might imagine everything will respond to him. It doesn't. Yet what touchstones can he use to work out what will and what won't?

The bright child might infer that, if something moves, it is more likely to respond than something which doesn't. He might learn then to distinguish between those things that move because he pushes them, slowly recognising the various ways by which objects can be propelled, leaving just those creatures that do genuinely generate their own motion - some of which will respond. Yet the force that allows something to move on its own is as mysterious as that quality which makes something a potential respondent. Whatever it is, it is effectively invisible.

Looking up from the world of the little child, science has given us a language with which to talk about these fundamental aspects of nature that are life and consciousness. An expert can refer to them with some measure of fluency, yet he still can't explain them. Though they are constantly revealed through nature's self-expression all around us, and their processes can be described in some intimate and beautiful detail, the essence of what they are remains frustratingly beyond our reach. Philosophers have struggled for millennia to understand them, pushing to the limits their capacity to abstract ideas, employing the strictest rules of rationalism to create conceptual explanations about what they might consider and declare to be true. Furthermore, over centuries, thinkers have done their utmost to pull these mysteries away from the custody of the priests and theologians - for whom that magical quality is easily interpreted as *soul*, a tiny droplet of God. Yet nothing can be proved.

Inexplicable at its essential level, yet perpetually experienced, perhaps it is natural to imagine that the property which allows something to respond is in fact magical, that it is made of something quite different from the solid tangibility of matter. I am not saying that such an idea is accurate or exact, simply that it is *natural* that one might imagine the distinction to be so. It is an easy and instinctive dualism that we feel, and one that could be (and most often has been) stated as the evident and inevitable conclusion to the mind-body question, even when thoroughly considered both empirically and rationally. Our experience of the world *implies* it to be so.

Unsurprisingly, the majority of religions and spiritual traditions concur, referring to the soul as separate from the body. Yet even where such teachings were not part of our childhood culture, an intuitive conviction about spirits and ghosts is hard to dislodge, rooted in those first mystifying lessons about what might respond and what will not. As adults, whatever our beliefs, our native language confirms the separation between mind and matter. We use the possessive when we speak of our physical bodies. Medicine still diagnoses and prescribes based on an understanding of that separation, however hard holistic practitioners and thinking doctors try to do otherwise.

While followers of the Abrahamic religions happily own it, where there is a rejection of those faiths it is common to blame them for this dualism within our culture. Christianity has so saturated our islands' mindset over the past thousand years that every aspect of our lifestyle is imbued with its metaphysical perspective. However, I would suggest again that dualism is actually more instinctive than that. Cultural norms must, of course, influence our metaphysical convictions, but my sense is that human nature provides the underlying template for a belief in dualism, because of the way a child learns. Whether we see spirits, souls, minds or just atoms in oak trees and puppy dogs, or solely in human beings, it is the observing *I* that is perceiving, and digesting that perception. As we grow from child to adult, our bank of experience increasing our ability to perceive and understand, the observer remains, his position becoming increasingly entrenched.

Turning inwards then, what is it that we feel or believe is looking out at the world? What is it we think we are?

Souls

In his book, *Seeing Red*, theoretical psychologist Nicholas Humphrey proposes that nature has provided the illusion of a mind-body duality specifically to allow us to feel confident within the chaos of nature. Imbued with a sense of being a soul within a body, we naturally feel somehow more significant than the world around us. It is an evolutionary trick: nature is suggesting to us that as human beings what we are is 'something extra-special to preserve, even beyond death', so we better be careful. Our instincts for self-protection and self-importance are magnified.

It's an interesting perspective. Considered within the process of evolutionary selection, where resources are scarce, where the human population is growing and forcing competition and adaptation, perhaps those most likely to survive and thrive are indeed the ones who believe themselves sufficiently distinct from nature's mud and flesh to feel able to take not only what they need but what they want, and without concern. The sense of being special permits an individual to sate his desires to the detriment of others, clambering over those around him to secure a better position. Where the religious or philosophical language of *soul* has slipped away, this crucial arrogance and assertion can perhaps be seen as clothed in the language of the ego and its rational mind, allowing ambition, personal achievement and other medallions of secular and capitalist culture. We are led to believe we are special because we have wit and reason, and can use it consciously to our own advantage.

Through millennia, thinkers have explored this quality, striving to understand nature, its creation or creativity, its expression as life, or wishing simply to affirm the distinctiveness of humanity. However, to look back in search of the emergence of a coherent concept of our conscious being is interesting. In the ninth century BCE, for example, in the earliest written material of our Western heritage, the poet Homer used various words that we might now understand as soul, mind or consciousness, but they were all constitutive of the physical body. Often in the chest, the *nous* or *thymos* were connected with experience and expression of emotion, intuition, and the intelligence that is interwoven with that, the *kradie* or heart being the well of our passion. The lungs or *phrenes* held vitality and consciousness. It was through the *psyche* that we are able to think, but this was not the rational mind; integral to breath, even if it survived death there was no assurance of the *psyche*'s continued cogency, for it may simply drift as a wisp of smoke, unable to function without the body.

In Homeric culture, with no mind-body differentiation, there was less of a distinct notion of the individuated thinking self as separate from nature. While Homer's characters do express themselves as individuals with will and purpose, there is also an assumption that they are subject to the whims and demands of the gods. Over the following centuries, lyric poets began to speak of the experience of inner conflict, the heroes self-reflecting on blame and justification, but it was a slow process. Around the turn of the sixth century BCE, Solon wrote of the *nous* in a way that implies a thinking, reflecting mind, and soon after the *psyche* and *nous* appear to merge into one idea. The competing forces of gods, instincts, needs and desires, began to come together, as the individual emerged, considering his own experiences as paramount. The independent and subjective observer was born.

No doubt pondering his own experience of the world, Anaximander, possibly a student of Thales, observed that everything in nature appears to be in a state of constant opposition, every element pushing against another, provoking the changes of growth and decay. Because this conflict is all that we know, filling our world so comprehensively, he proposed that the single substance from which all nature emanates had to be something entirely beyond our comprehension: ἄπειρον (*apeíron*) was the originating and essential boundless mystery. A young man from Samos, said to be one of his students, took this idea and ran with it.

By all accounts, Pythagoras was an extraordinary man. Known now for his discoveries as a mathematician, in his day it was his 'golden thigh' and miracles that were most talked of within the general population. Indeed, though evidently a charismatic leader, tales of eccentricities left him and his adherents ridiculed, even persecuted, and his teachings were for a long time dismissed. However, amongst the more deeply thinking of his era and those that followed, it was his metaphysics that was interesting. Anaximander's *apeíron* may have been beyond the human mind's ability to grasp but it was a monist idea: although at its origin it may be too vast, too pure, too subtle to imagine, all of nature was still constituted of a single substance. Emphatically differing from these monists whose thinking was still the norm, Pythagoras was a dualist: the divine universal soul was a different matter altogether. What is more, he said, a small part of it exists in each and every individual. This notion of an immortal *psyche* was radically innovative: a little spark of soul ever yearning to reconnect with the universal whole, this *psyche* was more real than anything that could be perceived in the material world.

Always seeking the certainty of absolute truth, in the uncompromising and immutable logic of mathematics Pythagoras found harmony in the patterns he perceived as underlying nature's apparent chaos. A few hundred years later, in his *Metaphysics*, Aristotle related the vision of the Pythagoreans: 'all other things seemed in their whole nature to be modelled after numbers, and numbers seem to be the first things in the whole of nature, they supposed the elements of numbers to be the elements of all things, and the whole heaven to be a musical scale and a number'.

If Pythagoras had not spoken out, if his teachings had not been heard or survived, another might have stepped forward with the same idea: the source and destination of the universe is a perfect and unchanging super-nature just beyond our perception. In *The Golden Ass*, in the second century CE, Apuleius proposed that Pythagoras learned his wisdom from the Jews and Persian magi, the Zoroastrians in Chaldea, and in India, amongst the Brahmins and gymnosophists. In the little we know of the ancient Orphic religions rooted in the second millennium BCE, there are devotional whispers of the earth as sensuous body and the skies as pure immortal soul. Wherever it came from, his influence can now be seen as pervasive. In the words of the English philosopher, Bertrand Russell: 'The whole conception of an eternal world, revealed to the intellect but not to the senses, is derived from him'.

It wasn't immediate. Heraclitus, a generation or so after Pythagoras, criticised his society for continuing to seek wisdom in the words of the poets and storytellers, such as Homer. An angry man, his thinking often bitterly obscure, he declared the primary and fundamental substance to be fire, an ever-living and perpetually moving force that contained nature's intelligence. 'Soul is the vaporisation out of which everything else is composed', he stated. The Athenian, Anaxagoras, a few decades later, believed nature to be made of an infinite number of 'seeds' which are mixed and separated again and again, expressing the processes of change and decay. Using the word *nous*, he said that the mind of nature had power over these seeds, entering into the mix and asserting order and coherence of form. Together with most of their contemporaries, both philosophers were still exploring nature's essence as wholly embodied.

Plato, however, strode right onto the pathway that had been cleared by Pythagoras. Declared by many to be the next great philosopher of the Western tradition, for those happy to accept the dualism of much of the past two millennia Plato is indeed a man to be celebrated. The degree to which he has affected our philosophical heritage, and hence perhaps our history as a whole, is worth considering. In *Process and Reality*, the mathematician and philosopher Alfred North Whitehead stated that the course of European philosophy 'consists of a series of footnotes to Plato'. In his book on anarchy, *Demanding the Impossible*, Peter Marshall wrote that Plato 'stands at the fountainhead of the great authoritarian river which subsequently swamped Western thought'. Taking Pythagoras' eccentric visions, and developing them through his system of meticulously rational dialogues, it is this dualism that is the intrinsic and guiding structure of his thought.

Tired of the fires of Heraclitean change, Plato was reaching for certainty and, like Pythagoras, he found it beyond the material world. The essence of the universe is not, he declared, made of elemental forces but ideas in the perfect mind of a single creator god, abstracts that are essentially unchanging and immortal. What we perceive in this world through the flawed media of our senses are tangible, mortal and corrupted copies of this divine perfection that underlies nature.

The German philosopher, Arthur Schopenhauer, outlines it in *The World as Will and Representation*; it is worth transcribing it to include Plato's pertinent Allegory of the Cave found in the *Republic*.

The things of this world, perceived by our senses, have no true being at all; *they are always becoming, but they never are.* They have only a relative being; they are together only in and through their relation to one another; hence their whole existence can just as well be called a non-being. Consequently, they are likewise not objects of a real knowledge, for there can be such a knowledge only of what exists in and for itself, and always in the same way. On the contrary, they are only the object of an opinion or way of thinking, brought about by sensation. As long as we are confined to their perception, we are like persons sitting in a dark cave, and bound so fast that they cannot even turn their heads. They see nothing but the shadowy outlines of actual things that are led between them and a fire which burns behind them; and by the light of this fire these shadows appear on the wall in front of them. Even of themselves and of one another they see only the shadows on this wall. Their wisdom would consist in predicting the sequence of those shadows learned from experience. On the other hand, only the real archetype of those shadowy outlines, the eternal Ideas, the original forms of all things, can be described as truly existing, since they *always are but never become and never pass away*. *No plurality* belongs to them; for each by its nature is only one, since it is the archetype itself, of which all the particular, transitory things of the same kind and name are copies and shadows. Also *no coming into existence and no passing away* belong to them, for they are truly being or existing, but are never becoming or vanishing like their fleeting copies. Thus only of them can there be a knowledge in the proper sense, for the object of such a knowledge can be only that which always and in every respect (and hence in-itself) is, not that which is and then again is not, according as we look at it.

This, he stated, was Plato's teaching.

Like Kant after him, Plato is affirming that our perception is not of nature in its essential and noumenal actuality. However, for Plato, because the soul belongs to the world of Forms or Ideas, it is able to access that knowledge, at least in part: if we live a life of study undistracted by the sensuous world, we can intuit aspects of that perfect knowledge. The role of the virtuous individual is to work with the principle of Good in order to create within this world of material copies in a way that is as close as possible to the original, ideal and immortal Forms.

Phaedo is Plato's first text to explore the debate thoroughly, and the first of his dialogues that is now well known. Just before his execution, Socrates is laying out his argument for the immortality of the soul, stating that it is through this conviction that he is able to face death without fear. His first justification is simply the cyclicity of nature: life emerges out of death as wakefulness comes out of sleep, and if a soul is to return to live again, it must continue its existence between physical lives. Addressing how we appear to hold a knowledge within us that is deeper than our life's learning or our ability to experience, he explains that we bring with us into each new life the teachings gained from previous lives. True knowledge is knowledge of the Forms, Socrates declares: in the world of the senses, we perceive nothing to be exactly the same, yet we have an idea of equal length, equality in the abstract, or the Form of Equality, an intuition we bring into life without needing to learn it.

In what is known as the Affinity Argument, he then describes how the soul or intelligence is able to understand such abstract ideas, for both are invisible and incorporeal; the body, being material and visible, engages with sensible, tangible, visible matter. The visible, prone to decay, is mortal, but the invisible, the abstract, is unchanging, and thus immortal. In Socrates words: 'is not the conclusion of the whole matter this? - that the soul is in the very likeness of the divine, and immortal, and intelligible, and uniform, and indissoluble, and unchangeable; and the body is in the very likeness of the human, and mortal, and unintelligible, and multiform, and dissoluble, and changeable'. In words that resonate with later Christian doctrine, he expounds that it is only by focusing on wisdom, living a life of virtue, and releasing the bodily distractions, that a man can have the potential to find 'the knowledge of true being' and an afterlife of peace. The soul of the person still craving physical pleasures will be punished in Hades and impelled to return to live again and again.

In a characteristic trick of Platonic logic, he finally states that, because the soul is what creates or animates life, the soul is connected to the Form of Life, and therefore cannot be death: 'the soul will never admit the opposite of what she always brings'. The soul is therefore immortal.

In *Phaedo* the soul is effectively the rational mind within a dualist metaphysics, but in the *Republic*, Plato extends the idea. Debating with the writer's older brother, Glaucon, Socrates argues that, because an individual's thinking can be torn in different directions, there must be more than one aspect to the soul. Through his interlocutors, Plato presents the tripartite soul: at the lowest level is the appetitive soul, the many-headed beast, the well of desire, the part of us that hungers and lusts, feeling the drives and forces of nature. The spirited soul is the aspect that holds volition, the active part of the mind that carries out our willing; this is the inner lion that provides us with assertiveness and courage, feeling indignation and craving justice. In many ways, its role is to enact what has been decreed by the highest part of the soul, the rational mind or the intellect. In *Timaeus*, he located the three within the body, while affirming their essentially immaterial nature. The rational soul in the head was separated and protected by the neck from the spirited soul beneath, the diaphragm acting as a barrier between that and the appetitive soul in the belly.

Living through a period of great upheaval, the Peloponnesian War raging throughout his childhood and into his twenties leaving crisis in the Athenian empire and political upheaval all around him, Plato was driven to understand what made men behave as they do. In his utopian *Republic*, there were three classes of people - the labourers, the warriors and the rulers -

correlating with the three aspects of the human soul. Like the philosopher kings of his *Republic*, the rational mind needed to dominate the rest if order and justice were to be in evidence. Indeed in the dialogues of *Phaedrus*, his analogy is even clearer: the rational soul is a charioteer, his vehicle employing two winged horses, one as unruly, irrational and hungry as the appetitive soul, the other noble, righteous and obedient like the spirited soul.

Having studied under Plato, Aristotle moved in a slightly different direction. Uncomfortable with his mentor's outright dualism, he questioned how the Forms might be connected to the mortal universe without their own purity being diluted. Seeking to integrate body and soul once more, in *De Anima* he states that while the soul is the *form* of the body, the body is also the *matter* of the soul. Integral to nature, not transcendent of it, the soul is the 'first actuality of a natural organic body'. Whether or not the soul is separable from the body, or survives bodily death, he dismisses as not crucial to answer, suggesting that the form or shape of a candle may indeed in some respect survive the melting of its bodily wax. Far more important is the unity of body and soul, for here is the utility, where the *telos* is expressed, the inherent purpose of a creature's form which was fundamental to his thesis.

Providing scope for later Islamic and Christian scholars, and other dualists, however, and frustration to those who would prefer a consistently integrated metaphysics in his work, Aristotle retained the idea of an immortal *nous*. Concurring with the tripartite nature of the soul, he believed that the two lower aspects were mortal; they are found in plants and animals and humans, providing their focus, vibrancy and *telos*. The rational *nous*, however, is part of the divine perfection of nature, and thus immortal. This part of the soul is exclusively human.

Aristotle always sought the most beautiful and practical

answer. Determining that knowledge could be found empirically not just rationally, he explored the world with his hands and feet, writing a huge number of books on everything from geology to metaphysics, a fraction of which have survived. Indeed, in his *History of Animals*, he wrote, 'nature proceeds little by little from inanimate things to living creatures, in such a way that we are unable to determine the boundary line between them'. Here was his *scala naturae*: each creature given its place along the spectrum of life, according to the refinements of its soul and its associated potentiality.

Finding many creatures with negligible brains that were equally able to function according to their own needs, instead of the head he chose the heart as a more dignified, central, well-shaped and coherent place for the rational soul to reside. Blood vessels he suggested were the conduits of perception and intelligence. As the heart produces heat, which he understood to correlate to intelligence, he concluded that the role of the brain was simply to temper and cool, balancing the system.

Shortly after his death, however, taboos changed, allowing the dissection of human bodies, and in the fourth century BCE physicians discovered the ventricles of the brain. Here they found empty spaces within the physical form and, as the rational soul was non-material and therefore, it was assumed, required space not matter to be housed, it seemed obvious to many that the location of intelligence had been proved at last. Eighteen hundred years later, it was discovered that these ventricles are only empty when a person is dead: in the living, they are filled with cerebro-spinal fluid.

The *soul*: it would be useful to pause briefly on this journey through history, and consider the word within the context of our own language, for where I have referred to the soul it has been as a translation (the most common translation) from the old texts. Yet, the English word *soul* has no Latin or Greek origin. Coming through the Old English as *sawol*, the meaning of which is as vague as the modern *soul*, its roots before that remain quite obscure. Some suggest it is linked to the sea, both words rooting in the hypothetical Proto-Germanic in the form of *saiwaz. Whether this is about the waters of birth and the place of death, implying the mysteries on the edges of corporeal life, or the tides and currents that reflect our own emotions and drives, isn't clear. Despite this, its use is widespread, the word found in various closely connected forms throughout Northern European languages; in German it is *Seele*, in Dutch *ziel*, Norwegian *sjel*. The Finnish is *sielu* and so on.

Allowing the developing discourse of Western philosophy to provide a definition has been a somewhat oblique tack. My justification is that the ongoing understanding of the soul as the intangible and invisible aspect of our human form has allowed the views put forward by Plato and Aristotle to remain current for well over two thousand years. Furthermore, that they focused on the importance of the rational soul was not just a way of glorifying humanity in comparison with the rest of nature, but a genuine fascination as to the process of thought, and it is natural that those for whom thinking is life's purpose - the philosophers of our heritage, the scientists and other intellectual explorers - will emphasise that quality of our inner being over any other. Such a focus has remained for most, if not all, of the intervening years.

The *OED* defines *soul* as the principle of life, thought and action, as the vital, sensitive or rational part of a person, and is 'regarded as an entity distinct from the body'. Note the Platonic tripartite and dualistic understanding is still irrefutably evident. There are also entries that talk of deep emotional engagement, the moral centre of an individual, and the personification of a quality, among others. Like the key words defined in the previous chapter, there is so much breadth in the definitions given that a specific use of the word is impossible without articulating one's own parameters. Psychologist Carl Jung clarified the term by talking of the soul as the functioning personality, as distinct from the *psyche* which included the unconscious as well. My instinct has been to go in the other direction.

In *Living With Honour*, I spoke of the soul as the wholeness of a being. In the poetry of animistic language, it can be synonymous with what is called the *song*, which in turn comprises all that could be said to make up an entity at a particular moment: the entity's expression or exhalation, if you like, which places it within a context. As an initial definition, that is probably as far as I can go at this point. It must stand as sufficient. For, like a song, it is neither entirely material nor immaterial. What it *is* will become clearer in future chapters. I mention it here because that non-dualistic nature directs us to another term in urgent need of definition, and one that again holds unavoidable connotations of metaphysical dualism: *spirit*.

Spirits

Other than as the chapter title, this is a word I have barely used, and for good reason. It is another minefield of assumptions. Dictionary definitions start by describing *spirit* as the principle that animates within nature, but quickly move to ideas that seem much closer to or synonymous with the soul. For a moment, I shall set aside the latter and focus on the former.

From the Latin *spiritus*, the fuel within the word is its root in *spirare*, meaning to breathe, underlying which is the PIE **pei-*, meaning to blow. Its arrival into the English language came directly through Christian scripture: when the Bible was translated into Latin in the late fourth century, the Greek *pneuma* and the Hebrew *ruah*, both of which speak of breath and air, were rendered as *spiritus*. Over the centuries of developing translations from the Latin Vulgate into Old, Middle and modern English, *spiritus* became spirit, at first simply meaning that force which breathes, or creates life through breath or blowing. It is a lovely image to find within that ancient text, of spirit and Holy Spirit being life-giving forces, vitalising through the gift of breath; it is an image that makes more sense to me than the more conceptual Ghost with its implications of an invisible (ever-judging) omnipresence. Indeed, Anaximenes, the last of the three Milesian philosophers whose work survives from the sixth century BCE, and possibly writing at about the same time as Genesis was first scribed, declared the primal substance of nature to be *pneuma*: breath and condensation are what create and sustain. Air is everywhere, allowing motion, providing energy, momentum and continuity, allowing us language with which to communicate, inspire and create. John's Gospel, written six centuries later but reaching back through the teachings of the same tradition, beautifully expresses the wholeness of that breath as the animating story of creation or creativity, told and retold through generations: 'In the beginning was the word, and the word was with God, and the word was God'.

When we talk of what *animates*, we find another word wholly entangled within the issue. The Latin *animus* is usually translated as the mind or rational soul: to the Greeks the soul, even the rational soul, was a feminine noun, but for the Romans it was categorically masculine, a linguistic form that profoundly influenced thinkers for millennia, proclaiming an indivisible connection between rational thought and the nature of man. The *anima*, on the other hand, spoke, and continues to speak, of the feminine aspect of being, the emotional soul, even life itself, remaining as it does much closer to its kindred words, all rooting into the same PIE base, *ane-*, meaning to breathe or blow.

Muddied by those bent on discarding it as irrational, the word animism has struggled to find clarity amidst all these definitions. The *OED* explains it as the 'attribution of a living soul to plants, inanimate objects and natural phenomena'. Deconstructed to the simplest level, this could be construed as the belief that some parts of nature may still be considered alive, even if they do not breathe; but to make any sense of that, we'd need a definition for *life*. However, the more common interpretation leads the casual reader to question how something that is *not* animate could possibly have a soul, as the latter definitively necessitates the former.

Equally confused is the common lay definition that the animist believes there is 'spirit' in everything. On that basis, animism is often deposited into the box of dualistic faiths without further consideration. For such spirits are not thought of as breath; here *spirit* and *soul* are conflated and the spirit of a mountain, a waterfall, a tree, is imagined to be a discarnate soul, resident in - but separable from - the physical form. While the dualist of a monotheistic tradition may consider the immaterial soul to be found only in human beings, and occasionally more recently in other mammals, the animist is assumed to believe that same concept of soul present in a much wider selection of bodies within nature, perhaps every body. To someone looking at animist ideas from outside, such beliefs may seem close to the immature response of a little child still wondering at how the world around him might respond. Yet such a view of animism *is* childish; it equates to the notion of Yahweh as an old man on a cloud. It is religious metaphysics drawn with fat, colourful crayons. Such a cartoon begins with an entirely erroneous understanding of *spirit*.

Considering the *soul*, I suggested in Chapter One that my use of the word would become clearer through the course of the book, for it is as central as *mind* to this thesis. The word *spirit*, however, I would like to place here within the bounds of an initial definition, in order to ensure that it doesn't sabotage with unhelpful connotations. Taking the two aspects offered by dictionaries above, I put to one side the latter, and here I would like to discard it completely: where spirit becomes synonymous with soul, both seem to suggest the immaterial and ghostly figures of dualistic superstition.

Spirit, then, in as much as I shall use the term here, refers to that particular quality of energy that animates, quickens or vitalises. The exploration of whether that is a rational or feasible thesis and, if it were, how that may be, continues to be the aim of this book.

Theophrastus was a philosopher and naturalist who worked with Aristotle, sharing his profoundly empirical approach. Aristotle bequeathed his library and writings to the younger man, and much of their work sits comfortably together. Where he differed from the Philosopher - as Aristotle came to be known - was with regard to motion: Theophrastus didn't perceive an inherent *telos* within nature. Instead he felt that nature simply had its own way of working, each creature functioning unguided by any specific inner purpose, just moving upon the currents of nature's broad design. It was he who first put forward the idea of 'animal spirits' to describe and explain these flows of motion. That the term now provokes images of ghostly scampering mice is indicative of just how the word *spirit* has been portrayed in those fat crayons.

Spiritus animalis in Latin, the idea was taken up and developed by Galen, a Turkish physician living in Alexandria in the second century CE. Still working within the structure of the tripartite soul, Galen believed nutrients from digestion were taken up by the liver, which produced 'natural spirits', the blood conveying these to the heart which then transformed them into 'vital spirits'. These were carried up to the brain where, blended with the air that is inhaled, the 'animal spirits' were formed. Stored in those apparently empty ventricles of the brain, he proposed that it was by the movement of such spirits flowing through the hollow tubes of the nerves that we are able to generate motion and feel sensation.

Aristotle had questioned how Plato's Forms could be in sufficiently affective contact with the material world while not being tainted by it, and similar questions have been asked of dualists ever since: if the soul or spirits are made of an entirely different stuff than the substance of matter, how can one communicate with the other? It is the key philosophical crisis of dualism. Galen's answer was presented as this animating inner breath of *spiritus animalis*. Being part spirit and part matter, these spirits bridged the gap between the two.

From the perspective of the twenty first century, it seems obvious that his solution was no solution at all, but at the time it was sufficiently supportable to be taken on board: in fact, Galen's work became the liturgy of Western physiology for the following fifteen hundred years. In the mid sixteenth century, the Dutch physician Andreas Vesalius published his text *On the Fabric of the Human Body*, in which he made it clear that Galen's anatomical drawings were actually incorrect. With contemporary taboos disallowing him from dissecting the human body, it is no wonder Galen made mistakes; the majority of his work was based on the carcasses of pigs and monkeys. Vesalius, on the other hand, considered now to be the father of modern anatomical science, was free to explore the human corpse with his collection of knives. Branded a heretic for questioning Galen though, his findings were dismissed, and in the early sixteen hundreds René Descartes was still working within the parameters of Galen's thesis. Indeed, in a number of his books Descartes wrote with intricate detail and conviction about 'the subtle wind' that was the flow of animal spirits through the nerves of the body, adding a system of tiny fibres that ran from sensory organs to the brain and stimulated the release of these essential spirits.

One of the founders of the Royal Society, Thomas Willis expressed beautifully the cutting edge of ideas within the seventeenth century: man was 'double soul'd', one mortal, corporeal, physical, 'sensitive', the other immaterial. The sensitive soul in humans and other animals was made up of these fine spirits that flowed through the nervous system, travelling 'the king's highway', the spine, to 'the soul's palace' in the brain. Although he had managed to bring the sensitive soul very close to the physical, through his dissections he couldn't discern sufficient difference between an animal brain and a human brain, and concluded that, because animals have no rational soul, the rational soul had to be wholly immaterial, and thus invisible in every way. In *Two Discourses Concerning the Soul of Brutes* (1683), he described how the process must work: 'The rational soul, as it were presiding, beholds the images and impressions presented by the sensitive soul, as in a looking glass, and according to the conceptions and notions drawn from these, exercises the acts of reason, judgement and will'. In other words, the rational soul has no direct knowledge of the world, but instead took in what the sensitive soul presented it, processed the raw input into reasoned information, and then directed the sensitive soul as to how to respond.

It wasn't until the eighteenth century that animal spirits were discarded. Willis had described explosions in the body caused when the animal spirits encountered sulphur, and in 1729 Isaac Newton suggested that the nerves carry vibrations. However, it was in the final decade of that century that the Italian physician Luigi Galvani presented his thesis of the nerves carrying electrical currents. By the mid nineteenth century, electrical impulses removed animal spirits from modern physiology completely. Their expulsion was a crucial statement in our cultural understanding of nature, suggesting that nothing that cannot be perceived - no souls, spirit or spirits - may be needed in order to explain the mechanics of life. With each significant stride made by the scientific explorers of our heritage, the fastidiously empirical approach was asserted to be more valuable than the purely rational. Answers to the fundamental questions of nature deduced solely through rational methodology were no longer seen to be enough: some of those answers, even long held answers, had now been proved entirely wrong.

Dualism

Amidst the apparent chaos of nature, the desire for certainty is keen in the human soul, and for centuries the West had been given that certainty in the form of Christian doctrine. Teaching within the mediaeval scholastic tradition of the Church was about rigorously rationalist dialectics, where the purpose of debate is not to explore possible answers but to find the logically inevitable path that reaches the answer which is already assumed to be correct. This is, again, Plato's influence, for the technique is entirely in tune with his portrayal of Socrates. What it allowed for in Christianity was the rationally irrefutable belief in an all-powerful, supernatural and imperceptible deity.

Educated by Jesuits, Descartes spent his life fighting an internal and external battle between ingratiating himself with the scholastic establishment in order to gain their protection and support, and pushing at their beliefs which he perceived as out of date. At the beginning of his first book, *The World*, he questioned the certainty that still so firmly underlay their theological tradition: that what we perceive is what there is. The book wasn't published until after his death, for when he heard of Galileo's trail in Rome he feared for his own freedom and postponed its release, indefinitely.

Descartes wasn't the first to question the Church's certainty. In 1580, fifty years earlier, in *Apology for Raymond Sebond*, Michel de Montaigne presented serious doubts about what we know of the world. That our senses regularly deceive us is well known, but in dreams we are also fooled: consequently, we can never know if in fact we are asleep. Furthermore, because we can only seek to prove our thoughts by the process of thinking, thought can prove nothing. For Descartes, though, such philosophical wiles lacked gravity. His ability to think was indeed what allowed him to find the certainty he was seeking. His argument began in 1637, in *Discourse on Method*, where he stated that the only thing about which we can be certain is the *I* that thinks. It is here that he first puts forward the phrase that sums up his conclusion, '*Je pense donc je suis*': I think, therefore I am. As a declaration of existence, he was affirming not the reality of the world, nor even his own physicality or its ability to perceive, but simply that thinking proves the existence of a thinking thing which we may refer to as *I*.

His position is beautifully extended in his *Meditations on First Philosophy* written at the end of the decade and first published in 1641. Previously writing in French to maximise his audience, trusting 'that those who use only their pure natural reason will be better judges of my views that those who trust only ancient books', he made the decision to write his *Meditations* in Latin and dedicated it to the theologians of the Sorbonne. By now a semi-recluse living in rural northern Holland, he was looking for a response from those who still held power.

Like de Montaigne, he recognised that it is not possible to be sure we are awake, for even as we reach for surety, a dazed feeling comes over us. Further, because we can't be sure of what we perceive, he questioned the validity of the empirical sciences - astronomy, physics, medicine - suggesting that there can only be certainty in arithmetic, geometry and other areas that don't depend on whether 'they really exist in nature or not'. This confirmed his certainty that he himself existed, as a thinking being. Something 'which I thought I was seeing with my eyes is in fact grasped solely by the faculty of judgement which is in the mind', he wrote, and the 'idea I have of the human mind, in so far as it is a thinking thing, which is not extended in length, breadth or height and has no other bodily characteristics, is much more distinct than the idea of any corporeal thing'.

Accepting God had created the world 'to correspond exactly with my understanding of it', he reasoned for the clear difference between body and mind: 'on the one hand, I have a clear and distinct idea of myself, in so far as I am simply a thinking, non-extended thing; and on the other hand I have a distinct idea of body, in so far as this is simply an extended, non-thinking thing. And accordingly, it is certain that I am really distinct from my body, and can exist without it'. His pronouncement is a celebration of the thinking *I*.

In many ways, Descartes was reworking the teachings of his Jesuit education. In *Nichomachean Ethics*, Aristotle had written, 'to perceive that we are perceiving or thinking is to perceive that we are in existence'. Seven centuries later, and still twelve hundred years before Descartes, Augustine of Hippo had walked through a parallel flow of questions and conclusions. Writing at the end of the fourth century in what is now Algeria, in his exquisitely devotional and self-reflective book, *Confessions*, he wrote that 'nothing can be more present to the mind than the mind itself': one can only know about one's own thinking with certainty, and because such knowledge doesn't confirm our physicality, our thinking self must be incorporeal. Without access to Aristotle's works, and only a limited amount of Plato, Augustine's ideas appear to have been original; he credited the Neoplatonists of the previous century for inspiring him to explore so deeply and sincerely.

Through the millennium that followed Augustine, it was in the Islamic world that learning survived and thrived. Through the tumultuous upheavals of the collapsing Roman then Byzantine empires, as most of Europe struggled under the oppression of wars, poverty and Christianity, the extraordinary ninth century caliph in Baghdad, al-MāAmūn ibn Harūn, demanded that every text be gathered from the ancient imperial libraries that wavered on the brink of disappearing. Commissioning the texts to be translated into Arabic, his gift of reclamation included the works of Aristotle, Plato, Ptolemy, Euclid, Galen, Hippocrates, Archimedes and more, all of which could have been lost forever. As the caliphates flourished, opening up the world with trade routes that stretched from

China to Spain, this rediscovered knowledge made Arabic the language of civilisation, and so it remained for the next six hundred years. While a wealthy European monastery may have proudly possessed a few dozen texts on Christianity in Latin, in libraries throughout the Arab world there were tens of thousands of books on philosophy, theology, science and mathematics, poetry, history, together with stories, folktales and songs.

Around the turn of the first millennium, the extraordinary Persian philosopher and physician Ibn Sīnā - his name later Latinised as Avicenna - would probably not have read Augustine's Latin. In his treatise incorporated into a Latin translation as *De Anima*, he presented the idea of the 'flying man': suspended in mid air, he wrote, although an individual would have no sensation of his physicality, he would nonetheless have an experience of himself as existent simply because he was thinking. Again this was seen as proof for the non-corporeality of the soul as distinct from the material world. Needless to say, his argument, like others in the same vein, provoked the question: what is the *I* that is thinking?

The life of Thomas Aquinas is also interesting at this juncture. A Dominican monk in thirteenth century Italy, he was one of the first generations of a Europe in touch with a wider world. The first universities were being established and a radicalism was rising as a result, not least within his own monastic order, inspired by the knowledge evident within the Islamic and Arabic world. In response to the first Latin translations of Aristotle the Church had quickly banned them, but Aquinas wondered if these ancient Pagan texts were in fact not a better basis for understanding the world than the Bible. As al-Kindī had done three centuries earlier for Islam, Aquinas set about exploring just how Aristotle could be made compatible with Christianity.

Discarding Aristotle's idea of natural *telos* so as to allow God alone to bestow purpose, Aquinas affirmed that only the immortal soul was capable of thought. However, as Aristotle had earlier proposed, it was the unity of body (matter) and soul (form) that created the functional intellect: the discarnate soul was no longer a person. Platonic Christianity had presented man as a spiritual being, but to Aristotle he was a natural being. Plato's focus has been an abstract world of reason allowing a Christian focus on heaven, but Aristotle had written of a universe that could be empirically explored. With a new era encouraging study of the material world, Aquinas' genius was the bringing together of faith and reason within the experience of living, seamlessly interweaving them, and so allowing for a fully reasoned dualism in a more Aristotelian and integrated world.

I began this chapter by suggesting that the empirical evidence is rather in favour of dualism: dualism seems to make *sense*, for our experience of being tends naturally to feel as a distinct inner observer. Over millennia, countless thinkers have added to that empirical bias, putting forward rational proofs in support of the thesis.

Yet, as I mentioned above, the key problem with dualism has always been the issue of interaction. Indeed, some thinkers have declared this to be the crucial factor within the mind-body debate. As the philosopher Susan Blackmore put it recently: 'The key (foundational) question with consciousness is the interface between mental and physical worlds. If you ignore this, you are not dealing with consciousness as a philosophical issue'.

The majority of philosophers who have referred to themselves as dualists in the past century or so are proponents of *property* dualism. Often called emergent materialists, their position begins with the belief that there is only matter in the universe, which develops in different ways to produce physical and mental realities. As a monist metaphysical view, their conviction sidesteps the problem of interaction. The gist of the current chapter, however, has been the purer form, still found within Christian and other theologies: *substance* dualism. The physical matter of nature being constituted of an entirely different stuff from that which makes up the mind or soul, the question remains as to how one can affect the other.

Determined to find a simple, mechanical answer, Descartes identified the pineal gland as the medium, clarifying why in a letter written in December 1640 (AT III:264, CSMK 162). Using calves' brains and Galen's erroneous drawings, he was mistaken about its location in the human brain, but declared that as 'the only solid part in the whole brain which is single' it would have the ability to bring together the information coming in from two eyes and two ears. As such, he concluded, 'it must necessarily be the seat of the common sense, i.e., of thought, and consequently of the soul; for one cannot be separated from the other. The only alternative is to say that the soul is not joined immediately to any solid part of the body, but only to the animal spirits which are in its concavities', a notion which he thought quite absurd. Having struck up a correspondence with him after reading his *Meditations*, Princess Elizabeth of Bohemia asked Descartes to explain further, believing he had not in fact answered the critical incompatibility; in his response he suggested that the interaction is more like gravity moving matter, than mind moving matter - while at the same time admitting that science had as little understanding of gravity. The princess considered his answer to be most unsatisfactory.

Later in the century, the Viscountess Anne Conway was exploring the same issues. One of the few female philosophers of our heritage, she lived her life in crippling pain and, when no medical treatment could be found to ease her condition, she sought answers through faith and philosophy instead. If the soul were separable from the body, why could she not disconnect herself from the excruciating experience of its physicality, and why did that pain make her feel such despair? Writing of the soul, she asked, 'If, when united to the body it has no corporeality or bodily nature, why is it wounded or grieved when body is wounded, whose nature is so different?'

The answer she came to was that the absolute distinction between body and soul was mistaken. There was no need to find that elusive point of connection, for matter was 'condensed spirit' and spirit was 'subtle volatile body'. In this way spirit became a substance as divisible as matter, and equally matter was now varyingly penetrable. In her only book, *The Principles of the most Ancient and Modern Philosophy*, published after her death, she spoke of three 'species' of being along that spectrum. God was immutable, infinite, singular, alive, constant and pure; creation and all its creatures were crafted of living particles, mutable and in constant change; between the two were the 'middle spirits', the mediators, the Christ. In an era and culture where dualism saturated thought, her ideas were fascinating, suggesting as they did a monism that might be said to be closer to idealism than anything else.

Idealism

Metaphysical monism is the belief that there is only one substance out of which everything is crafted. In Chapter Three, we'll look at the monism that is materialism or physicalism, the belief that there is only matter. Gently nudged by the viscountess, however, I shall end this chapter with a little idealism.

Bearing similar connotations, the Greek ιδέα can be translated as the form or appearance of something, while the Latin *idea* means a figure or symbol. Both are rooted in the PIE as *weid-*, to see. In Samuel Johnson's dictionary of 1755, an idea is defined as 'something of which an image can be formed in the mind', and given its common usage now it is easy to forget just how fundamental the visual is to the word. Understanding idealism philosophically, the roots of idea are important: simply, it is the conviction that nature does not comprise any matter at all, but is constituted solely of the stuff of mind. We must then recall that the mind is comprised of all that allows us to comprehend the world we perceive.

So far we have encountered a good number of what may be called epistemological idealists, whose assertion is that we can be certain of nothing but ideas: our subjective experience of mental processes or thought. In 1739 David Hume declared that the question was not whether matter exists, but 'what causes induce us to believe in the existence of body'. Because our sense of matter is entirely based upon perception, 'all knowledge degenerates into probability'. That we are able to function, he proposed, is simply because we are naturally programmed to believe in the actuality of the world in which we live. If we were not, we would not survive.

Kant termed his own metaphysics transcendental idealism. In his *Critique of Pure Reason*, he stated that without 'the thinking subject, the whole material world must at once vanish because it is nothing but a phenomenal appearance in the sensibility of ourselves as a subject'. Like Hume, though, he wasn't asserting that the universe had no independent existence, simply that our perception of it was wholly subjective and formed by our understanding.

In many ways, Georg Hegel presented the strongest form of pure idealism within the Western philosophical tradition. A man whose work I have found desperately hard to read, his words often as dry and arrogant as a desert wind, his systematic approach is nonetheless fascinating in its meticulous comprehensiveness. His thesis seems founded on the idealist assertion that nature must be rational if it is to be viable, and must therefore be essentially immaterial. Inspired by the sixteenth century thinker Giordano Bruno, he spoke of its natural logic as dialectic, explaining and extending Bruno's systematic process: a *thesis* immediately suggests its *antithesis*, this conflict then dissolving into a higher *synthesis*. He believed this process of intrinsic development to be in operation from the smallest discrete entity to the totality of the whole, communicating in its every respect the flawlessly rational constitution of reality.

He spoke of the *Geist*, a word which frustratingly has no true equivalent in English; it is rendered as either mind or spirit depending on the translator. *Geist* flows like a river, with individual lives like eddies and whirlpools giving the appearance of coalescing into form, yet merely crafting momentary patterns that soon return to the flow. In terms of the dialectic, he described the world as no more than the contents of an individual's subjective perception, that reality being regularly shaken with doubts as to the reality of the objects that are perceived; the synthesis that comes, that is needed for viability, is the broad awareness the individual then feels of being an integral part of the common whole. Being opposes Nothing, yet is ever Becoming: the world soul perpetually in a state of unfurling. At the purest level, Idea, the abstraction of thought, is opposed by Nature, the world beyond understanding, yet what ultimately exists is Spirit, and in the greatest sense, the self-knowing, self-actualising totality of the Absolute, or God. Indeed, as such, we are all simply a part of the mind of God. It's an extraordinary, quite glorious vision and impeccably reasoned; perhaps it is no wonder he is felt to be somewhat inaccessible as a result.

Influenced by Kant and/or Hegel, idealism in Europe has most often been within the German philosophical tradition, British empiricism being for the most part too grounded to allow for such thinking. Notable exceptions were a good number of the Romantic poets and thinkers such as Samuel Taylor Coleridge who, towards the end of the eighteenth century, reacting to changes incited by the Industrial Revolution, was heavily influenced by the German idealists. I shall speak more of them in a later chapter.

Living earlier in that century, George Berkeley, an Anglican bishop in Ireland, is considered to be another pure idealist. An *immaterialist* in his own words, he had written his key texts by the time he reached his mid twenties, waging a campaign against the increasing focus on matter which he felt was distracting from the sovereignty of God. More accurately, what he objected to was the assumed actuality of mind-independent matter, in other words, material things that would exist even if nobody were there to see them. It's a game we might play in our teens, regressing in some state of intoxication to flickering memories of the infant's reality, where nothing exists beyond that which makes up the immediate self. I don't dismiss Berkeley's arguments, for they are beautifully presented in a logic that is hard to refute, but they are also wonderfully counter-intuitive.

Questioning what it means to say that something exists, he answered with the now familiar *'esse est percipi'*: to be is to be perceived. Affirming that the soul (he tends to use the word *spirit*) must exist in order to be the subject of perception, he stated, 'if there were external bodies, it is impossible that we should ever come to know it'. Like others, he recognised that our only access to knowledge is 'by sense or reason', and as such we cannot think of an object without thinking. According to Bertrand Russell, Berkeley 'thinks he is proving that all reality is mental; what he is proving is that we perceive qualities, not things, and that quality is relative to the percipient'; it is possible to critique his position, but there is no doubt that his intention was idealist. He not only saw no reason why the material world should exist, he felt it compromised the authority of religion to do so. His faith was both his motivation and the solution he put forward to counter his detractors: if there were no matter to trigger sensation, ideas must be caused by another idea, spirit or mind. Given the exquisitely complex nature of our mental experience, he resolved that the cause could only be God, the most powerful, wise and benevolent spirit.

Another problem presented by idealism is how two individuals might have a shared reality; without jointly perceiving an external material object, how can two people both have the same idea of, for example, a tree standing before them?

Berkeley's response was that God provides us with those ideas, but he went further, explaining that the problem is not only for the idealist to answer. Materialists, he said, 'own themselves unable to comprehend in what manner body can act upon spirit, or how it is possible it should imprint any idea in the mind. Hence it is evident the production of ideas or sensations in our minds, can be no reason why we should suppose matter or corporeal substances, since that is acknowledged to remain equally inexplicable with, or without this supposition'. In other words, in the early seventeen hundreds thinkers could not explain how consciousness works; nor can they now.

The experience of being alive as a human being is certainly a puzzle. The sensation of being an individual observing the external world, contemplating our physicality and mental processes, very easily gives rise to an instinctive dualism, which is further enriched by the sense proffered by the *I* that we are at the centre of our world, and to some extent holding the reins of our reality. It is also rationally sound to recognise that this experience of the *I*, or our thinking about the *I*, is perhaps the only certainty we can have in a world that is offered us through the veils of our perception. Furthermore, imagining this *I* to be fundamentally different can be instinctive, particularly in a world where life seems harsh and transient. Indeed, in such a difficult reality, it is reasonable to wonder whether all there might be is the realm of thinking, imagining, and matter is no more than an illusion.

Such metaphysics of the soul have inherent problems, however, problems that have not as yet been resolved. In the next chapter, we will explore another possibility: that the universe is made of nothing, in fact, but matter.

Chapter Three

Matter

From the reader anxious for an exposition of animism, I ask for a little more patience. My route may seem unnecessarily protracted and oblique but, as I have earlier explained, it is for good reason. The scale of misunderstandings prevalent about modern animism, and the depth of prejudice that allows such misunderstandings to be held with such conviction, requires me to approach the subject from what may at first seem an overly indirect tack. Yet, as I have shown, definition is so often at risk of infinite regress, whereby the language used to define one word is littered with words that themselves need to be defined if the first definition is not to be left devoid of meaning, or distorted by some foundational yet unexposed assumption. My strategy has been, therefore, to address at the outset the whole notion of the ethereal spirit or soul: terms that carry all varieties of subjective opinion, from childhood conditioning and instinct to adult reasoning.

However, before I suggest just where those words sit with philosophical cogency in an animistic worldview, I must address the other side of the argument presented in any debate about the mind-body question: matter must be placed upon the scales, that we might weigh it in reference to mind, spirit or soul. To some, there will seem an immediate and instinctive imbalance. The material world is assumed to be a heavy, solid and definitively measurable concern, while the other is insubstantial, sometimes to the point of irrelevance. Yet I hope in my words so far I have at least provoked a line of thought that can be extended here: if the veil of perception denies us any certain knowledge about the apparently tangible world, what do we mean by matter? Can we assign to the word a definition any more objective than we have to the word *real*, or must we acknowledge its nature as wholly subjective?

Empirically our experience of life provides us not only with the sense of a physical world, but with a simple method of learning about our environment that further confirms and compounds that intuition. In other words, it isn't necessary for us to use our human ability to reason consciously in order to hold to a reality of the physical world. Indeed, it is only by implementing an intricate reasoning that we reach a point in scientific exploration where the common sense view of matter is turned upside down. Copernicus' idea that the earth was not actually stationary was, no doubt, a ludicrous suggestion to folk of his time, and now we are informed with all seriousness that this planet is spinning at just over a thousand miles an hour, whilst haring through space at over a thousand miles a minute, ideas that make no *sense* to us whatsoever. There is much scope in Hume's suggestion that we only believe the world to be as solid, coherent and continuous as we perceive it to be because our human nature programmes us to do so. Yet, can we dismiss the material world as no more than a belief generated by our own minds, in part perhaps even if not in its entirety? If rational thinking confirms that we can be sure of nothing but that we are thinking, the question is not only *what* is matter, but *does* it matter?

The Illusion
Matter matters because it is problematic.

It is all too easy to become entangled in the physical clutter of life. Indeed, our Western culture is now dependent upon the majority of its population believing that they are ever in need of yet more of it. As human beings, our basic requirements are actually very few: food and shelter, the simple stimulus of the natural world and a little company are enough. Such ideas are presented by most spiritual and religious traditions, counselling us not to seek happiness in the stuff of matter. The key word is often desire: there may be a recognition that wanting is inherent within nature, but our human ability to consider consciously is said then to bring with it the responsibility to ensure that there is sustainability, and so to limit our desires to within the bounds of ethical action. Further, many traditions are equally or more concerned with the attainment of an inner peace, pointing out that the desire to *have* is accompanied by the suffering evoked by the *not* having. The aim is thus to overcome the longing to be led by our hunger, and especially so when it meanders from need into the realms of desire.

Underlying such teachings is often the understanding that the world we perceive is no more than an illusion anyway. The forces of life incite a desire, yet when that ache is sated it doesn't take long before another craving kicks in: not only is satisfaction fleeting, but nature's perpetual state of change makes every interaction momentary and insubstantial. Mystical traditions go further, stepping with calm determination from the psychological into metaphysics: as Kant too explained, any sense that we have of a soul or self is also part of the phenomenal world, the world *as we see it*, and therefore must be placed into the same category. The Sanskrit word *māyā*, used in many Eastern traditions, has no translation as sweet in English: a beautifully pertinent negation, it refers to the phenomenon of life while, in two short syllables, simultaneously marks it through as an illusion.

Beyond is the noumenal, the essence or source of the phenomenal world, what Kant called *das Ding an Sich*, the thing in itself: nature as it actually is. Some assert that, trapped within the bubble of our perception, we can have no knowledge of that. Others speak of deep introspection allowing us brief but significant glimpses: Schopenhauer wrote, 'Here, therefore, alone lies the datum capable of becoming the key to everything else, or, as I have said, the only narrow gateway to truth'. Though writing before the sacred texts of Eastern philosophies became available in his native Germany, there are many similarities between Schopenhauer's thought and the teachings of Hinduism and Buddhism. Reflecting the singularity of Brahman, he explained how Kant's *noumenon* could only be a oneness: outside time and space, it can have no past or future, so must lie beyond any process of change. Formless, it can hold no distinction between subject and object, so can be neither knower nor known. If the actuality of nature, the universe, were such a unified whole, our perceived world must indeed be entirely illusory.

Considering the issue with such a rationality, although our perception presents us with countless separate things, the fundamental monism is evident. Even if we are unable to know more of this metaphysical truth, the oneness can guide us in terms of ethical behaviour and the search for peace, allowing a suggestion of coherence from which can emerge a sense of integration within the human and nonhuman ecology of an environment. As Schopenhauer says, concurring with many Eastern and mystical spiritual traditions: if in essence we are all one, then when an individual is wounded, deep within we all feel the pain.

Yet, though reasoning may help to guide the ethics of our actions, it may not satisfy the yearning to understand what nature actually is. On a profound and intuitive level, through deep meditative practice or the inner exploration of intro-spection, we may reach visions that support the fundamental illusion of matter - but *empirically speaking*, the evidence is not sufficient. When it comes to our survival instinct, it is the physical world that provokes us to respond, however illusory the philosophers and priests declare it to be.

Mechanism

However we may question the values and tenability of our modern world, we cannot deny how the physical realities of our lives have changed in comparison with those of our ancestors. It is our ability to manipulate the tangible stuff of matter that has been the foundation of that material development, and particularly so over the past four centuries of radical scientific and technological change. As such, matter matters.

The belief that we can understand the physical world is not only instinctive but *useful*. Greek philosophers may have been high intellects, but the Roman Empire was a practical force, underpinned by the thoroughly grounded perspectives that allowed it to accumulate so much material wealth. In first century Hispania, the rhetorician Quintilian wrote, 'We may regard as certainties first those things which we perceive by the senses, things for instance that we hear or see'. This was the position taken up by the Christian scholastics, a canon disseminated through Europe's illiterate populations, bound up with the idea that God has provided us with truthful senses. Where the authorities require the people to engage with the practicalities of life, there is no benefit in supporting doubt: the world is what you see it to be, by the grace of God, and no more.

The emergence of European philosophy from the broad embrace of mediaeval scholasticism seems, in hindsight, unhurried. The thinkers of the Renaissance tended still to perceive the natural world as a complete entity created by God, ensouled by God, and teeming with spirits. Seeking ways to read the subtleties of nature's patterns, their aim was to understand the harmony of divine reason, and so to uncover the design used by God in its creation. Many employed alchemy, astrology, Cabbala, high magic and other mystical systems: the equivalent of applied physics, these were the most exacting tools available, guiding the explorer to dissect the forces and elements of nature in his quest for the source of life. Some thinkers remained within the scholastic tradition, asserting the primacy of their religious convictions, but others found themselves on the outside. A Dominican friar inspired by pre-Socratic writers, newly available Arabic teachings and translations, Neoplatonism and

Hermeticism, Giordano Bruno believed that Christianity had cast a veil over the true knowledge taught by the ancient philosophers, leading humanity away from the integrated fabric of God's creation to a cult of the dead. In the words of Bruno scholar Hilary Gatti, he described a 'new infinite universe, composed of a single homogeneous substance that is both material and spiritual and that links all things within it into a harmonious whole, that will save a new era from despair'. In Copernicus' new vision of planets circling in perfect harmony, the earth fully incorporated within that motion, Bruno saw the possibility of a glorious return to an understanding that perceived and revered the living natural world. After a long and horrendous trial, in 1600 in a market square in Rome, he was burned at the stake.

At a time when so little of nature had been probed, it is easy to imagine how much would have felt incomprehensible, unpredictable, supernatural, magical. Changing attitudes towards witchcraft are revealing. In 1486, when the scientific knowledge of the Arab world was still only touching the edges of Christian Europe, Pope Innocent VIII commissioned the *Malleus Maleficarum* as an account of contemporary witchcraft: guided by the devil, sorcerers were able to learn the inner workings of nature, to bend its rules and, collaborating with spirits and demons, manifest changes in ways others were unable to do. In 1542 in England Henry VIII passed the first law against 'conjurations, enchantments and witchcraft'. A few years later, the Council of Trent declared that only religious elders could interpret the Bible, and as the scriptures confirmed such practices were possible, to doubt it was blasphemous. When those laws were brought under the jurisdiction of the common courts in 1604, the power of judgement was removed from the Church in an attempt to offer a fairer hearing to those accused; the height of the Witch Trials took place between 1580 and 1650.

Alongside this fear and brutality, slowly European thinkers were beginning to consider the world in new ways. Genuine in their beliefs or scared to step across the line, many continued upon the same paths as their predecessors, celebrating God's reason within their mathematical and early scientific findings. Soon, however, such works were allowing insights into nature that provoked increasing discomfort for those who demanded truth should remain in the hands of the Church: in 1559 Pope Paul IV published the *Index Librorum Prohibitorum*, and many of the books emerging in this first flush of science were listed in it. Beliefs about knowledge were now coming from three different directions - the scholastic Aristotelianism of the Church, the alchemical magic of both high intellectuals and frauds, and the new visions of the emerging scientists - and the tension mounted.

Like so many of his contemporaries, the physician Robert Fludd, working at the turn of the seventeenth century, stood doggedly within the thick of this tussle. Fludd was keen to differentiate himself from the scientists, saying, 'it is for the vulgar mathematicians to concern themselves with quantitative shadows; the alchemists and Hermetic philosophers, however, comprehend the true core of the natural bodies'. William Gilbert, whose *De Magnete* was published in 1600, leaned the other way. Writing of how matter is drawn to matter, not through Aristotelian teleology nor divine decree, but by the embrace of nature's inherent soul, he described how everything has 'a propensity towards the body, towards a common source, towards the mother where they were begotten, towards their origin, in which all these parts will be united and preserved and in which they all remain at rest, safe from every peril'. Celebrating the vibrant order of a world alive with spirits, he was keen not to be seen as a magician, and avoided words associated with alchemy such as *attraction* and *revulsion*. Yet when Gilbert wrote that 'the moon causes the movement of the waters and the tides of the ocean', another great contributor to the new worldview, Galileo, ridiculed him for suggesting something so obviously supernatural.

Both commenting upon and adding to these crucial narratives, around 1610 Shakespeare was presenting *The Tempest*, pertinently expressing these contemporary conflicts between magic, science and those who held the power of governance. At first he appears to contrast Prospero with Sycorax in favour of the former, presenting him as a rational magician while she is a demonic sorceress, a witch, but by the end of the play the two seem less dissimilar; the morality of intrusive and manipulative magic is questioned and Prospero renounces his craft.

Ecclesiastical dominion over truth was being increasingly shaken. Francis Bacon, another contemporary of Shakespeare, actively revolted against the Aristotelianism that was still so embedded in attitudes of the era and the Church, including once again the Philosopher's principle of teleology. Aristotle, he declared, was a dictator. Purpose, both inherent and consciously directed, was the prerogative of mankind; the natural world was entirely soulless, but with hard work man could learn how to 'conquer and subdue her, to shake her to her foundations'. He encouraged his associates to 'bind her to your service and make her your slave'. The feminine association is important, for nature, like woman, was seen as existent entirely for the benefit of the rational, white, human male. Indeed, the question was still debated as to whether a woman had a (rational) soul. Bacon measured truth by power in action: 'For truth is rather revealed and established by the evidence of works rather than by disputation, or even sense'. As the writer Roy Porter said in *Flesh in the Age of Reason*, this new philosophy of science and mechanics sought to replace the scholastic view 'with a fruitful utilitarian philosophy of works not words'. The intuitive and empirical tangibility of matter was indeed *useful*.

Pure rationalism was not the way forward.

In the early to mid sixteen hundreds, Descartes had explained how metaphysics needed to be based on reason, but it was the practical application of this belief that had the most profound impact. Slamming in the nails with his systematic rational methodology, Descartes created a philosophical structure that became the foundation of a new mechanistic worldview which, over the coming centuries, was to oust both the ecclesiastical and alchemical.

Aristotle's view of the physical had clearly been relative: the interplay of matter and form happened within a broad context, with inherent, perpetual and mutual influences, the intrinsic purpose of each entity emerging as a directive force, that purpose finding fulfilment as a result of its contextual whole. Descartes, however, freely discarding this two thousand year old doctrine of *telos*, perceived matter very differently. Matter was simply mechanics. With no inner drive, nature was inert, always requiring an external force if it were to move and, as part of the universal mechanism crafted by God, the matter of nature was in a constant state of collisions which provoked such movement. With no inner purpose, the external world offered an entity no purpose either, other than the use made of it by the actions of rational man.

Nature, matter, body, as machine, required no soul, for its mechanics alone were sufficient to keep the system in operation. In *The World*, Descartes explained that, if the rational soul were remembered to be of a non-material substance and thus distinctly separate, when assessing the body 'it is not necessary to conceive of any vegetative or sensitive soul, or any other principle of movement or life, other than its blood and its spirits which are agitated by the heat of the fire that burns continuously in the heart'. In his *Treatise on Man*, he further wrote, 'I should like you to consider that these functions (including passion, memory, and imagination) follow from the mere arrangement of the machine's organs every bit as naturally as the movements of a clock or other automaton follow from the arrangement of its counter-weights and wheels'.

As analogies in the late twentieth century were all about computers, the image of our culture now being the internet's web of connectability, it is worth remembering that in Descartes' era the development of reliable mechanisms was the very cutting edge of technology. The Arab caliphates had of course been playing with automata from as early as the ninth century, but mechanical toys and tools were still rather a novelty in northern Europe; the dependable clock was deemed the true goal of achievement, not least for its value in navigation as parties of royally-commissioned pirates set off to explore lands beyond the ocean's horizon. To speak of matter as machine was to infer its extraordinary precision, and thus the ingenuity of God the creator, and indeed the intellectual capacity of those scientists who were at last stumbling upon the intricacies of that holy design.

The comprehensive efficacy of Descartes' thesis was based upon the principal distinction between body and soul. Once the God-given substance of thought had been removed, what was left was empty. The spirits of the wildwood, the personality of a dog or horse, the heavy presence of a thunder storm, the striving growth of the barley, the irrational and thoughtless urgency of human love-making, all were no more than the clunking of levers and gears in nature's various array of mindless machines.

In his final book, *The Passions of the Soul*, he wrote, 'anything we experience as being in us, and which we see can also exist in wholly inanimate bodies, must be attributed only to our body. On the other hand, anything in us which we cannot conceive in any way as capable of belonging to a body must be attributed to our soul. Thus, because we have no conception of the body as thinking in any way at all, we have reason to believe that every kind of thought present in us belongs to the soul'. In other words, effectively he removed from the notion of matter everything other than that which was 'extended', or had form and took up space. Mechanisms, having no interiority, no perception, no sensation, had no free will, but were instead entirely subject to the pushing and pulling of their mechanised systems. As Roy Porter wrote, 'In a single intrepid stroke of thought, Descartes had disinherited almost the whole of Creation – all, that is, except the human mind – of the attributes of life, soul and purpose, which had infused it since the speculations of Pythagoras and Plato, Aristotle and Galen'.

A century later, Isaac Newton was standing at the centre of that ongoing wrangle between magic, science and religion. Dismissed as a magician by mechanists of his time, he seems to have been a man willing to delve, or indeed dive deep, into any possible well of understanding, seeking above all the 'seeds' or forces that were the active principles of creation. At a time when science was primarily focused upon the mysteries of motion, he explored the new mathematics, presenting the world with a battery of physical equations that seemed only to confirm Descartes' vision. A dedicated Christian, however, he worried that a mechanistic view of matter was opening a door to atheism, and with good reason, 'because we have an absolute idea of it without any relationship to God'. We may now recognise how much his work gave to scientific development, but he did not find what he himself was searching for; dedicating the latter part of his life to the intricate experiments of alchemical exploration, he continued seeking those 'seeds' of life that would guide him closer to the mind of God.

Perhaps the world could and would be explained entirely by a series of scientific laws: many were beginning to believe that possible. In 1682, the French king Louis XIV passed a Royal Decree saying that witchcraft was based on no more than delusion: witches and conjurors could be punished as charlatans and deceivers, but not sorcerers. The laws against witchcraft were repealed in England half a century later; indeed, according to Brian Easlea in *Witch Hunting, Magic and the New Philosophy*, 'As if to enable future historians to be able to locate within a ten year period the edge of one era and the beginning of a new one, the English government introduced the death penalty for frame-breaking in 1726 and abolished the crime of witchcraft from the statute books in 1736'. The trouble was no longer from demons and nature spirits, and those who apparently commanded them, but from the impoverished in a land that needed a compliant workforce. Slowly, both the religious and the rational were ceding to the authority of empirical science, where logical deductions were being made from repeated experimentation and observation, the new machine of industry growing all the while. Indeed, Bertrand Russell, writing of Spinoza, described his purely rational approach as 'incompatible with modern logic and scientific method'; in a world that was increasingly demanding progress, 'facts have to be discovered by observation, not by reasoning'. Presenting its results as *objective*, and thus dismissing Kant completely, science proudly and confidently declared that it had now found the actuality beneath subjective perception, what the twentieth century philosopher Thomas Nagel called the elusive 'view from nowhere'.

Certainly, science had found a way of measuring what it could capture of nature, but had it done more? To say so was, and still is, a matter of belief.

Materialism

Despite being mechanists and scientists, the credo of Descartes and most of his contemporaries was still dualism. As they laid out their new philosophy of matter, all the while they affirmed that the human mind or rational soul was constituted of a very different stuff. It *had* to be, after all. Descartes knew full well that if he were to consider the mind as physical, as a mechanical apparatus, there would be no reasoning upon which to maintain the belief that human beings were different from the rest of nature, from the 'brutes' grazing in the pasture. All across Europe, brilliant men were hanging by their thumbs in the Inquisition's dungeons for making suggestions that were less contentious.

Some philosophers perceive doubts within Descartes' writings, and question whether it was fear that stopped him from expressing them. His friend and student, Henricus Regius, presented ideas that were clearly sourced within Descartes' thinking but, taking a step further, he found himself in the dilemma of his era, between Cartesian mechanism and Christian scripture. In *Physical Foundations* he described the soul as 'organic as long as it exists in the body' and was joined to the body 'in a single substance', yet as if backtracking then affirmed it to be 'really distinct from the body and is separable from it in reality'. Desmond Clarke narrates the debate between the two, suggesting that 'Regius was not disagreeing with Descartes but articulating a view that resulted from Descartes' own work', a view that Descartes himself was too scared to point out. Known to be an inveterate liar, and terrified of being connected with the book, Descartes broke off all relations with his old friend.

Few were willing to risk upsetting the Church. One of the exceptions was the truculent English radical, Thomas Hobbes. In common with most of his seventeenth century contemporaries, his thinking was influenced by the atrocities of the Thirty Years War in Europe, and the English Civil War with its ensuing shift from incompetent monarchist decadence to puritanical republican tyranny. That these conflicts were so unnecessary, provoked by the religious and monetary demands of the governing elite, made their tragedy even worse; tearing apart ordinary communities and families, destroying ancient loyalties, battles left starvation and madness in their wake. Wholly sickened by the barbarity around him, Hobbes laboured to understand the clumsy mess of human nature and its bloody civilisation.

Into his forties when he first read Euclid, its exquisitely

rational clarity offered him the tone he had long been searching for. As Spinoza was doing at around the same time in the Netherlands, Hobbes based his text, *Leviathan*, upon this beautiful mathematical reason. Instead of a pantheistic celebration of God as nature, however, what Hobbes apprehended was a mechanical world that was entirely physical: all the world 'is Corporeall, that is to say, Body', 'and that which is not Body is no part of the Universe'. Even God, he stated, was made of matter, albeit too fine to be visible and no longer interested in his creation. Such words effectively branded him an atheist, an indictment that he denied passionately, and not only to protect himself from charges of heresy. His sincere belief that even the ultimate must be a material entity only emphasised the completeness of his monist metaphysical conviction.

In twenty first century Britain, the associations we hold about nature's physicality include its potential for pleasure, sensuality and satisfaction; the majority have access to the necessities of life whether through work or welfare, and still have a little left over for the unnecessaries - and healthcare provided by the state. In Hobbes' time there was little such comfort. The body bore the fragility of damage and disease, ever prompting awareness of its mortality, the very tangible realities of hunger, plague, fire and violence always close by. A simple fever was a potential killer, a broken bone or deep laceration could mean a permanent and crippling disability that left a family homeless and destitute. Hobbes sums it up in Chapter XIII with a phrase that has become well known: 'And the life of man, solitary, poore, nasty, brutish, and short'. For him to unite the mind or soul with matter was contentious in a way that can hardly be imagined now. God had provided the challenge of a physical world, but with it he had promised the rarified intangibility of the soul for which, if one behaved according to strictures laid out by the Church, there awaited the sweet salvation of heaven after the physical horrors of life on earth. If the mind, however, were made of the stuff of matter, it would be as mortal as the body that slaves, suffers and hungers, dies and decays. That would remove the sweet whisper of hope and scour life of its purpose. Furthermore, as Descartes, Bacon, and their contemporaries knew, if all were made of the same stuff, then the door would be open to debate whether all men might be equal; in a society based on divisions of class, heritage and race, that would be revolutionary. Even more problematic, perhaps, all mankind would be brought down to the level of the rest of nature. The seventeenth century pamphleteer, Richard Overton, one of the Levellers, declared that Adam's fall was complete, body and soul, and for his words he spent much time behind bars. In his time, such ideas were just too hard for most to accept.

Yet, slipping forward four hundred years, through the Civil War and the slow changes of parliamentarian government, through the extremes of Georgian to Victorian imperialism and the rise of abundance, the notion of the world being made of nothing but matter seems not so challenging. I don't deny the obscene and divisive gap between the wealthy and the rest, nor that there are pockets of desolating poverty where individuals and families fall through the net of social security, nor indeed that depression and other mental afflictions are not an epidemic in our culture, but lives are easier now than perhaps they have ever been in Western Europe - in *material* terms. That increasing plenty has helped loosen the need for a paradise after death available to the immortal soul: for some, if this life is all we have, if this body is all we are, perhaps it is enough.

So came the spread of the monist view that is materialism: metaphysically, the belief in a universe constituted of just one substance, matter.

Presenting his own position, the English philosopher Galen Strawson put it succinctly: 'My faith, like that of many other materialists, consists in a bundle of connected and unverifiable beliefs. I believe that experience is not all there is to reality. I believe that there is a physical world that involves existence of space and of space-occupying entities that have non-experiential properties'. Extrapolating, he goes on to present a peculiarly materialist image: 'I believe that one could in principle create a normally experiencing human being out of a piano. All one would have to do would be to arrange a sufficient number of the piano's constituent electrons, protons, and neutrons, in the way in which they are ordinarily arranged in a normal living human being'. Beyond what we perceive of the tangible world, then, the materialist asserts that the entirety of nature is constituted of the same material stuff, including our processes of thinking and feeling. As Strawson says, 'Experience is as much a physical phenomenon as electric charge'. But how could that be?

The word *matter* has an interesting root. Its earliest citation coming from the thirteenth century, it reached our language through the Anglo-Norman *matere*, the root of which is the Latin *materia*. Although used to denote physical substance, more specifically *materia* meant the hard heartwood of a tree out of which the rest of the tree grows. It is easy to see its origins in the Latin for mother, *mater*. Poetically, words meandering through centuries like rivers, the word's feminine roots allude to mother nature, the irrational and unpredictable yet fertile wholeness that Bacon sought to beat into submission. Now, soulless, matter is defined by physical science as that which has mass and occupies space, while materialist philosophy includes that which thinkers have for millennia referred to as definitively having no extension (taking up no space at all): spirit, soul and mind. More accurately, the materialist believes matter carries out the functions that were before attributed to spirit, soul and mind. With the *soul* dismissed as mythological, the frustratingly elusive *mind* provokes fiery debate and an ever increasing catalogue of theses from those determined to explain its apparent existence with the rational arguments of materialism. As for *spirit*, the wizardry of electromagnetism has taken care of (most of) that.

With my finger tips tapping the keys of the computer, pausing to drink, feeling the cool water in my mouth and the fullness it brings to my belly, the materialist perspective can seem simple, particularly if we are able to disregard the Kantian revolution and concur with the old scholastics, believing our senses do indeed provide us with an accurate picture of the world. If we are more comfortable without the notion of a creator deity, with effortless reason we may still understand how as a species we could have evolved specifically and successfully to survive and thrive: regardless of what nature actually is, we perceive the world in a way that enables us to function effectively. Even if our senses do proffer a vision of nature that is not absolutely exact, it is good enough to believe we can perceive and manipulate an objective reality. Compared with dualism, the instinctive simplicity that comes from its empirical tangibility makes materialism appear to be the populists' thesis, taking power away from the priests and putting it back into the hands of the people. No doubt adding to the rate at which it has saturated our culture, its proponents portray it as *the* scientific, logical and reasoned approach: as fact, not belief. However, there are serious problems with the materialist view, problems that have not yet been solved, by scientists or philosophers.

As I quoted in the previous chapter, Susan Blackmore states that it is *the interface between mental and physical worlds* that needs attention if we are to address the issue of consciousness at a philosophical level - in other words, if we are to face the questions which have no scientifically verifiable answers, and where we are not willing to sit back on jargon, assumption or belief. Guided by their conviction, however, materialists have a tendency to expound their ideas as if they were philosophical, but in focusing purely on the physical in search of the mental they are repeatedly failing to tackle that interface.

In the four centuries since Descartes described animal spirits in the pineal gland, neurology has developed into an extraordinary science: medical technology can now provide scanners to show the firing of neurons in patterns across the brain. This is physiology: it tells us which part of the brain tends to be active when the subject is engaged in a particular thought or activity, but it says nothing of what it feels like. Today's science tells us that myelin-sheathed nerve fibres can carry a message from a squashed finger to the brain in about twenty milliseconds, that unmyelinated C-fibres take about 500 milliseconds (half a second); we know that the subject will consequently experience a sharp pain followed by a deep ache, and we can reason out the evolutionary purpose of those messages and sensations - but we don't know what *pain* is. Equally, we know that human sight operates between 390 and 740 nm, or 400 and 790 terahertz, being the spectrum of our visible rainbow, but the processes that go on in the occipital cortex are not the same as the experience of seeing red, green or violet. Our human hearing works between twelve hertz and twenty kilohertz, the main area of sensitivity being between one and five kilohertz. Sound vibrations move down the ear canal, hit the drum, the hammer, anvil and stirrup bones, reaching the cochlea which is filled with liquid and tiny hairs; here the vibrations are changed to electrical signals that move down the auditory nerve to the brain, which then seems to provide us with sound as we know it. As American cognitive scientist Daniel Dennett asks in *Consciousness Explained*, 'When, after all, do these toneless signals get their final translation into subjectively heard sound?' Indeed, with his characteristic self-confidence, at the start of the book Dennett warns his readers that the mystery of consciousness was about to be mercilessly taken away from them and replaced with 'the rudiments of scientific knowledge'. Having read the book, I was still wondering when, and how, that translation might yet be explained, for his materialist thesis was no more than another discourse on neurophysiology.

A common thread of materialism is identity theory, the belief that mental states equate with brain states. The buzz term is NCC: neural correlates of consciousness. These are the physical events that can be observed and measured in the brain and the nervous system which appear to be linked to various experiences of consciousness. However interesting the neural correlates seem to be, however, what we are perceiving is brain activity, not consciousness. We are still stuck in physiology. Furthermore, that the same areas don't always seem to be activated in different subjects under different circumstances, or where there are brain abnormalities or damage, throws up significant doubts, as does the question of perception (however primitive) in organisms that have much less complex brains, or indeed no brain at all.

Addressing some of these problems, in the late twentieth century a handful of philosophers developed the theory of functionalism, focusing on the purpose of mental states in relation to each other rather than simply with respect to the brain; avoiding the need to base these functions in specific neural locations, however, it may have been a practicably useful thesis but it didn't support the materialist belief.

The process theologian David Ray Griffin is a philosopher very aware of the problems inherent to materialism. In *Unsnarling the World Knot* he describes it as a 'decapitated version of the worldview created by the dualistic naturalists', those whose philosophy spoke of a mind (not soul) that directs otherwise inert matter. Thinking about his statement, it is useful to remember that - and how - the idea was developed out of dualism. The original mechanists were keen to remove the Aristotelian *telos* that allowed for the belief in a tripartite soul, but they were still not willing to deny the presence of God. Those who followed wanted first to exorcise what remained of the anima, the rational soul; then they turned to God, dismissing the transcendent creator together with anything else that suggested the supernatural or was beyond the reach of scientific measurement. By the mid twentieth century, when it became clear that the interior self was not going to reveal its workings as the atom had done, it was inevitable that *mind* would be the next to go.

Eliminativists, like dualists, assert that there are no neural correlates to consciousness. However, unlike the dualists, they are not looking to find the interface between the physical and the mental; instead, they disregard the latter completely, regarding it as a natural deception. An analogy often used takes us back to those changing laws about witchcraft: our ancestors used to negotiate with demons and angels, until civilised society decided that such creatures didn't actually exist. Eliminativists, such as Paul and Patricia Churchland, declare that all interior experiences, from beliefs to emotions, do not actually exist. They are no more than illusions generated by the mechanisms of the physical brain.

Like many evangelical materialists, what this American duo are fighting is what they refer to as commonsense or folk psychology. Sounding at times like a secular Inquisition, they advise to be profoundly suspicious of taking as real any experience of interiority. Of course, the obvious argument against such a standpoint is that it is clearly a belief which declares that beliefs don't exist, but the determined materialist seldom accepts that his stance is based on anything but manifest fact. All that exists to the eliminativist is the physicality of nature. Indeed, ironically, the intricate functionality of nature is celebrated by some such thinkers with as much passion as by any devoted animist.

Wilfrid Sellars, exploring philosophical pragmatism and intuition in the mid twentieth century, suggested that the experience of an inner self or mentality is entirely cultural; we learn it in our earliest years as we are taught how to make sense of the world around us. To Daniel Dennett, though, the concept of qualia, the *what it feels like to be something,* is simply incoherent.

He perceives its inescapable subjectivity as a perpetual stream of inconsistencies, concluding that the idea of consciousness is thus inherently flawed, and as such not sufficiently robust to pose any threat to comprehensive materialism. Instead he presents a 'heterophenomenology', a 'neutral portrayal of exactly *what it is like to be* that subject' (his italics). Creating a notional third-person objective observer through what he sees as a muscular scientific methodology, he believes he is avoiding the apparently invalidating reference to first person subjectivity - while all the while presenting his own personal perspectives, thoughts and beliefs, and asking that we agree with them in order to give the illusion of rational objectivity.

The American philosopher, John Searle, comes at the problem from a different perspective. In a 1980 edition of the *Behaviour and Brain Sciences* journal, he wrote that when discussing the mind one must 'always insist on the first person point of view. The first step in the operationalist sleight of hand occurs when we try to figure out how we would know what it would be like for another'. To reach for the objective, in the way that Dennett does, is a 'category error', hopelessly muddling what is empirical and what ontological, what is objective and what subjective. Whether it is possible to be anything but subjective is a problem that many materialists would prefer to disregard.

An additional problem with the materialist belief is cohesion. On a physical level current understanding tells us that nature is made up of numerous seriously small particles. The human brain is said to contain around a hundred billion neurons, each one forming clusters that connect to the synapses of up to ten thousand neighbouring neurons. In one cubic millimetre of the cortex there are a hundred thousand neurons with a possible ten million synaptic connections. There are a hundred million neurons in the gut, and more in the oesophagus, the stomach, the small intestine, the colon. Additionally, those NCC scans indicate that different elements of perception - the visual, auditory, and so on - can be seen as electrical activity in different neural areas around the brain. We have no understanding of how our various diverse experiences of a moment are unified into coherence. This is further complicated by our ability to multitask on both a physical and mental level: talking business on the telephone while walking down a crowded pavement, scratching at an itchy nose, we manage still to be wondering what we'll eat for lunch (with the average busy woman worrying about a child, thinking about a lover and mentally completing her tax return at the same time too). Organising the numerous electrical firings into distinct and comprehensible ideas and sensations without a soul or mind that, constituted of a stuff not limited by mass or form, can act as an overall embracing and cohering force, the physical universe seems quite magically unfragmented.

Contributing further to the problem is the issue of free will. I shall go into this crucial issue more deeply in Chapter Eight but, suffice to say here, if there is no self-directing soul or mind, no overseer, we are left with an entirely deterministic universe: a physical mechanism whose processes are assumed naturally and inevitably to follow their own flows of cause and effect, affording neither need nor opportunity for decision-making. If the mind is illusory, the experience of free will must be equally so.

Quantum

Faced with these rational snags, the supporting arguments put forward by the materialist again and again are those based on an absolute faith in science and technology. The line taken is that, although we may lack the understanding now, with rapid developments in the field it surely won't be long before our measuring devices will be subtle enough to reveal the answer to every question.

Reflecting this conviction, the term used more commonly now than materialism is physicalism. The word spins us into regress in most dictionaries which define it as pertaining to matter or synonymous with materialism. It is a broader term, however. Physicalism is not just about substance; the feminine Latin noun *physica* speaks of the study of nature, the Greek Φύση (*physi*) being nature itself. The ancient PIE base for the word is **bheu-* meaning to live, to exist, to grow, from which the Old English *beon*, to be or become, also derives. Again though, nature here - and thus the term physicalism - is now soulless. Use of the word allows the materialist simply to include more subtle levels of what is perceived empirically or abstracted rationally: energy, space-time and the new landscapes of subatomic particles.

Yet if nature is to be crafted entirely of matter, what is this substance that, in essence, can provide the capacity for both physicality and consciousness? At a fundamental level, to the dualist the stuff of mind may be intangible and even imperceptible, but for the materialist the stuff of matter must surely be distinct, concrete and discernible.

Materialist views can be found as far back as pre-Socratic Greece; in the fifth century BCE the Athenian philosopher Anaxagoras suggested the universe was infinitely divisible and made up of an infinite number of elements or 'seeds' which, by mixing together and separating, generate the perpetual process of change. Towards the end of that century, Leucippus talked of nature consisting of tiny, indivisible and indestructible units, an idea that was developed by his more celebrated student, Democritus, who used the term άτομα (*atoma*), meaning that which cannot be cut or divided. These atoms came in various shapes and weights, each containing soul and fire; in constant motion, they moved through what is otherwise empty space. The solidity of the phenomenal world, the reality we perceive, he concluded, was an illusion created by the movement of these tiny atoms.

Plato's ideas were typically more rationally elaborate: in *Timaeus* he wrote of perfect geometric solids that fitted together to create the harmoniously aesthetic order of the universe: the tetrahedron, hexahedron, octahedron, icosahedron and dodeca-hedron, relating to the four elements of fire, earth, air and water respectively, the fifth being the stuff of the wider universe through which the stars moved. Aristotle rejected this vision in his writings, outlining the earlier thesis of Democritus but not concurring with that either. In the first century BCE, the Roman philosopher and poet, Lucretius, presented atomism once again. In *On the Nature of Things* he wrote of the Epicurean belief in *primordia rerum*, the indivisible and indestructible primary particles that make up the universe, also using the word *materies* with its allusion to *mater* or mother. Affirming that there could be nothing supernatural, he believed nature emerged simply out of the random movement of these fundamental particles, circling, colliding, breaking apart and recombining.

With Aristotle's work forming the basis of Western scholastic thinking, his refutation of atomism meant the theory was not considered for some fifteen hundred years or so. It was perhaps the rediscovery of Lucretius' work in 1471 that fuelled a new interest in atomism, notably the French philosopher and priest, Pierre Gassendi, in the following century. Gassendi described these perennial atoms as created by God, with some making associations that he called molecules. Even the sensitive soul in humans and animals was composed of atoms, comprising the brain and nerves, though for Gassendi the rational soul was wholly immaterial. In various forms the theory spread through seventeenth century Europe, with Bacon, Bruno, Galileo, Hobbes and the alchemist Robert Boyle all exploring similar ideas, seeking ways in which to differentiate the stuff of matter from both void and thought. Newton believed these primary particles were uniform, his laws of motion, inertia and mass applying to the atomic level. Yet, however brilliant these early scientists and thinkers were, they were still discussing particles well beyond the reach of observation: it took another three centuries of developing scientific experimentation and technology before this foundational premise of materialism shifted from the realm of pure philosophical rationalism into the rational deductions generated from empirical science, each step along the way answering the challenges raised by the previous position, each explorer reaching for the base building blocks of nature and the certainty that such knowledge would surely provide.

Of course, where we stand now, at the start of the twenty first century, although we do have more knowledge we have no more certainty. Newton believed light was made of particles, but when James Clerk Maxwell was exploring the connections between magnetism and electricity in the mid nineteenth century, he discovered light behaving not as a particle, but an electromagnetic wave. In 1900, Max Planck's declaration that 'electromagnetic radiation is emitted in discrete packets, or quanta' was a huge breakthrough in the understanding of matter: within three decades quantum theories were transforming into quantum mechanics. Soon light would be deduced to be a wave *and* a particle. Just when many felt science was on the brink of revealing the blueprints of nature itself, uncertainty poured back into physics like a surging spring tide.

To some extent this was due simply to scale. Work with subatomic particles allowed the empirical to slip away once more, scientists meandering back into their old dependency on the abstract and rational. Indeed, in 1930 Paul Dirac referred to quantum physics as no more than mathematics - not reality. Looking at the numbers involved, the mundane world of perception is quickly lost: Planck's Constant, reflecting the size of a single unit of energy, is 6.626×10 to the minus 34, revealing just why the gaps between the quanta and their unpredictable behaviour are not part of the real world within which we have evolved to live and thrive. They are unimaginably small.

Working with these new micro dimensions, it was assumed that inconsistencies and unpredictabilities at first seen with regard to the location and causality in these tiny particles were due simply to an inadequacy in the tools of measurement: it was the German theoretical physicist Werner Heisenberg who claimed the phenomena were actually inherent in nature. His Uncertainty Principle described how the photons used to find other particles influenced the behaviour of those particles: a small wave packet of photons could identify where an electron was but in doing so it pushed it off course and therefore couldn't identify its velocity, while a broader wave packet of photons allowed the scientist to measure its momentum, but wasn't able to show exactly where it was. With the involvement of the observer so crucial, all hope of objectivity was lost. Towards the end of his remarkable career, in the mid 1950s in his Gifford Lectures at St Andrew's University in Scotland (later published as *Physics and Philosophy*), Heisenberg wrote, 'The conception of objective reality of the elementary particles has thus evaporated not into the cloud of some obscure new reality concept but into the transparent clarity of a mathematics that represents no longer the behaviour of particles but rather our knowledge of this behaviour'.

For some, this was too frustrating: questioning the inherent uncertainty of the observer-centred approach, physicist David Bohm put forward an interpretation of quantum data that focused on the essence of the electron rather than its potential inconsistencies of position and momentum, and so 'does not need to abandon the precise, rational and objective description' of the system. For others in the field, this observer-involvement is crucially instructive, for they affirm that it is the act of obser-vation that collapses the probabilities inherent within the wave, allowing the particle to find its moment of actuality. Whether quantum physics is simply epistemological (how we see it) or could be accepted as ontological (how it is) is still fiercely debated. Many physicalists remain fully convinced that what they are deducing from such experiments is nature *in itself*: even where they are wholly conceptual and theoretical, scientific facts are deemed to equate to how the universe actually is.

Leucippus' theoretical and definitively indivisible *atom* was no doubt minute. Along the journey of discovery, however, the word became entangled in the language of chemistry, now describing a unit that is vast in comparison with the nucleus, protons and electrons that are understood to make up its mass. When Heisenberg was lecturing in Scotland, these were the extent of the known subatomic particles, yet now there are many more basic elementary particles, the quarks, leptons and bosons, with hypothetical additions such as photinos and squarks also moving around somewhere in the brew. Perhaps what I find most delightful in this storm of mathematical possibilities is that these tiny entities are usually considered as *point* particles, in other words, they are given no dimensions - taking us straight back to the stuff of the soul which also, definitively, has no extension at all.

Of course, that is not the only commonality, for while the scientist may declare that soul substance has not been empirically proven, nothing has been revealed in these primary particles of matter that even begins to hint at what consciousness may be or how it might work. To the physicalist, this is not a problem, for there is no expectation of an inherent quality within matter that allows for consciousness: it is how these particles behave together that is assumed to be the key. While some thinkers question whether events on the quantum level can have any effect on the macroscopic world of our experience, there are now significant physicists stepping into the mind-body debate, bringing with them their metaphysical monism, asserting that quanta could explain not just the experience of qualia, but the whole gamut of non-sensory perceptions, from aesthetic experience and abstract thought to memory, intuition and telepathy. The strangely mystical process whereby the electron remains in its probabilistic form, called its superpositional state, until some trigger collapses the wave into a particle, is considered by some to be indicative of how consciousness might function. For example, neuroscientist and psychologist Karl Pribam, together with David Bohm, some decades ago developed what they called a holonomic model of the brain, using quantum mathematical principles to understand how mental experience might emerge from wave patterns in the physical matter of the brain.

Theoretical physicist Roger Penrose has also proposed that the collapse of waves into particles could explain what he called the *non-computable* abilities of the brain, the ways in which the brain works that cannot be replicated through mathematical algorithms. Instead of relying on an external observer, he believes the quantum wave collapses by 'objective reduction', provoked into instability by a process inherent to its immediate space-time geometry. Having read his theory in *The Emperor's New Mind*, American anaesthesiologist Stuart Hameroff suggested that such an idea could function by way of the microtubules of the brain, the tiny cytoskeletal tubulin through which molecules travel, made of a mesh that Hameroff believed would allow for 'π electron resonance clouds', or wave coherences that would rise to the experience of consciousness when they collapsed. Yet the language of quantum neurology is moving at such a pace that new theories negate and override old ones all the time. Indeed, just as one group dismisses Penrose and Hameroff's idea as no longer scientifically viable, a new generation of neurologists sets forward another idea about waves, called Quantum Brain Dynamics. With its acronym so essential in the twenty first century, QBD suggests that it is the water content of the brain that creates the quantum field; the quanta, here termed corticons, move through the neuronal network upon the hum of electromagnetic waves. Indeed, other bands of brilliant young minds have no doubt already ousted QBD and are presenting their theses with the sparkling confidence of their determination.

Certainly quantum physics reminds us what Einstein had mathematically confirmed, that matter and energy are interconvertible. Fifty years ago, Heisenberg explained that:

> collisions between two elementary particles of extremely high energy would be the only process by which the particles could eventually be divided. Actually they *can* be divided in such processes, sometimes into very many fragments; but the fragments are again elementary particles, not any smaller pieces of them, the masses of these fragments resulting from the very large kinetic energy of the two colliding particles. In other words, the transmutation of energy into matter makes it possible that the fragments of elementary particles are again the same elementary particles.

As such, he goes on to suggest that quantum science reveals 'the primary substance of the world' to be energy:

> if two such particles, moving through space with a very high kinetic energy, collide, then many new elementary particles may be created from the available energy and the old particles may have disappeared in the collision. Such events have been frequently observed and offer the best proof that all particles are made of the same substance: energy.

To suggest now that the search for consciousness might be better placed in the wave, rather than the particle, or in the transformation from one to the other is fascinating. In the sensible world, the world we can sense through conscious experience, energy feels very different from matter. From the Greek, ἐνέργεια (*energeia*), a word found in our written heritage from as early as Aristotle, it is easy to understand how it may be equated with spirit and purpose, the 'soul and fire' of Democritus' atoms, and indeed the animal spirits of Galen's physiology. We can feel it, measure it, we can perceive it everywhere in nature, describing it as the fuel needed for work to be done; we know how to generate it, store it and conserve it, yet still it feels elusively abstract. To find consciousness, or the facility for consciousness within it, can seem rather like, in a moment of desperation, looking for one's partner at home when we know they're not actually there - evidence of their presence fills our senses despite reason telling us we are wrong. Yet science is not about what feels reasonable. Empirical as it may seem in its simplicity, to maintain the materialist stance takes a feat of hyper-rationalism. Physics is founded on ideas: mathematics, electromagnetic fields, particle waveforms, are all mental constructs describing what things *do*, not what things *are*. In other words, science may know how the mechanics of a process operate, but not what propels them to do so.

As a basis for a perspective on the mind-body question and consciousness, as Bryan Magee says, 'a materialist view of total reality is a metaphysics, not a scientific theory. There is no possibility whatsoever of scientifically proving, or disproving it'. If materialism is to find a firmer ground, by its own standards of scientific certainty, or accountability, perhaps a radically different account of the substance of matter needs to be found. At present, I tend to agree with Griffin when he says:

The idea that physics by itself could predict, or even causally explain, all the movements of living human bodies is a pure pipe dream. Contemporary physical theory is not even remotely close to such a capacity. The idea that physics ever will have such a capacity, or even the more modest (and completely unverifiable) idea that physics in *principle* has such a capacity, is radically underdetermined by the evidence.

Building a philosophical foundation of understanding, in this chapter and the last we have looked at the metaphysical beliefs that have maintained a dominant position in our Western heritage over the past few millennia - dualism and materialism. I have presented their basic tenets, together with ideas as to why they are problematic. In the following chapters, my focus will move to describe accounts of the stuff of nature founded on different premises, each step taking us closer to a metaphysics of animism.

With his inimitable skill as a wordsmith, Schopenhauer described materialism as 'the philosophy of the subject that forgets to take account of himself'. As so many philosophers have known, the separation between subject and object is one cleaved by a blunt axe, leaving rational tatters and empirical confusion. In laying down a possible path to guide the reader towards animism, the first step would be a simple word: *integration*.

Chapter Four

Integration

It is a beautiful word. Associated with the movement against racism and other forms of social prejudice, integration is often used to imply the process of bringing together disparate elements in order to create something unified. Its etymology, however, takes us to the Latin *integer* which simply means whole, and my use of the word taps into those roots. In other words, the act of integrating is not about gathering up various discrete entities and drawing them into one, but recalling an innate wholeness that for some reason we have grown to imagine is not there. Breaking the word down further takes us to the Latin *tangere*, to touch, and its PIE base *tag-* which also speaks of touch or handling, while the negating *in* prefix addresses that apparent divide. Instead of two or more distinct entities reaching across a chasm of separation to make contact, there is an integrated wholeness. Being whole, there is indeed no separate other to reach to and touch.

We are not talking about a singularity. In an earlier chapter, I mentioned how Schopenhauer, critiquing Kant's thinking, had pointed out the inevitable oneness of the noumenal. His reasoning was a direct progression from Kant's proposition that time and space have a rational foundation: constructs of the mind, they are tools of perception, and thus in his terms they are fundamentally synthetic *a priori*, in other words, beliefs that help us to create our worlds, beliefs without which we could not function. Certainly, if time and space are not ontologically true, there can be no separation in the noumenon. Nature *in itself*, nature beyond our perception, must be a single undifferentiated unity.

When later in his life Schopenhauer began to read Hindu

texts, he found a spiritual counterpart to what had been his own rationally-based insights. The complete disparity between the noumenal oneness and the plurality of our perception is accounted for in the oriental traditions through the metaphysics of idealism: the perceived world, including the individual mind, is an illusion generated by the mind of the one.

The universe may indeed have an integral spatiotemporal structure which may or may not accord with our own perception of it; if we take Kant's words seriously, we cannot know. Instead of declaring the actuality of nature an undivided unity, the words I use are integration and wholeness: each and every divide created by the senses of the observing *I* is questioned on the basis of nature's ontological integrity. On what evidence do we assert the existence of that integrity? The answer to that question will be explored over this and the following chapter.

Let me pause for a moment briefly to clarify another handful of terms, however.

The collection of words based upon *real* I have explained are all here to be read as associated with the subjective and phenomenal world. Equally, although used for many centuries to imply an independent and objective actuality in line with scholastic beliefs, the roots of the word *world* are very much about humanity. The Old English *woruld* meant human existence or the affairs of mankind: the Proto-Germanic *wer* meaning man combines with *ald* meaning age, giving the age of man. In this text, the word is used to encompass the reality that we perceive, whether subjectively and individually, or as a collective and agreed reality.

What lies beyond our perception I have referred to as nature *in itself*. Nature: this potent word is debated passionately by everyone for whom the politics of value are important, particularly when it comes to environmental sustainability and the ethics of human influence and intervention. That argument is one I addressed in *Living With Honour*. Here, however, where I use the word it is within a purer metaphysical context. Without need for complication, I am referring simply to the actuality. Rooted in the Latin *nasci*, meaning to be born, its more ancient root comes from the PIE *gene-*, to give birth. As such, the multitude of words around natal and nation, genus and genius, are all related, speaking of the essential and inherent qualities that we might believe have been present since the beginning. Removing any anthropocentricity, nature then describes the entire context of our existence without the intrusion of our human perception.

The other word I have used already to intimate nature's actuality is *universe*. Its implications of wholeness are satisfying; the Latin *universus*, meaning all together, comes from *unus*, one, and the past participle of the verb *vertere*, to turn, implying the action of having turned towards a unity. Indeed, through the Greek its deepest roots are in the PIE base *sol-*, which simply means whole. To me it is a word that unconditionally embraces everything, and in this context usefully so. The universe proffers an idea more vast perhaps than nature, but nature is no less comprehensive; I use the latter to emphasise its rich content while the former alludes to its possibly boundless expanse.

Kant's word, on the other hand, connotes the mystery, and in using either nature or the universe I am conscious of being repeatedly at risk of implying that I know something of that actuality beyond perception. Primarily my intention is in tune with Kant, however, who defended his use of the distinction between the phenomenal and the noumenal by calling it a limiting concept, *ein Grenzbegriff*, a wonderful, almost onomatopoeic word. This limiter declares a boundary that keeps reminding us that we cannot know what is truly there, and consequently to think more carefully, avoiding the easy mistake of assuming that we do.

Animism neither contains nor requires any such assumptions.

An aspect of animistic traditions that Christians and other monotheists can find challenging is the way in which the animist embraces the darkness. Although often mistakenly conflated with animistic Paganism, New Age philosophies and spiritualities tend to be religiously focused on their quest for the light, defining the darkness as the negativity to overcome. Undisputedly, a craving for the light is entirely natural. In the light there is the opportunity to see, and of all our senses our visual capacity is predominant in our conscious awareness, allowing us the possibility of knowledge. At least for those without a sight impairment, although we may touch, smell, taste and even hear something, seeing it with our own eyes extends a different level of surety. The desire is fundamental to human nature as we seek out what we need in order to survive. When facts about nature were provided by the Church, its scriptures and preachers were proclaimed to be the source of light. As science has stepped forward, with its supply of information and promise of salvation, it is the strip-lights of the laboratory that are now providing the focus for many. Light is judged then to be *good*.

To the animist, a state of permanent en*light*enment is not considered natural. His senses inform him that, firstly, life is sustained by a balance of light and darkness, and, secondly, it is lived for the most part in neither darkness nor light, but in varying degrees of twilight and shadow, of half knowing, believing, assuming and concluding. The aspiration for fluency and lucidity, another light-derived word, is firmly established within our culture though. Literally and figuratively, in darkness we are denied the safety of certainty. As dusk comes and the light slips away like an outgoing tide, edges begin to dissolve. In darkness, our senses more easily blur, leaving us potentially deceived. If we are dependent upon knowing, this can leave us confused and fearful. The not-knowing is judged as ignorance;

darkness is declared *bad*, and to be avoided as dangerous. As the deep wellspring of wickedness, any who embrace the darkness must be equally spurned.

If, however, our aim is not a knowledge-based certainty, what the darkness provides is delicious and necessary release. In the dark, the separation created by edges is no longer relevant to our perception and reality, allowing entirely new parameters of freedom. Though naturally we do need light, we do also crave the darkness, for we need a place into which we can withdraw, relaxing from the stimulus of our senses and sinking into the dissolution of sleep. We need moments within which we can dissolve all we are and all we know, that we might find the nourishment for new inspiration and realisation. Over the course of the year, day and night are balanced, and in these temperate zones within which my animism is rooted the seasons unfold and dissipate providing another balance. Our climate generates ecologies that move in pace with the changing light and temperature, the herbaceous plants and deciduous trees expressing the journey step by step. As summer peaks, the flowers turn to seed to be shed into the breeze, grain dries to be harvested, fruit swells and falls, the leaves dry and let go to dance in the wind, and when frost comes the landscape fades to brown and grey, life withdrawing, sinking into the mud to wait until the cycle allows for growth once again - and indeed it does, with the first green shoots pushing through the cold hard earth, as the days again begin to lengthen.

Based upon the experience of perceiving nature in his surrounding and immediate environment, the animist doesn't work on the assumption of polarities. Crucially, nature appears as tidal, not digital. Although there is light and dark, our lives meander across the spectrum, most comfortable in the half light chosen by our distant ancestors down the tracks of our mammalian evolution. Extremes are seldom experienced, for they are not sustainable. Instead of black and white, there are a thousand colours. Instead of good and bad, there are the broad and tangled contexts of each thought and interaction. Instead of fact and fiction, there are the subjective experiences of each individual, the phenomena of their own world based upon their own beliefs and expectations: the stories of our people. Indeed, any such oppositional notion feels like a childish yes-no confrontation.

The suggestion that nature is constituted of two distinct substances - the stuff of mind and the stuff of matter - seems an equally unnecessary polarisation, and one that has over centuries brought about violent confrontation and brutal repression. Out of that dualist conflict, four hundred years ago the materialist stance began to emerge, eventually slicing off the soul/mind to retain only the material body; yet as such, it is but half a metaphysics attempting to present itself as comprehensive. Overlaying a Hegelian dialectic pattern, one might say that the dualist thesis, opposed by the materialist antithesis, has naturally presented the synthesis expressed by modern animism, but the animist's metaphysics is not a bringing together of disparate concepts; its integration is a remembering of an inherent wholeness. For the individual living in a Christian or secular culture where dualist and materialist beliefs are pervasive, it is a rediscovery of an ancient and very natural understanding.

Just what that understanding is will begin to unfold in this chapter.

I shall take a winding course once again, like an old river through its floodplain, picking up and analysing assumptions, expectations and language along the way. An important element must now be borne in mind though: so far for the most part I have presented the ideas of other thinkers and philosophers, the majority of whom spent their lives in the search for certainty. As an animist, I have explored their work, walking the journeys of their stories, picking up pebbles that sparkled in the sunshine, watching the breeze in the trees along the way. As yet through these pages I have not presented my thesis as if it were absolute truth, nor will I do so now. Rationally sound argument is crucially important, as is an empirical justifiability, if we are to find inspiration, insight and agreement and so share ideas in a way that is tenable and nourishing, allowing for practical ethics and morality to become clear. However, declaring universal truths on the basis of one's own reality is neither necessary nor wise. The reader whose quest is for certainty may feel unsatisfied by my words. What I hope to achieve, nonetheless, is an exposition of the integrated view where the light of certainty will be like dappled sunshine through the woodland canopy, and areas of deep shadow are not evaded nor denied but instead brought right into the heart of our understanding.

Mindedness

As have been described, there are problems intrinsic to the dualist and materialist metaphysical hypotheses that have yet to be overcome, or indeed may never be overcome. At the simplest level, the interface between the mental and physical substances in dualism seems still rationally insurmountable, and the explanation for subjective experience or qualia, let alone consciousness, has not yet been adequately addressed by materialism. However, as David Ray Griffin put it, the debate between these two is essentially 'a family quarrel'. Both sides assert that nature is inert.

The fissure cleaved by Descartes was not simply between the mental and the material. For Descartes the only mental state worth considering was the rational human soul, in other words, the educated human mind capable of conscious reasoning and self-reflection. Everything else could and should be swept into the category of insentient, mechanical matter, including every other aspect of human nature. It was this view that was so comprehensively taken up by Western philosophy, followed by its science and culture, and still provides a foundation for contemporary capitalist morality.

It is no wonder the layman's view of animism is still stuck in the playground. When the idea is put forward that mental states may be present other than in human beings, there may be a discussion of higher animals, albeit with a curiosity soused in scepticism, and with heavily limiting conditions once we move from great apes to dogs and lab rats. The suggestion that fleas or earthworms may have some form of subjective qualitative experience is generally dismissed as ludicrous. To speak of mindedness in a landscape is decried as a mad proposal about ethereal spirits in the mud and stone. The integrated worldview is thus dismissed as laughable, a primitive or childlike metaphysics. Yet, with the notion of mind still packaged as if it were *human* experience of awareness and reason, of course it is preposterous to suggest it exists anywhere other than in human beings.

Such misassumptions are typical within the debate, and they negate the validity of many critical perspectives. Indeed, there is a remarkable lack of semantic clarity in a great deal of the narrative literature, terminology being used with truly indolent imprecision in order to establish quick and witty dismissals, while displaying a paucity of philosophical rigour that should in fact shame the critic.

In Susan Blackmore's *Consciousness: A Very Short Introduction*, there is one brief mention of this standpoint in the book's 133 pages. Addressing the thesis as *panpsychism*, a term commonly used to express the metaphysics of some aspects of philosophical animism, her words are revealingly simplistic: 'panpsychists believe that everything in the universe is conscious; so for them, there are no unconscious creatures, and consciousness was there from the start'. Words are important. Like spirit and soul, consciousness can be used broadly in poetic and spiritual contexts, but to bring such terms into philosophical argument without clear definition or consistently relevant application is simply poor scholarship. Blackmore's example is not highlighted as an outrageous example, but as one amongst many such perfunctory judgements, and in that vein succinctly put.

Let me here propose a definition of animism then, using a few references already explored, in order that we may look more closely at these crucially relevant words. Honing it down to one sentence, we might begin with this: *animism is a monist metaphysical stance, based upon the idea that mind and matter are not distinct and separate substances but an integrated reality, rooted in nature.*

As a monist stance, in other words, I am implying that the belief recognises the existence of only one essential basis to nature. Note, however, that I am not yet suggesting another substance, just an integration.

Many definitions of animism speak of the physical world being comprehensively enspirited. Beginning to clarify terms, a good start may be to revisit the word *spirit*. Acknowledging its evolution through the course of our philosophical and theological heritage as sketched out in Chapter Two, early as we are in the text it is possible now to bring the word a little more into the context of animism. Spirit can be seen as comprising those essential forces and energies that, moving within particular structures or patterns, vitalise and empower. Not only its qualities but its very existence are generated wholly by its context, and as such, though it may differ considerably in accordance with its immediate and influencing environment, it is not a distinct entity or even a substance. As such, the implications of dualism, expressed only in the most simplistic of animistic theses, are here fully discarded. Spirit is integral to nature, an aspect of its wholeness. Nature is not inert.

In presenting such a definition I am aware that I have stepped over the line of Kant's prohibition: I have suggested what nature actually is. Bear with me, for there is more to say before I can justify such an action.

The second word commonly found in definitions of animism is *soul*. As quoted earlier, the *OED* declares the animist to attribute 'a living soul to plants, inanimate objects and natural phenomena'. Again, the word implies a dualism that is not found in the philosophically cogent tradition. Throughout most of its history, however, the word has referred to interiority as a whole, including our drives, desires, memory and reasoning, and on this understanding it is possible to equate the soul with the mind. As such, the definition then becomes dependent on a fuller definition of *mind*. Where the soul refers only to the rational thinking mind so important to Descartes, needless to say, the *OED* definition loses its validity entirely. Yet, in order to understand how the word sits fully within animism, a good deal more work must be done on the foundation.

Both words are not yet then defined sufficiently to contribute to a definition of animism.

One more word will bring us to a definition of mind: *psyche*. It is not a term I tend to use, but as the core of panpsychism, it is worth addressing. Panpsychism, literally translated, describes there to be soul everywhere: while this *psyche* (ψυχή) is seldom equated with *nous* (νους), the rational mind, what psyche actually does mean is left open to an individual's own interpretation. Employed as a philosophical term that evades the spiritual associations of the word soul, panpsychism does not necessitate an integrated metaphysics, only the pervasive presence of what we might call mind within nature. Again, we return to *mind*. In his 2010 book, *Becoming Animal*, off-beat philosopher and cultural ecologist David Abram expresses the perspective beautifully in his question, 'What if mind, rightly understood, is not a special property of humankind, but is rather a property of the Earth itself - a power in which we are carnally immersed?' What then is mind, rightly understood?

Accepting the importance of the word, I propose the following development of my earlier definition: *animism is a monist metaphysical stance based upon ubiquitous and integrated mindedness.* As such, mind is the term that now needs to be considered.

Mind is often used to imply our thinking self. It seems like a more modern word, for it is often used now instead of soul specifically in order to evade any religious or spiritual connotation, but it is an old word too. The mind is that part of a person that allows them to think, to feel and remember, the word *mental* having the same root to the Latin *mens,* meaning mind. The PIE base *men-* encapsulates the same idea, inferring all that happens in the mind, the Old English *gemynd* implying thinking, memory and intention. Yet, mind, like soul, has a broader general definition than just the rational. The emotional drives, and the deeper hungers of our belly and groin, may feel more tangible because our sense of them is more visceral, yet some would still argue that, but for the actions they provoke, these forces are also invisible, and as such they are also elements of the non-material soul.

Allowing meaning to course through the etymology and into present use, I propose that both mind and mentality encompass all that happens in that interior realm of subjectivity. Using its many tools of perception, a mind takes in information about its environment and processes it through its various mental states, creating the phenomenal world of its reality. This includes the acts of perceiving, experiencing, sensing, feeling, thinking, emoting, knowing, anticipating, intending, remembering and more. All involve, at some point, interaction with an external world and nearly all include a level of reflection; information gained generates a reaction or response, to whatever degree that is consciously or intuitively processed. Obviously, for there to be mind, there does not need to be the capacity for every variation of mental state, from the simplest and briefest perceptive reaction, to the most complex processes of intellectual interiority.

Yet, is there a limit, a necessary minimum?

The word used by Blackmore in her definition of panpsychism was consciousness. If that word were synonymous with mind as I have here described it, then her definition would hold some validity. However, this would both overextend the word's meaning while limiting its depth when used more specifically. According to my preliminary definition at the end of Chapter One, consciousness denotes *knowing*, implying a measure of self-reflection in the digestion of information, whether with awareness or in the darker subconscious. As such, consciousness cannot be all the mind comprises. Defining animism as the belief that the capacity for such self-reflecting knowing is present in every 'creature' or distinct entity within nature is both misguided and misguiding. It is entangled in that anthropocentricity which glorifies the mind by restricting it to the educated, rational self. We have tripped again into philosophy written in crayons, imagining rivers and trees that think and speak in human tongues, and primitive folk who believe such things to be true.

Indeed, if we are willing to state that a specific level of intelligence is necessary for mind to be present, then we are left with the problem of declaring the line between what has capacity for mentality, for subjective qualitative existence, and what is merely mechanical passivity. This is the line I pointed to in Chapter One, the line that marks out those parts of our world that are worthy of consideration, and those which are objects whose value only accrues for how useful they are to humanity.

Descartes required the presence of the thinking *I*. Maintaining his conviction about the superior nature of human reason, in tune with so many men of our Western scientific and scholastic heritage, Dennett speaks of the need for language: it is only through the development of language that consciousness appears, all else being simply the mechanics of non-minded nature. Like others, he allows for no possibility of a consciousness or mindedness that is unlike that which we experience in our own human nature. Even if we can accept that a dog has an ability to remember and anticipate but deny it the ability to self-reflect or consider, its language being too primitive to allow for developed interior dialogue, does that mean it has no consciousness? Dennett would say it has no consciousness. Does the dog have mind or mentality, the capacity for mental states? The words are important.

A less anthropocentric measuring device is based upon qualia. The question is answered by deciding whether or not there is present in an individual the subjective awareness of what it feels like to exist as that individual. As Nagel pointed out, it is just not possible for us to know whether another creature has a sense of what it is like to be itself, let alone what that sense may be. Human beings spend the majority of their wakeful hours with no self-awareness, merely moving upon the currents of reaction based upon varying levels of awareness; it is impossible for us to get inside the mind of another human, even one with whom we have lived most of our lives, with whom we communicate openly and fluently. Pondering the subjective mental states of a wood pigeon or stag beetle is surely beyond our scope. Considering the issue on the basis of observing behaviours, Colin McGinn suggests the dividing line may lie somewhere around 'the fancier models of mollusc'. Yet an amoeba, an organism of a single cell with no sense receptors (in as much as we understand such things), appears to have the ability to learn to avoid a toxic substance: can we call this mentality? We might say that there is here evidence of perception, experience and possible recall, beyond which we must admit there may be more that we cannot know. DS Clarke speaks of mind 'as the having of a qualitative perspective … in all natural bodies with unity of organization and the capacity to maintain themselves against potentially destructive environmental forces'. Again, with no apparent sense receptors, bacteria appear to organise themselves according to their immediate environment in order to survive and thrive.

Indeed, how far *can* we simplify the parameters in order to use the term mind and succeed in drawing a justifiable dividing line? The answer given by the animist is to decline the invitation to draw that line at all.

Perception I have defined as the gathering of information by simply being attentive. Attention we could now further define without slipping into the error of limiting it to human experience. In Chapter One, I related perception and attention to the observing *I*, but that observer need not be consciously aware of being attentive. I would now sharpen the definition by simplifying it: attention is the state of being *awake* to our environment. That wakefulness is what allows for perception.

A tree perceives the world around it. It is aware of gravity, light and temperature, the resources within the soil into which it roots, the availability of water. By the way in which it adapts in order to make the most of its environment, we might say that the tree senses the changes of the seasons, for its perception is experienced corporeally. In human terms we would talk about visceral sensation, and there is nothing in those words that definitively limits their use to human experience. Through our limited perspective, we can see how the tree retains evidence of that experience, its memories revealed in its shape, in the rings of its trunk, in the information it stores and passes on in its seed and fruit. Like the woodland it may be a part of, it has inherited and adapting strategies for its own protection and survival, a self-organising entity within its immediate ecological context. As to what subjective awareness it has, we just cannot know.

What of the water that is flowing from the hills to the sea, the rock in the river bed, the storm accumulating in the skies above, the midges flitting over the water's surface, the swallows darting to catch them before the rain comes in? Where is mind here within these interacting organisms and systems of nature? Furthermore, without a line now drawn, we have no choice but to consider what science tells us about matter: can we talk of mindedness in the water molecule, and consider its mental state as it is torn apart by an atom of potassium?

Such questions only retain validity where we are fully able to discard all the assumptions that come with the blinkers of anthropocentricity.

The history of dualism and materialism has asserted that the mind is connected with the human body, more recently broader agreement linking it to the human brain. If we accept there is more to mind than rational consideration, self-awareness, consciousness, we are released to acknowledge the presence of mind in creatures without brains, or even nervous systems. If we allow mind to be where there is the simplest level of perception, we are drawing closer to an understanding of its definition within animism.

The physical brain, however, provided a substance of which it was constituted, as did the soul or mind, and I have as yet offered no such substance with regard to animistic mindedness. Indeed, I can go further in suggesting that there may be neither mental nor material *stuff* at all. Stuff: that may seem a strangely informal word to use in the context of a serious philosophical discussion about nature, but its use highlights how close we are to the edge of usable language. The extraordinary young mathematician and philosopher, William Kingdon Clifford, coined the term 'mind-stuff' in the late nineteenth century, the American William James spoke of the 'stuff' of the universe, and Colin McGinn refers to consciousness as 'a kind of stuff'. I like the quality of frustration that can be heard in the word.

There are many questions as yet unanswered then, not least about the essence of a reality that is minded, and whether this is purely epistemological or if I am speaking of nature *in itself*. Before attending to these questions, as I shall do in Chapter Five, I am aware that this mindedness may seem unfamiliar. In order to aid me in my explanation of the thesis, I shall turn again to other thinkers, those who have shared such ideas, presenting a very brief history of animism, panpsychism and integrated metaphysics.

A History

Animism is broadly accepted as humankind's oldest religion. Indeed, there is no reason to imagine that animist views have not been held since the earliest days of *Homo sapiens*.

For two hundred thousand years and more, in family units, in clans and tribes, our ancestors lived in a manner that required them to be thoroughly involved and connected with the landscapes through which they moved. Their success was wholly dependent on their wakefulness to the idiosyncrasies of each ecosystem, ensuring that their interaction with each place, its climate, its earth and water, its flora and fauna, was sufficiently erudite and respectful to provide them with safety and nourishment, and tenably so. Life was tough, resources no doubt at times scarce, power struggles erupting into brutal conflict: I have no wish to sentimentalise. However, such a vast span of time, over half a million generations, makes the past five to ten millennia of civilisation somewhat fleeting, and the last fifteen hundred years of widespread monotheism a blink. On such a scale, the last four hundred years of growing materialism should be wholly insignificant - but that those four centuries tally with the exponential surge in human population, its irreparable impact on the planet and consequent collapse in long-term sustainability.

The modern animist is proud of his tradition's immensely ancient roots. Being the oldest religious tradition, it is easy for others to deride it as primitive, yet the twenty first century animist isn't regressing to join his neolithic ancestry, re-enacting a lifestyle of hunting mammoth with flint-knapped arrowheads. Over many thousands of generations, as our human ability to communicate has been honed, as we have learned to abstract and reason through floods of reactive emotion, as our technologies have improved offering stronger and more specific tools, so equally has our thinking evolved. There is nothing naïve or unsophisticated about the philosophy that now underlies animistic beliefs; while retaining its fundamental tenets of integration and participation, animism has developed along with other aspects of human thinking.

What we know of this gentle evolution is limited, however, and not least because documented history has most often been written by the dualists and materialists whose beliefs have been politically more acceptable to those holding power over the past fifteen hundred years. The co-operative, participatory attitude of the animist is not one that inspires or fuels the gaining of power over others. It is nonetheless worth picking out what history we can.

When we are considering the distant past, much available evidence comes through archaeology, a good deal more by way of anthropology, both from modern studies and from observations made in post-mediaeval centuries when explorers were first encountering tribes outside Western civilisation. Additionally, there are the oldest writings, the lyric poets of lands around the Mediterranean and, some seven hundred years or so later, adventurers from those lands narrating tales about our more northerly tribes. From such sources we are able to craft ideas about how our ancient ancestors saw the world; that they believed gods, spirits and souls to be present everywhere within nature is wholly beyond doubt. Whether these were perceived as ethereal and incorporeal beings, connected to but distinct from matter, simply cannot be known for certain.

As described earlier, the Pythagoreans were understood to be dualists, but we know their beliefs were entirely out of synch with their contemporaries. The Druids of north western Europe were said to hold similar ideas, believing, for example, in the transmigration of souls at death. Such early thinkers and theologians were reaching out of the mud and pain of mortal reality for a purity of form and purpose. Plato followed in these philosophically ambitious footsteps, as did Christianity after that. For our ancient ancestors, educated by nature, these were high ideals quite possibly outside the conceptual scope of the vast majority of people.

Where glimpses of dualism could (and can) be found at ground level within animist cultures, I would suggest these derive not from abstractions of purity, but from mundane fears and superstitions about the dead. In many simple animistic traditions, the only entities perceived to be wandering without bodily form are those who have been torn from their physical integration through violence or other severe trauma: here is psychosis, madness and rage, and all the more dangerous because such souls are believed to crave the release that can only come from regaining the natural state of integration. This is evidence of superstition, found within any religious tradition, not a tenet within a considered metaphysics: such fears kick in instinctively. What is more, the indication for substance dualism is negated, for the state of peace is understood to come only where that soul/body unity is maintained or reattained.

Nonetheless, it is still easy to impose or presume a dualistic interpretation of animist traditions as a whole, or indeed to imagine that dualism was (or is) the norm within animism, particularly if the paradigms and language of integrated metaphysics are wholly unfamiliar to the individual asking the questions. Yet to do so is to misunderstand the nature of mind and matter within a metaphysical position rooted in nature. Forces, energies, patterns repeating, flows of causality, all intimate an inherent purpose, a guiding intention or fate, and these may be languaged as gods or spirits or souls, depending on what is understood to be their power and scope. However, other than the broken and unhappy exceptions, these cannot be said to be discarnate beings: they are thoroughly integral to the tangible world of fire and flesh, of barley and river. Even using the term *discarnate* defines matter too specifically here, and in a way that is too distinct from soul or mind to be valid.

Clarity is, however, contingent upon what is understood to be the essential substance of matter, of spirit, of soul, mind and god, or indeed the stuff that allows for an integration of all these. The further back in history, the more dependent we become upon how other thinkers have construed the evidence and translated those key words across centuries and languages. The remainder of this chapter reviews the history as we can extract it, albeit with an awareness that often that crucial *stuff* remains undefined. Nonetheless the tracks are useful to survey, leading us as they do towards those more recent thinkers who are able better to articulate just what that stuff may or may not be.

As civilisation took root, settled communities growing larger, thinkers began turning to understand more deeply the essence of nature. In lands around the Mediterranean, the surviving work of the earliest lyric poets reveals those basic and ancient animistic beliefs to be still fundamental to life and culture. Slowly the gods were coming to be represented in more human forms: nature, including human nature, with its storms and wars, its famine and floods, its lusts and jealousies, was depicted in the tales with all its brutality and injustice, stories being written that in one form or another had no doubt been told for millennia. Such stories are indeed still the bedrock of human culture, as mythologies consciously and unwittingly are retold in novels and operas, in ballads and films, the forces and patterns, the drives and spirits of nature explored, lambasted and celebrated, as ever.

In the sixth century BCE Thales had affirmed there to be gods in all things. A century later the Sicilian Empedocles was teaching that soul must be integral to the four elements that comprised nature - earth, air, fire and water - for if it were separate from nature it could not *know* nature, and definitively it did. With soul integral to nature, everything in the universe contained a measure of wisdom and intelligence. A few decades later, Democritus was speaking of those tiny spherical *atoma* of soul and fire which he believed fuelled movement. In humans and other animals, the atoms entered the body through breath and so maintained life. As Aristotle made clear in his writing about the thinker, this soul was not just *psyche* or *anima*, but *nous*, the rational mind as well, and it was universally present as the very principle of nature. Such ideas, he related, were commonly held by many thinkers of the day.

Aristotle himself, however, felt that soul in any form was a principle not of nature but of life. In *De Anima* he wondered at those who 'say that soul is intermingled in the whole universe', suggesting that this cannot be true, as not all that he saw around him could be said to be alive. The Stoics though, whose focus was upon the *pneuma*, the creative blend of fire and air, presented another strongly integrated view: mind was not separate from body in their teachings, for the universe was crafted of natural reason. Consequently, it was decreed, mind or reason was an essential, integral, indeed structural component of matter.

The philosophy of the Stoics, together with various other Hellenistic ideas, held sway until the beginning of the Christian era, when what followed was well over a thousand years of European thinkers unable to step outside the preoccupation with Christianity. Aristotle's clear distinction between the lower souls and the *nous* - which 'cannot reasonably be regarded as blended with the body' - allowed his work to become foundational to scholastic dualism with its predominant concern with the immortality of the soul. So did philosophical thinking remain fettered by these dualistic and liturgical chains throughout mediaeval Europe. Indeed, it wasn't until the early sixteenth century that thinkers were again finding the language and courage to explore ideas of integration that had been so unacceptable within the bounds of Church dogma.

Five philosophers of the Italian Renaissance lit the way. Gerolamo Cardano, born at the turn of the century, was a philosopher, physician and mathematician who spoke of the soul as the principle within all matter that provided coherence. The southern Italian, Bernardino Telesio, declared that nature was imbued with perpetually opposing forces of (expanding) heat and (contracting) cold. Soul was the embodiment of these active forces, and thus nature was inherently sensate, feeling and responding, changing and creating. Further, because soul is influenced by matter, to evade the problem of interaction he stated that it must also have a material existence. Towards the end of the century, it was Francesco Patrizi who coined the term panpsychism, though his vision was more dualistic in terms of substance. A defender of Plato against Aristotelianism, his system was a hierarchy of nine levels, from the wholeness of the world soul, to the human soul, and the soul which imbued the animals, the plants and the stones of the earth, all of which were constituted of an elemental yet divine and immaterial light.

Giordano Bruno was not the only one of the five to get in trouble with the Church, but only he, standing unrepentant, lost his life to the Inquisition. As mentioned in the previous chapter, he perceived the world as a vibrant and integrated whole, composed of countless individual atoms or *minima*, each containing an innate intelligence that together made up the world soul. Perceiving humanity as neither special nor central within nature, in 1584 in *De La Causa, Principio, et Uno* (or *Cause, Principle and Unity*) he wrote, 'there is nothing that does not possess a soul and that has no vital principle'. Written in the style of a Platonic dialogue, in response to whether shoes, or clothes, or the dead, have soul, he wrote, 'in all things there is spirit, and there is not the least corpuscle that does not contain within itself some portion that may animate it'. Equating the world soul with God,

Bruno is now described as a pantheist, but like many animists who recognise the wholeness of the universe as divine it is entirely reasonable to refer to him as an animist as well.

The final of the five was Tommaso Campanella who also espoused a belief in the sentience of matter: 'It is an error to think that the world does not feel just because it does not have legs, eyes and hands', he declared. His thesis was based upon the 'three primalities' of power, wisdom and love, where the process of awareness allows a state of becoming, a developing knowing and direct relationship with the world. These were based on the old Stoic triad of knowledge - physics, logic and ethics - which Augustine of Hippo had moulded in the fourth century to a philosophy that could be applied to all creation: being, knowing and love or willing. Although no animist himself, Augustine's ideas were accessible and, drenched in devotional enthusiasm, they were extremely influential. As qualities of the soul, Campanella believed they were integral to every part of nature from stones to God, allowing everything 'the sensation of their own being and of their conservation'. Describing him as an Hermetic magician, as was Bruno, Brian Easlea wrote, 'Campanella's animism is not only explicit but once again a dangerous connection must have been drawn in the minds of ruling elites between animism, magic and political subversion'. Imprisoned for twenty seven years and repeatedly tortured by the Inquisition, he escaped death only by faking insanity. It is easy to understand why some of his less audacious contemporaries, such as the elusive and evasive Descartes, behaved as they did, compromising their work to play it safe.

Yet, despite all the efforts of the Church, despite the very public persecution and execution of Bruno and others, I would suggest that animism remained a natural and instinctive belief across Europe for a very long time, most particularly amongst those whose rural lives were guided still by the tides and cycles of nature more than by a human-mediated and transcendent god. In tune with its own character, it continued almost unspoken. Even now, it is possible to talk to people whose livelihoods are largely or wholly dependent upon the land and find that, just beneath the surface, there is an animism that guides both their decision-making and sense of gratitude: a belief in the inherent intelligence of nature.

One of the pleasures of Shakespeare is his ability to describe the perennial crises and drives of human nature which are as relevant today as they were in his era, while at the same time revealing beliefs and attitudes that were prevalent in the world around him. In many of his plays there are references to spirits or ghosts, with clear direction that ignoring such presences can only bring disaster. Belief in the discarnate souls of the discontented dead was a common fear, an intuitive superstition reinforced by a judgmental and condemnatory Christian dualism. Yet there is an easy paganism in his writing as well, whispers of animistic belief emerging, sometimes with a beautiful simplicity. Often his words voice what were still very different realities between rural lives and those in the crowded noise and human politics of the burgeoning towns. Written in the last decade of the sixteenth century, in *As You Like It*, wandering the forest his Duke Senior declares:

And this our life, exempt from public haunt,
Finds tongues in trees, books in the running brooks,
Sermons in stones, and good in everything.

Here there is a romantic tone to his words, but with an animistic lack of sentimentality, spirits of nature are presented with as much charm as malice across his work: Puck in *A Midsummer Night's Dream* is clearly a troublemaker, a sentience within the natural world that isn't limited by a human morality. Indeed, the play could be interpreted as an exploration of humanity's turbulent relationship with nature, including the drives and hungers of human nature. In *The Tempest*, the magician Prospero is well aware of the inherent intelligence of nature, summoning spirits to do his bidding:

Ye elves of hills, brooks, standing lakes, and groves;
And ye that on the sands with printless foot
Do chase the ebbing Neptune.

The air sprite Ariel is an ethereal creature that personifies a natural sentience, both brilliant yet fragile; without the rational wit to evade the magician's power, he is once again tricked and enslaved. Shakespeare is returning to nature its voice, which Christian anthropocentricity has so determinedly tried to remove.

To a twenty first century audience, such stories are rich with fantasy, but reading it alongside contemporary texts that impression is diluted. In *De Magnete*, published ten years before *The Tempest*, Gilbert writes with a beautiful enthusiasm, 'we deem the whole world animate, and all globes, all stars, and this glorious earth, too'. Gilbert's animism challenges the position of humanity as the crucial centre point of the Great Chain of Being, based upon Aristotle's *scala naturae*, above which there is only soul, below which there is only matter.

The poet John Milton does the same. For him too, the flesh and mud, the water and blood, the stones, the trees, the angels and minds that make up the natural world are comprised of a single primary substance - and it is inherently animate. In *Paradise Lost*, written during Cromwell's puritanical republic but not published until the Restoration in 1667, Milton's angels are not all ethereal soul, but deliciously tangible. Raphael shares a meal with Adam in *Book V*, and in *VIII* he even reveals how angels make love, with an exquisite connectedness:

Whatever pure thou in the body enjoy'st
(And pure thou wert created) we enjoy

In eminence, and obstacle find none
Of membrane, joynt, or limb, exclusive barrs:
Easier then Air with Air, if Spirits embrace,
Total they mix, Union of Pure with Pure
Desiring; nor restrain'd conveyance need
As Flesh to mix with Flesh, or Soul with Soul.

Two hundred thousand years are not easily swept aside where nature's voice is still heard.

Like Bruno, Baruch Spinoza is referred to as a pantheist, for he asserted that God and nature were a single unity. Radically monist, his seventeenth century philosophy was based upon a rationale about God, the perfection of whom must entail an indefinable or infinite number of attributes. These attributes, however, cannot be expressed through a variety of primary substances, for his definition of substance didn't allow one to interface with another; he concluded that there must be only one. If we are not to slide into idealism, this substance must be, as Spinoza described, *Deus sive Natura*, translated as 'God, or nature'. Of the countless attributes this divine substance must have, it appeared to our human perception as only two: thought (mind) and extension (matter). Although these seem distinct, they are constituted of the same stuff; thus every thought or idea has its corresponding extension or material form. Consequently, every object can be said to have its own mentality or mind. Mentality and physicality are intrinsically one. Spinoza presented this as an ontological truth, so allowing for even the tiniest particle to have its own mindedness.

A complicated character with perpetually conflicting objectives, politically ambitious and socially grasping, Gottfried Leibniz could hardly have been more different from the quiet and contemplative Spinoza. Also writing in the late seventeenth century, his ideas have been equally influential in the history of panpsychism. Objecting to Spinoza's monist stance, Leibniz asserted a philosophy based on the existence of an infinite number of primary substances, each a minute and indivisible unit with a 'plurality of properties and relations', each capable of perception and sensation, appetite and agency, 'so that we must conceive of them on the model of the notion we have of *souls*'. As a mathematician, he proposed that these were point units, in other words, as if one dimensional they were entirely without extension. As such, they were effectively outside of time and space, yet each contained a comprehensive knowledge of the entire universe. At first he called them entelechies, simple forms, *unité substantielle, point metaphysical*, and *forces primitives*, but after hearing of Anne Conway's work he came to use her term *monad*, from the Greek μονάδα (*monada*), meaning a single unit.

In a letter to the English theologian Thomas Burnett in 1697, he expressed his conviction that 'everything takes place according to a living principle and according to final causes - all things are full of life and consciousness'. His paper, *Monadology*, eventually finished in 1714, clarified further: 'Every being in the universe from living animals down to the simple monad was alive or composed of living parts, there being nothing fallow, sterile or dead in the universe; no chaos, no confusion, save in appearance'.

It wasn't integration Leibniz was seeking. Born at the end of the Thirty Years' War, the population of Germany having been almost halved through conflict, poverty and famine, his father dying when he was just a young boy, Leibniz came into a world that was in ragged disarray. His goal was to 'calculate' the nature of order and order within nature. Avoiding the problem of the interface, his perfect monads, created by God, did not interact with each other nor with the physicality of nature, but instead smoothly ran in parallel, according to a 'pre-established harmony' set into motion by God. It was a beautiful system, suffering only from that great divide which, while scattering soul or mentality across the entirety of the universe, is not an integrated or monist system, effectively still favouring the mental over the physical.

Indeed, here we see clearly how panpsychism diverges, on one side stepping into idealism where the mind is definitively present everywhere, but where matter is illusory. Where it does not retain its dualism, on the other side it steps into the mud and blood of integration. Two eighteenth century French philosophers who took the second route were, perhaps not surprisingly, known for their poetic sensuality. In his blend of science, philosophy and erotica entitled *Vénus physique*, philosopher and mathematician Pierre Louis Maupertuis explained how, at its most fundamental level, matter contains a self-organising intelligence. These 'percipient particles' are essential for the generation and sustainability of life. Six years later in *On the Interpretation of Nature*, the liberal thinker and dramatist Denis Diderot was expressing what is termed his vitalistic materialism: keen to dismiss established notions of the supernatural and transcendent, he explored ideas of inherent intelligence. If religion hadn't taught us that God had made everything, he suggested that the philosopher would surely speculate 'that animality had from all eternity its particular elements scattered in and mingled with the mass of matter'. Animality: a wonderful old word interpreted today too simplistically as the behaviour of a nonhuman animal, what Diderot meant here was that wakeful perceptiveness, sentience and ability to respond, the mindedness of nature as a whole. In his later work, *D'Alembert's Dream*, not published until well after his death, he repeatedly refers to the sensitivity of matter, its capacity for sensation, as its key quality: 'From the elephant to the flea, from the flea to the sensitive living atom, the origin of all, there is no point in nature but suffers and enjoys'.

As the eighteenth century clattered into the Industrial Revolution, significant change moved more quickly through Europe than it had ever done before. Fuelled by the rising tide of science, over the course of a century the landscape was transformed, as quarries, mills and factories, railways and enclosures relocated growing populations and recontextualised poverty. The reactive cries of revolution, that in some nations broke into the violent clashes of protest and civil wars, were accompanied by an outpouring of art, literature and music railing against both the old order who were indignantly holding to their wealth and power, and the new intellectualism that was forging new brands of exploitation and brute inequality.

In his radical and revolutionary prose poem, *The Marriage of Heaven and Hell*, written in the early 1790s, the Londoner William Blake speaks of matter and desire as part of the divine order, dismissing the dogmatic philosophical habit that is dualism, and celebrating the intense sensuality of life.

All Bibles or sacred codes, have been the causes of the following Errors.

1. That Man has two real existing principles Viz: a Body & a Soul.
2. That Energy, call'd Evil, is alone from the Body, & that Reason, call'd Good, is alone from the Soul.
3. That God will torment Man in Eternity for following his Energies.

But the following Contraries to these are True.

1. Man has no Body distinct from his Soul; for that call'd Body is a portion of Soul discern'd by the five Senses,the chief inlets of Soul in this age.
2. Energy is the only life and is from the Body and Reason is the bound or outward circumference of Energy.
3. Energy is Eternal Delight.

This Romanticism revered raw inspiration and imagination, the untamed and undeveloped, seeking out the vital principle in the natural world: that which gave it not only life but *wakeful* life. As such, nature, venerated as sacred, was perceived to be humming with its own sentience. The devotion in poetry such as that of William Wordsworth is more than sentimental poesy. Like others, he is expressing a Spinozistic pantheism, acknowledging nature as divine, ensouled and minded, expressing its innate passion through its vibrancy of colour and form, its wild storms of desire, its many gods and spirits, all of which the open heart and mind can experience as nature's sweet and painful ecstasy. In 1798, in *Tintern Abbey* he writes,

And I have felt
A presence that disturbs me with the joy
Of elevated thoughts; a sense sublime
Of something far more deeply interfused,
Whose dwelling is the light of setting suns,
And the round ocean and the living air,
And the blue sky, and in the mind of man:
A motion and a spirit, that impels
All thinking things, all objects of all thought,
And rolls through all things. Therefore am I still
A lover of the meadows and the woods,
And mountains; and of all that we behold
From this green earth ...

In a letter to his brother George and his wife in 1819, just a few years before his death, John Keats wrote, 'Intelligences are atoms of perception - they know and they see and they are pure, in short they are God', going on to explain how such atoms are honed by nature to create each individual soul. Not conventionally thought of as philosophers, writers such as Percy Shelley, Alfred Tennyson, Johann von Goethe and Friedrich Schiller, and the

Americans Ralph Waldo Emerson, Henry David Thoreau, Walt Whitman, are men whose writings are drenched in the exhilaration and despair of their love of nature, a nature that is shimmering with perception and drive. To many modern animists and other Pagans, this Romanticism is acknowledged as a key part of their heritage.

The strength of idealism in German philosophy, particularly that of the nineteenth century, has been another influence on the evolution of panpsychism. I shall sketch only briefly this trend, and where thinkers seem to me to be far closer to animism than panpsychist idealism, for it allows me to mark out a path towards the end of this chapter, opening the door to the next.

Characters like Friedrich Schelling were heroes of the Romantic movement, passionate idealists reaching for propositions that embraced the boundlessness of natural deity while not rejecting out of hand all that science was beginning to uncover. In *Ideas for a Philosophy of Nature*, Schelling wrote of an organising principle in nature, an intelligence or soul, which expressed itself as consciousness in humankind, and was experienced as thought, direction and sensation. So integral to nature was this principle that it led Schelling to his essentially monist position: 'one can push as many transitory materials as one wants, which become finer and finer, between mind and matter, but some time the point must come where mind and matter are One'. His writing was perhaps profoundly influential on the English poet Coleridge who, in his *Biographia Literaria*, was concerned with the role of imagination as the creative force, making meaning of and so giving life to the raw data of perception.

Goethe and Schopenhauer both wrote of how matter cannot exist or function without soul (*Seele*) and vice versa, but more uncompromising in his philosophy was the German experimental psychologist Gustav Fechner. Born at the beginning of the nineteenth century near to what is now the Polish border, he had written a good number of scientific works, completing many translations and innovative investigations, before he succumbed to a crippling neurological illness. For three years he struggled, for long periods losing his will to live, but when at last he did recover, his attitude and insight were profoundly enhanced by the experience. His is a vision as passionate as that of the Romantic poets: 'Is it not more beautiful and glorious to think that the living trees of the forest burn like torches uplifted towards heaven? To be sure, we can only think this: we do not directly see anything of these soul-flames of nature; but since we *can* think it, why are we not willing to?' In *Über Die Seelefrage*, he wrote: 'I asked myself how the opinions of men could ever have so spun themselves away from life so far as to deem the earth only a dry clod, and to seek for angels above it or about it in the emptiness of the sky'.

For Fechner, there was one basic substance which viewed from the outside is matter, and from the inside is mind. As we cannot be both inside and outside simultaneously, it is not possible to perceive both the mental and physical aspects at the same time. He recognised that, with no possibility for proof, it takes faith to accept that another entity has a soul; the point he raised was that this is as true for one's brother as it is for a nonhuman animal, or a plant, or planet. On that basis, in *Nanna* he argued that the question of whether plants have souls has been 'treated too lightly', and that 'what has been said with regard to this matter suggests a desire to justify a preconceived opinion rather than to scrutinise it'. Asking what are the *'essential* signs' that reveal the presence of soul, he pointed out that plants are as effectively self-organising as animals, and if we allow that they are alive, why should they not be animate? Both plants and animals, after all, 'derive by a remarkable process of multiplication from a single original cell'. His poetry is exquisite: 'in addition to the souls which run about and cry and devour might there not be souls which bloom in stillness, which exhale their fragrance, which satisfy their thirst and their impulses by burgeoning? I cannot conceive how running and crying have a peculiar right, as against blooming and the emission of fragrance, to be regarded as indications of psychic activity and sensibility'.

Fechner saw the earth as a whole as minded, and by analogy again he extended that out to the stars, expressing that long term perspective often used by animists: 'The view that in the heavenly bodies there dwell heavenly souls is so strange to the world of today that we cannot but wonder why it could seem so natural to an earlier world - and we shall cease to wonder only when in a later world it will again seem just as natural'.

Rudolf Hermann Lotze was a contemporary of Fechner, a philosopher and scientist, whose thinking also added significantly to the development of psychology. In his *Mikrokosmus*, he called for 'a thorough-going revolt of the heart against the coldness of a theory that transforms all the beauty and animism of forms into a rigid physico-psychical mechanism'. Instead, he sought a way of perceiving the world as a relationally vibrant whole. What we comprehend as laws of nature he suggested were the fabric of ecological relationships: these connections he saw as the world mind, the absolute, God. As our own minds are integral to that whole, and our inner mind is the only thing about which we can have certainty, it is valid to perceive these connecting relationships of nature with surety. Although he saw beauty in this vibrancy, and nature's rationale for such beauty, he recognised too that such a view would not be acceptable in the growing materialism of his era: who could bear to imagine 'there is everywhere present the fullness of animated life'?

Like many Germans of his era, living through the process of national unification in 1871 which so painfully highlighted cultural diversity, ideas of *Heimat* and identity were important to Lotze. The animistic perspective provided a powerful sense of home and belonging through his understanding of connectedness, not only within landscapes but through the fabric of communities, crafted by shared culture and history.

Ernst Haeckel was a German naturalist and philosopher whose animism was beautifully overt. Also writing in the late nineteenth century, he popularised Darwin's work in Germany, himself describing hundreds of new species. Defining himself as a monist, he believed all matter to be capable of perception, of sensations of pleasure and pain, and of response or motion. This he took down to the chemical level, writing in 1895 that 'an immaterial living spirit is just as unthinkable as a dead, spiritless material; the two are inseparably combined in every atom'. I have no doubt that he would have extended his view to the subatomic level should science have offered him the opportunity to do so at the time.

In the first half of this chapter, I offered a few preliminary definitions of animism. Recognising that a significant reason why ideas of integrated monism and panpsychism are dismissed out of hand is because of the slack and ill-defined use of terms, I gathered up a number of the words generally used and deconstructed them, giving a clear description of my own use within this context. On that basis, I laid *mindedness* on the table as a key term in my ongoing process of exposition.

Acknowledging that animism is furthermore disregarded as primitive, or that modern animists are attempting to recreate an ancient philosophy, in the second half of the chapter I reviewed the history of such ideas, bringing to awareness the good number of thinkers who have had similar convictions. This was not so much to back up my own thesis or definition, for many of these presented metaphysical ideas that run somewhere alongside rather than in tune with my own. I paused in this review towards the beginning of the twentieth century and consciously so.

Integrated animism addresses the central problems raised by the three other generally recognised systems. Dualism: without the substance divide between mind and matter, there is not the issue of how the two might interact. Materialism: with mindedness always present, there is not the dilemma as to how matter might produce qualia or consciousness. Idealism: because nature is not considered an illusion generated entirely by the mind, the problem of shared reality is also resolved. However, serious questions about animism and panpsychism have not yet been answered. These will be the subject of Chapter Five. Those philosophers who have explored panpsychist and integrated metaphysics over the last hundred years will be called to aid me in crafting a satisfactory explanation.

Chapter Five

Moments

In *Panpsychism in the West,* eco-philosopher David Skrbina put forward nine comprehensive points to back the panpsychist thesis, the last of which he called the Argument from Authority. More of a seal of approval on the previous eight than an argument in its own right, Skrbina is reminding the reader that this view is far from naïve; brilliant minds throughout the history of Western thought have held convictions that concur with the animistic and panpsychist stance, including a great many during the last few centuries of increasingly complex scientific and rational thinking.

One such brilliant mind was the American scientist Thomas Edison, many of whose innovations are now integral to the structural framework of our world's technological and social fabric. Describing his own religion in terms somewhere between Spinoza's pantheism and the rational deism of Thomas Paine, and defending himself against the charge of atheism in just the same way, Edison spoke of nature as the supreme intelligence: 'what you call God I call Nature'. As Skrbina quotes, he went on to explain that belief in terms that satisfied his scientific instinct: 'I cannot avoid the conclusion that all matter is composed of intelligent atoms and that life and mind are merely synonyms for the aggregation of atomic intelligence'.

Another was the Englishman, Arthur Eddington. Another exceptional physicist whose insights changed our world, he saw that nature worked in a structurally consistent way, and concluded that mindedness must therefore be inherent throughout. In his *Time, Space and Gravitation* in 1920, he wrote, 'All through the physical world runs that unknown content, which must surely be the stuff of our consciousness'.

Exploring deeply the potential of consciousness in his extraordinary text *Tertium Organum*, the Russian philosopher PD Ouspensky described his own vision in 1912: 'A mountain, a tree, a river, the fish in the river, drops of water, rain, a plant, fire, each separately must possess a mind of its own'. Ouspensky was considered by many to be on the esoteric fringes of Western thought, but it is only the richer poetry of his language that sets him apart from highly respected and established thinkers for whom animist and panpsychist views were wholly defensible.

Where I might speak of perception or experience, in *A Contribution to the Theory of the Living Organism*, in 1943 English zoologist Wilfred Eade Agar used the term consciousness to describe the varying degrees of awareness evident within nature. Accepting the parameters of his own definition, his perspective was entirely in tune with the animistic: 'we must ascribe consciousness to every living agent, such as a plant cell or bacterium, and even (if the continuity of nature is not to be broken) to an electron'. A decade later in *Gene and Organism*, American geneticist Sewall Wright spoke of the earth as 'one great organism', a self-regulating structure the internal relationships of which provide its ongoing coherence. Mind, he suggested, might be found in the nucleoprotein molecules of genes, the very DNA of our physical being, consciousness being a fusion of these tiny cell-minds.

English evolutionary biologist, Julian Huxley, was another whose vision could be seen as essentially panpsychist: though he acknowledged it may be impossible to prove, the notion of mind or mindedness being inherent throughout nature he believed to be 'the most economical hypothesis'. An advocate of Pierre Teilhard de Chardin, the French Jesuit philosopher, in 1958 Huxley provided an introduction for the posthumous English edition of *The Phenomenon of Man*, in which de Chardin himself declared there to be 'some sort of psyche in every corpuscle', even those too small for us to perceive.

Such a handful is one of many supporting the integrated and panpsychist position, snippets of which could be scattered across these pages, the point being that serious thinkers have continued to consider the option. It genuinely offers an immediate and overt solution to many problems of the metaphysical debate.

There are a number of key questions here, however, that remain as yet unanswered, a principal one being the issue of substance.

I have reviewed notions of mind and of matter within other metaphysical theories. I have spoken of the animist belief as *a monist metaphysical stance based upon ubiquitous and integrated mindedness*; in other words, I have suggested that there is just one basic stuff of nature and that it is somehow minded. Taking mindedness to be the capacity for mind, I have begun to develop a definition of *mind* and spoken of how broadly it may be used, considering ideas of what it may include. However, I have not yet discussed what mindedness might be constituted of: I have evaded describing a primary substance, and consciously so. This chapter will face that question. I shall also address the question linked to it in traditional philosophical debate, that of how such a substance might originate or whether it has always been present.

Having placed ideas on the table, an equally inevitable question must be that which returns us to evaluate just what it is we can know. Having proffered the suggestion that all nature is minded, my next obligation could simply be to provide a feasible explanation as to why it may *appear* to the animist to be that way. However, having discarded the stuff of mind and matter and offered an alternative, I must address the question of ontology: am I talking of nature in itself, and if so, how can I do so justifiably? The divide between the phenomenological and noumenal then also needs to be faced, the chasm between the subject and the object, the issue raised by Kant that so acutely measures philosophical integrity.

Substance

In Spinoza's definition, 'a substance does not depend upon the conception of another thing from which it might be formed', for it is 'conceived in itself and conceived through itself': its nature is self-generated, self-perpetuating, and entirely self-contained. As a result, it cannot interact with any other substance. This is the basis on which the gentle thinker asserted there to be only one substance, which he called God or nature - and of course, being God, it *must* exist. Such a definition, although rationally acute, is more radical than most.

In philosophy, the word is considered more generally to mean that out of which everything else is comprised. The Latin *substantia* translates as substance, but its deconstructed root refers to *sub stare*, to stand beneath, giving the word its meaning of a base or essence. Consequently, a crucial quality is presumed to be its temporal durability: for something to underpin a reality it must consistently be there. Yet, I wonder if the etymological links with the Italian *stare* and Spanish *estar* offer more tones to the colour of this word; both these mean *to be*, but in the sense of being present and in a particular condition or situation. So substance implies not a passive state of intrinsic being but an active and immediate involvement. This is reflected in the fact that we know it only through its various properties, attributes or qualities, an issue that inspires constant debate as to the boundaries between a substance (what it *is*) and what might be said to be its properties (what it *does*).

Until now I have used substance and stuff fairly synonymously; from here on, I shall differentiate between the two, albeit with a fine line. While substance clearly points to that which is fundamental, underlying or primary in nature, it also brings with it associations of form and durability that can, to the modern ear, subtly imply something more *substantial*, i.e. matter. Stuff is less restricted. Its roots are in the Old French *estoffe*, meaning to furnish or equip, and tell stories of the padding used beneath heavy mediaeval armour. My use of the word is lazy with regard to these tales, I admit, but I am inspired by the way it sits within modern English and wonder if perhaps this usage reveals a little more of its history. The word has an energy and verve that celebrates the nonspecific: *stuff!* It is a word filled with bewildered and indignant amazement where there is found to be a lack of articulate understanding. It is this mystery I acknowledge in my own use of the word. Like substance, then, stuff is only really known to us through its apparent properties or qualities.

Taking these ideas fully in hand, when considering the mindedness of nature, I lay out another proposition, one that will be developed and adapted in pages to come: *in animism, mindedness is understood to be a property of the primary stuff of nature.* In other words, at this stage we might say that mindedness is what it *does.* We have yet to explore what it *is.* How we go about finding an answer to that is a journey that must again be, naturally, somewhat indirect.

When we feel wholly confident in our own perspective, there is always a risk that we may believe our understanding is definitive, and consequently unwittingly impose that definition where the context, and thus the appropriate meaning, is in fact quite different. While a liberal Christian or Muslim may accept the polytheist's reverence for many gods, he may still consider the reverence for a god of thunder or lust to be disturbingly dangerous, assuming that all religions require unconditional love for and worship of deity; the Western polytheist's devotion is not about submission though, but about studious attention and respect, as he strives to live honourably given such violent forces of nature are an integral part of our world. Projecting definitions between paradigms is an error of assumption.

The same problem can be found with regard to substance. Given mind and matter as we have seen them to be most generally understood, two distinct substances wholly saturated with dualist connotations, no combination of the two together could give us the animist's stuff of nature. The mixture would always be formed by and held within the basic paradigm of the two separate substances. Indeed, the result of such a combination is always going to look like - or to be - a form of property dualism based upon materialism: a belief that the foundation of nature is matter, but with two distinct qualities or functions, the mental and the physical. This is a not an integrated, animistic monism.

Of course, our language is limited, but more specificity than this is possible. The reader will note that I have never here referred to minded *matter*, instead talking of the mindedness of the broader and mysterious actuality of *nature*. Repeatedly, however, the language of property dualism is used by those considering and critiquing what they assume to be an integrated view. A perfect example can be found in Thomas Nagel's *Mortal Questions*, where he defines panpsychism using just such terms, stating that 'the basic physical constituents of the universe have mental properties'.

David Chalmers is an Australian philosopher who, from a young age, has made significant waves in the mind-body debate. Exploring the subject more comprehensively and with a mind more open than most, his words are carefully used, but still his perspective seems to me limited by the old paradigms. In his paper *Consciousness and its Place in Nature* (published in 2002), having considered every possible dualist, materialist and idealist configuration in search of a solution, the final option he calls *Type F monism*: 'the view that consciousness is constituted by the intrinsic properties of fundamental physical entities: that is, by the categorical bases of fundamental physical dispositions'. This, he says, could be a straight materialism or a property dualism, depending on just how the intrinsic 'psychical' or 'protophenomenal' properties are conceptualised. Substituting another philosopher's words is always risky but, to a good level of accuracy, for his *phenomenal* we could use my term mind, his *protophenomenal* being the capacity for mind. In other words, the closest he comes to panpsychism is still a materialist view, the basis of nature being essentially a material substance. As such he is not resolving the problems inherent within materialism.

The option, he explains, would mean 'nature consists of entities with intrinsic (proto)phenomenal qualities standing in causal relations within a spacetime manifold'. Acknowledging the distinction between what we perceive as mind and matter, he states that, 'Physics as we know it emerges from the relations between these entities, whereas consciousness as we know it emerges from their intrinsic nature'. He then secures its rational justification by confirming the view to be 'perfectly compatible with the causal closure of the microphysical, and indeed with existing physical laws'. As such, the view 'can retain the *structure* of physical theory as it already exists; it simply supplements this structure with an intrinsic nature. And the view acknowledges a clear causal role for consciousness in the physical world: (proto)phenomenal properties serve as the ultimate categorical basis of all physical causation'.

It is a thesis that Chalmers feels 'promises a deeply integrated and elegant view of nature' about which, at the time of his writing, nobody had 'yet developed any sort of detailed theory'. He recognises that it may initially seem counterintuitive to consider 'that there is something it is like to be an electron'; however, he adds, physics informs us that the world is strange, especially at the microphysical level, and 'we cannot expect it to obey all the dictates of common sense'. However, by remaining within the boundaries of materialism, he can't help but chain his proposition to the old notion of substance.

Galen Strawson is another proponent of panpsychism from a materialist perspective. Given that we are still not close to finding a provable solution to the debate, he suggests there is need for a radical rethink, including considering ideas that the establishment of Christian dualism and scientific materialism consider heretical, viz. panpsychism. His tack, however, is to challenge the definition of the stuff of matter from the outset, questioning 'the view - the faith - that the nature or essence of all concrete reality can in principle be fully captured in the terms of *physics*'. In other words, it is only the limited notion of a material substance that is describable within the language of physics and, if we are to consider a physical stuff with the capacity for mind, we need to broaden that definition quite considerably. In *Mental Reality*, he explains that 'a fundamental and universal property of all matter, from the smallest portion up, is that it is experience-realising or experience-involving', proposing a 'plurality of physical ultimates', some or all of which 'are intrinsically experiential'.

Using the same title as Chalmers' essay *Consciousness and its Place in Nature*, Strawson suggests in his 2006 book that, as a materialist, 'if you deny the existence of the phenomenon whose existence is more certain than the existence of anything else: experience, consciousness, conscious experience, *phenomenology*, experiential *what-it's-likeness*, feeling, sensation, explicit conscious thought as we have it and know it at almost every waking moment', then your materialist argument is already inevitably flawed. He uses the term *real physicalism* for a materialist perspective that fully includes the necessary capacity for interiority. In *Real Materialism and Other Essays*, published in 2008, he writes: 'I think it can be shown that something akin to panpsychism is not merely one possible form of real, realistic physicalism, but the only possible form, and, hence, the only possible form of physicalism *tout court*'.

With academic philosophy so dominated by fundamentalist orthodox materialism, his stand is audacious, but he is aware of the journey he has taken to reach such a conclusion: 'All physical stuff is energy, in one form or another, and all energy, I trow, is an experience-involving phenomenon. This sounded crazy to me for a long time, but I am quite used to it now that I know that there is no alternative short of substance-dualism'. Although expressing a clear panpsychist view, he is not abandoning the established ground of monist materialism.

The materialist approach, however, inevitably provokes the debate about the origin of mind. After all, in the early universe before the formation of planets, or on the earth before the first flickerings of life, or in the womb when the first cells are dividing, nature appears very different from the vibrant consciousness of a rational, adult human being. Intrinsic to materialist metaphysics is the belief that mind or mental properties (or the illusion of such) must then have emerged out of the material substance of nature.

The formal theory that encapsulates this belief, emergentism, describes how interactions can sometimes result in the emergence of an entity or property that can be considered to be more than the sum of its component parts. The English philosopher CD Broad, a serious proponent of the idea, wrote in 1925 that the properties of the emergent whole must not, *even in theory*, be deducible from the qualities of the individual components or their separate relations. So, for example, in the metaphysical debate, the interiority of mind is so radically different from all that we understand about matter that, given materialism, it must result from some as yet inexplicable transformation. Although the miracle is far from understood, the evidence of consciousness is enough for emergentists to believe the theory valid: in 1920 the influential but little known Samuel Alexander called emergentism a 'brute empirical fact, or, as I should prefer to say in less harsh terms, to be accepted with the *natural piety* of the investigator. It admits no explanation'. For Alexander, as others, the miracle of emergence was only explicable through God, and indeed its inherent hierarchy reached its pinnacle with God.

For many emergentists, various interpretations of the theory of evolution have proved useful. In the nineteenth century the idea was welcomed as another progressive stance, allowing philosophy and science to take further steps away from the old scholastic vision of a stable and unchanging universe. It is a picture book story, and one that most of us have been taught implicitly from an early age: the slow but sure generation of increasingly developed organisms provides the easy suggestion that mental capacity grows with biological complexity. Looking down at simpler and simpler creatures, the light of consciousness slowly fades, until eventually it goes out, leaving the darkness of inanimate matter. It is an anthropocentric perspective, still based on the Great Chain of Being with its spectrum of virtue, from the inert rock of the earth to the rational purity of heaven.

The South African politician and thinker, Jan Smuts, who coined the term holism so widely used in New Age circles today, was one such emergentist, believing that nature had an inherent tendency to create larger and more complex wholes with potential abilities greater than their individual parts. In his 1926 book, *Holism and Evolution*, he asked, 'Where was the Spirit when the warm Silurian seas covered the face of the earth?', 'Where was the Spirit when the Solar System itself was still a diffuse fiery nebula?' His response was clear: 'Mind or Spirit did not exist at the beginning, either implicitly or explicitly; but it does most certainly exist now'. A supporter of racial separation and indicted of brutality based upon his beliefs, he saw nature's creative evolution as a process of holistic synthesis, the crowning achievement of which was the rational, white, male human being. Dismissing panpsychism, he declared that, 'Mind is not at the beginning but at the end', and 'those who ascribe mind or even potential mind to the cell open the door to the most serious confusions'.

Nearly seventy years later, in *Consciousness Explained*, Dennett declared there to have been nothing but wholly inanimate matter on earth for a billion years. At some point the first tiny evolutionary steps were taken in the development of life, beginning with minute creatures that had no personal interests, no awareness or purpose. Then, he states, when 'an entity arrives on the scene capable of behaviour that staves off, however primitively, its own dissolution and decomposition, it brings with it into the world its *good*. That is to say, it creates a point of view'. This, he claims, is the gap that had to be faced; once bridged, consciousness was free to evolve. Yet, in his typical fashion, Dennett is proposing a rational answer to his scientific query without attending to the philosophical problem: why would such a leap be made? Rationally, as entities with awareness, we can appreciate the value of self-preservation, but no such appreciation can be present where there is no awareness.

Furthermore, if a thinker is to endorse the theory of emergence, he must be willing to draw a line marking the separation between matter with and matter without mental properties. It isn't easy to do. It is not a simple case of physical properties reacting and adapting. Supporting emergentism, Karl Popper used the analogy of water: liquids become solids when frozen without having latent properties of solidity. Equally, the two gases that are hydrogen and oxygen have no inherent liquid properties, but when brought together they can turn into water. Such analogies are wholly based within paradigms of physicality, to the extent that they are referred to be *category errors* by those who cannot support the thesis, for changes in physical properties are entirely different from the capacity for interiority. As Strawson says in *Consciousness and Its Place in Nature*, 'The experiential/non-experiential divide, assuming that it exists at all, is the most fundamental divide in nature (the only way it can fail to exist is for there to be nothing non-experiential in nature)' - and our experience of self denies that possibility.

Nor can there be a spectrum between the two: it is either there or it is not. Certainly, there is a development from basic perception to the complexities of conscious, self-reflective consideration that we can at times experience within our human selves. Further, there is no reason to believe such developments have not been in process within other species and systems throughout nature and the universe. This, though, is the evolution of mind, not its emergence. The American philosopher Catherine Wilson, in her contribution to Strawson's book just mentioned, acknowledges the issue as 'resistant to explanation because it seems impossible to have something on the way to an experience that isn't quite there yet'. An entity is either aware or not aware. Through biology, chemistry and down to the most microcosmic levels of modern physics, matter is reducible; experience is not.

While materialists debate at what point the capacity for mentality might have come into being, physicists worry that the fundamental laws about the conservation of energy, which maintain a steady balance in the universe, would not support the development of a wholly new form of interactivity: mind. It is a question irrelevant to the idealists, substance dualists, panpsychists and animists for whom mind has always been integral to nature. Indeed, a further element of Nagel's definition of panpsychism is that the mental component of matter must always have been present.

The non-emergence view is straightforward: mindedness could not have emerged out of non-mindedness or non-minded matter. Strawson's argument is also based on a conviction against the theory of emergence: 'You can make chalk from cheese, or water from wine, because if you go down to the subatomic level they are both the same stuff, but you can't make experience from something wholly non-experiential'. The view has a long heritage: in his epic poem written in the first century BCE, Lucretius wrote, 'Nothing can ever be created out of nothing even by divine power'. In the early seventeenth century,

Campanella affirmed it stating that 'sense does not come from nothing, the elements whereby they and everything else are brought into being must be said to be sentient, because what the result has the cause must have. Therefore the heavens are sentient, and so [is] the earth'.

Although panpsychist and animist philosophies had been evident in Germany for over a century, it was not until the last decades of the nineteenth century that such ideas started once again to be considered in the English-speaking world. The young genius William Kingdon Clifford was one of the first to do so. Referring to this issue of emergence and the process of evolution, he too argued that at no point could mental states suddenly appear. 'It is impossible for anybody to point out the particular place in the line of descent where that event can be supposed to have taken place. The only thing that we can come to, if we accept the doctrine of evolution at all, is that even in the very lowest organisms, even in the amoeba which swims about in our own blood, there is something or other, inconceivably simple to us, which is of the same nature with our own consciousness.' He continues, acknowledging that to stop at organic matter would be to ignore the fact that life must have evolved out of lifeless matter, writing, 'along with every motion of matter, whether organic or inorganic, there is some fact which corresponds to the mental fact in ourselves'. Recognising his heritage of European thinkers, he declared that his thesis 'is not merely a speculation, but is a result to which all the greatest minds that have studied this question in the right way have gradually been approximating for a long time'. In 1890 in his *Principles of Psychology*, exploring Clifford's ideas in depth, William James wrote, 'Consciousness, however small, is an illegitimate birth in any philosophy that starts without it, and yet professes to explain all facts by continuous evolution. If evolution is to work smoothly, consciousness in some shape must have been present at the very origin of things'.

Colin McGinn declares the issue of emergence to be the insurmountable dilemma at the heart of the mind-body question. Yet, like so many others, his critique of non-emergence is founded upon the idea of phenomenological complexity, all mental properties equating to a consciousness comprehensible to humanity. Furthermore, languaged in the terminology of property dualism, those extensive mental properties must be existent in the very smallest units of material substance. It is a lot to ask.

Or Stuff

If both mind and matter are discarded as primary substances, an obvious step may be to consider nature as constituted of another kind of stuff altogether. Mental and physical states could still be acknowledged as integral to the actuality of nature or perhaps simply the phenomenal world, but both would be reducible to this more fundamental stuff, and both be comprised of it. The philosophical proposition based on such a theory defines itself on the basis of this third alternative being crucially neither more mental nor more physical: it is the position known as neutral monism.

If the very rudimentary parameters above are taken as its broad outlines, neutral monism can sit comfortably with some animists. It has also been a starting point for a number of philosophers who, having delved into its metaphysical possibilities, went on to consider the validity of panpsychism. Many credit that gentle yet radical Scotsman David Hume with the initial inspiration. In 1739, he wrote, 'I shall at first suppose; that there is only a single existence, which I shall call indifferently *object* or *perception*, according as it shall seem best to suit my purpose, understanding by both of them what any common man means by hat, or shoe, or any other impression, convey'd to him by his senses'. In other words, if there is a difference between the actual shoe and the shoe that I am seeing, perhaps that is irrelevant. Shaking the established doctrines of mental and material substance, in his superlative style Hume was asking us to question just how we are putting together our ideas about nature at its most essential. Each bringing their own various ideas to pad out its bare tenets, neutral monists continued along this same tack.

Though some, like the English thinker John Stuart Mill, had continued to explore Hume's train of thought, considering how both our perception and understanding of an object are both in fact no more than intellectual constructs, it was the Austrian Ernst Mach who is often acknowledged to be the first neutral monist. Living through the second half of the nineteenth century, he was a truly fascinating man; better known for the legacy he left to physics, he declared himself not to be a philosopher, but his broad and penetrating intelligence embraced so many areas of interest that he couldn't help but weave the threads together. Observing the great divide between the relatively new and fast developing disciplines of physics and psychology, he naturally sought out the most economical solution to bridge that gap.

Profoundly affected by Kant as a youngster, Mach accepted that we cannot know nature in itself. He perceived the world instead as a perpetual flood of visceral experience, '*one* coherent mass of sensations', made comprehensible by the self. Writing in 1886, he discerned that these sensations, such as colour and temperature, have psychological as well as physical components. Calling them elements, he went on to suggest that they could be understood to be the principal stuff of nature: 'the world does not consist of mysterious entities, which by their interaction with another, equally mysterious entity, the ego, produce sensations, which alone are accessible. For us, colours, sounds, spaces, times ... are provisionally the ultimate elements, whose given connexion it is our business to investigate'. Under the scrutiny of such a perspective, the familiar concept of substance inexorably begins to corrode. Further he wrote, 'Bodies do not produce sensations, but complexes of elements (complexes of sensations) make up bodies'; in other words, 'The elements constitute the I'.

The notion that sense data could actually be the primary stuff of nature can seem strange to those used to relying on something more *substantial,* and indeed even to those seeking understanding about a variety of minded or 'experience-involving' matter. After all, the idea effectively turns the world inside out. Traditionally we might believe that we look at a tomato and consider its colour; Mach suggested that it is the redness that we are aware of first. The colour is not a physical property of the tomato, for colour can't be said to be a material substance, yet equally nor can it be said to be comprised of the stuff of mind. Instead, both the physical tomato and the mental state are created *out of* the sensory information.

He realised that 'the elements given in experience, whose connexion we are investigating, are always the same, and are of only one nature, though they appear, according to the nature of the connexion, at one moment as physical and at another as psychical elements'; how we perceive those elementary sensations is dependent upon the context. Yet he is emphatic that he is not proposing a materialist property dualism, nor does he wish his view to be interpreted as an idealism or abstraction of intangibles. His vision is wholly integrated.

We shall then discover that our hunger is not so essentially different from the tendency of sulphuric acid for zinc, and our will not so greatly different from the pressure of a stone, as now appears. We shall again feel ourselves nearer nature, without its being necessary that we should resolve ourselves into a nebulous and mystical mass of molecules, or make nature a haunt of hobgoblins.

Sensations are the primary 'elements of the world'.

William James cut a similar path through neutral monism on

his way to panpsychism. Unwilling to grapple with why or how consciousness could be so magically available in what is otherwise inert matter, he was as keen as Mach to dispense with the property dualism evident in materialist philosophies. Indeed, James took a further step, questioning the *insubstantial* character of what is generally referred to as consciousness: comparing it with the notion of the soul, he calls it a 'superfluity', a 'nonentity' used to explain that which is not otherwise understood, and consequently should be 'openly and universally discarded'. When we do let go of this ethereal container, what remain are what would have been considered as its momentary contents. It is these, or this, that he now puts forward as crucial. He calls it 'pure experience': the raw sense data of immediacy, of contextualised presence, unprocessed by any individual mind, 'it is plain, unqualified actuality, or existence, a simple *that*'. If there is to be interaction between the apparently distinct mind and matter, he knew that the two needed to be part of a larger whole: 'co-implicated already, their natures must have an inborn mutual reference each to each'. So does he propose this pure experience to be the fundamental stuff of nature. Like Mach, he suggests that it plays different roles within different contexts, in one moment being effectively a thought, and then a thing.

Breaking down the idea of substance was a task taken on by neutral monists such as Joseph Petzoldt in his *Das Weltproblem*, together with a small group at the start of the twentieth century known as the American Realists; their key aim was to dislodge German idealism by advocating in various ways this idea that nature's fundamental and neutral stuff could be empirical experience. In England, Bertrand Russell derided the notion of substance as being thick with assumption and 'savage superstitions'. In *The Analysis of Matter* in 1927, with his inimitable wit he described the idea of one substance with varying properties to be 'useful in practice, but harmful in theory'.

Influenced by Mach and James, Russell supported neutral

monism, at least in his earlier work. In his 1921 text *The Analysis of Mind*, he made a distinction between physical laws, such as the law of gravitation, and psychological laws, such as the law of association. Because sensations are found in both mental and material realms, they are subject to both kinds of laws, indeed sensations 'may be defined as the intersection of mind and matter', and are 'therefore truly *neutral*'. With this understanding, he shrugged off the problem of qualia still faced by materialists, for 'colour and our sensation in seeing it are identical'.

Significantly, in his later work, wanting to emphasise the independence of sensation, he referred instead to *percepts* and events, but the key was still experience. It is a shift often analysed with an eye that criticises his unwillingness to remain constant in his conclusions, but Russell was an inveterate explorer; he seems to me to have been a man filled with a mixture of passionate conviction, curiosity and indignation. He couldn't stand still. It is an important shift, for it takes us a step closer to an understanding of animistic metaphysics.

However clear we writers aspire to be, our everyday language has not evolved to facilitate metaphysical arguments. Unlike mathematics we haven't a separate set of symbols with which we can concisely describe complex philosophical abstractions. As a result, however much jargon is used, however specific the definitions offered, at times it is possible to read some thinker's words and immediately - as if intuitively, even viscerally - understand their meaning, while another thinker may as well be speaking in some unknown foreign tongue. What intrigues me is when I experience the former, but then find myself reading others' narratives on those same ideas that seem to misunderstand or very differently construe them, slicing them up with criticisms that make no sense to me whatsoever.

This was what happened when I first read of the fundamental

yet substance-less stuff proposed by Mach, James and Russell, in their own words and those of their critics. A pivotal argument put forward to undermine the thesis was repeatedly based upon the apparent need for there to be a perceiver (or, in philosophical terms, a percipient). Sensation or experience, it is assumed, requires a subject, and one of sufficient complexity to be capable of coherent mental states. If this is agreed to be the case, the asserted neutrality of their monism would unequivocally be proven false, for their primary stuff would clearly be *mind*, and thus the metaphysics effectively a disingenuous form of idealism.

I had seen no such flaw in the original argument. Reading from an animistic perspective, it hadn't occurred to me that independent sense data were not possible. In 1739 Hume had written that perceptions 'may be conceiv'd as separately existent, and may exist separately, without any contradiction or absurdity'. In the late 1950s, the English Taoist, Terrence Grey, known as Wei Wu Wei, wrote: 'there is no perceiver, nothing perceived, and only the perceiving really is. It is a manifestation of pure consciousness', which, in the very sensuous context of Taoism, I had not read as idealism. In the late twenties, rationalising his own thesis, Russell wrote, 'If we are to avoid a perfectly gratuitous assumption, we must dispense with the subject as one of the actual ingredients of the world. But when we do this, the possibility of distinguishing the sensation from the sense-datum vanishes; at least I see no way of preserving the distinction'.

That word *datum* or data is one that helps in the elucidation, for in our modern world data is something with which we are intimately familiar and involved. Although now used mainly to refer to digital information transmitted or stored by computer, its roots are in the neuter past participle of the Latin verb *dare*, to give, and as such it speaks of a thing or things that have been given. The French word for data is its literal translation *données*, emphasising this quality. When considering data as the primary stuff of nature, I like the sense of the word's passivity; it acknowledges the 'subject' or percipient as the recipient of that data. Indeed, taking the other word closely associated with data, the Latin *informare* literally translates as to shape into a form or idea. As the essential stuff of nature, information would comprise, would construct, would literally *form* the percipient of that information, the subject.

Differentiating from the realist empiricism of his forebears, sitting instead within what is once more the acutely rational world of abstraction in modern physics, the neutral monism of American thinker Kenneth Sayre is based upon information theory and inspired by Platonic form. In his thesis, in tune with Pythagorean teachings of two and a half thousand years ago, the ontological basis and structure of nature is presented as mathematical: it is pure 'information'. Writing in *Cybernetics and the Philosophy of Mind* in 1976, he suggested that not only do 'states of information' exist 'previously to states of mind', allowing the generation of interiority from simple perception to complex thought, but also that 'an ontology of information is similarly basic to the physical sciences' and thus the material world. Information creates the percipient and the perceived.

Although the idea was unique at the time of his writing, in many ways there feels an inevitability to it now - twenty first century thinkers have developed his thesis in countless ways. Our culture is saturated with information, not just from the natural world but through the written word, through audio input, with still and moving pictures, and the chatter of a densely packed and increasingly networked, growing population. Millions upon millions are in a position of constant feed, from the older style billboards to the latest pocket technology, the latter in a state of incessant change, stories developing, updating, adapting. Information has perhaps never made its omnipresence so evident. If this were indeed the primary stuff of nature, it feels as though it may be evolving its ability to generate complexity, on every level: not just creating mental-material entities such as human beings, it is cohering into massive entities such as the internet which, being closer to its essential nature, appear more powerful because of it.

Critical assessments of neutral monism are often focused upon whether or not the asserted neutrality is valid. The fastidiousness of some commentators on this point is really quite wearying, based as it often is on inflexible definitions and expectations of substance. However, when we are able to re-conceive nature's essence, replacing the familiar constancy of substance with the fluid transience of something more like data, possibilities open up.

How close are we then to a minded stuff of nature funda-mental to animistic philosophy? There is another journey to make before the answer becomes clear.

The Divide

For over a thousand years, the scholastics had declared the indubitable existence of the subject and the object, the former being accorded the ability to perceive the actuality of the latter, a worldview that has been studiously perpetuated by the majority of materialists to this day. In his revolutionary eighteenth century declaration, however, Kant had determined it to be the subject that constructs the object as it is perceived, while the *actual* object can never be known. Inspired by Kant's provocateur, Hume, the neutral monists turned it around once again, suggesting that nature is in its very essence purely elementary data, data out of which the subject is in fact comprised, data that the subject proceeds then to language as perception, sensation, experience or form. Nevertheless, Kant's question still remains: what, if anything, can truly be known?

Although Russell expressed a conviction that 'we know nothing of the intrinsic quality of the physical world', for William James, neutral monism based on the essential stuff of pure experience expounded just how it was possible to know nature *in itself*. Was he really disregarding Kant's prohibition? Not quite, for his basic premise was slightly different. Nature was to him not made of an external actuality of matter and an interiority of mental processes, the one ever isolated from the other: such distinctions he saw were made by us, not for us, according to the context and needs of each moment. Nature was instead comprised of the neutral actuality of experience, existent independent of and prior to the existence of the subject.

Unseating the subject can be a hard idea to grasp. In our perpetually polarising Western culture, the subject/object divide seems so entirely structural, to think differently is unusual, even outlandish. Indeed, Hume's brash act of removing the fundamental role of the *I*, picked up by the neutral monists, was not just radical but misunderstood or ignored by a great many thinkers, and still is. Descartes' *je pense donc je suis* reflects a powerful need for human self-realisation, after all; through the ceaseless noise of the rising tide of information, the subject, the *I*, is asserted to be crucial. In animism, as in neutral monism, however, that assertion is not held.

Within the context of philosophical exploration, that the subject's removal is, primarily, conceptual makes it all the harder. We *think* about the idea, considering it within the interiority of our mental introspection, yet such a process brings the thinking self entirely to the fore, giving the impression that it is the very foundation of being. As such, its removal is felt to be surely more than annihilating: to do so would destroy not just the self but the world in its entirety.

Let us pause, however, and recall our definition of mind. The thinking *I* is working on a level of self-reflective consciousness, entirely aware of its own existence, and such a degree of functionality can be placed towards the complex end of the mind's spectrum of ability. What I have previously called the observing *I* is far simpler. Here we have the recipient of perceptive data. Although it may still be valid to use the term *subject of perception*, it is useful now to remember the limitations of its capacity: the percipient does not *think*. Albeit to varying extents, perception is passive within its context of data, within the environment that is given. Here the individual *I* is not so prominent; it may barely exist at all. A fully integrated element of its immediate surroundings, it may have no lasting experience, merely perceiving through emerging and evanescing moments of presence. We may like to believe that as human beings our ability to think lifts us from such passivity, but a good part of our day and night is spent in such unthinking states. Indeed, in the previous paragraph I said that to *think* differently may be unusual: to *be* within a reality that is not divided into subject and object is not, both for human beings and within nonhuman nature. It is perfectly natural.

The phrase just used referred to a *reality* that is not divided. Is this then merely epistemology?

Given the fundamental tenet of animism is the ubiquity of mindedness, a statement that provides nature with a universal capacity for mind, it is necessary to acknowledge that minds are subjects, and definitively so. The strength and prominence of subjectivity differs, but minds are always subjects. I would then assert that the rational argument for the Kantian veil cannot be dismissed, and so the world perceived by a subject must be a phenomenal reality: no mind can perceive nature's actuality. What is perceived is nature's raw data processed through the filters of perception established by beliefs based on limitations and experience. In this respect, in the perceived world of our realities, in the phenomenal world, the subject/object divide does persist. Importantly though, the more conscious we are of what we perceive or have perceived, using the complex capacities of the thinking *I* and standing within the bounds of the individual self, the more distinct is that apparent divide.

However, the animist is no idealist: nature is not mind but

minded. Perceived through mental filters, our minds create the world as we see it, but nature itself is not an illusion. As a tradition, animism highly values the empirical, the experiential, the heuristic and sensuous, for these are indications of integration. There are, of course, animist philosophers, scientists and other thinkers for whom the beauty of rational thought is a driving force, but their work is always balanced by the visceral influence of the sensuous world, reminding them of nature's inherent integration. The animistic thesis is then not just based upon rational arguments against idealism and in favour of an integrated metaphysics, but is informed too by the profound and visceral experience of integration which, being so central to his worldview, is a focus of the animist's philosophical, ethical and spiritual practice of life. Furthermore, being fundamental, such beliefs are intrinsic to the animist's filters of perception, and thus contribute to how he sees the world, and what he is able to experience and understand about it.

Indeed, many are now drawn to the teachings of animism in search of that conscious sensation of integration which can be found within an ecosystem or community, a sensation that was once perhaps more widespread but has slipped away with increasing urbanisation, civilisation and technology. What the seeker strives to lose are the constraints of being locked within his own individual and subjective mind; instead of becoming passive, however, instead of simply switching off as is natural to do, relaxing and releasing oneself from the concerns of individual existence, the animist remains wholly awake and attentive to the experience of being. As such, he is able to break down some of those filtering beliefs that shape his own reality, allowing him to perceive very differently. Within animism this can be deep meditation or just a moment of sweet integration. I suspect this state of immediate presence is what William James refers to as pure experience, and retaining awareness of it, allowing the fleeting moments to flow into one another, offers the opportunity for insight and profound regeneration. So is the role of the thinking *I* seen to be as innate and important to human nature as is that of the passive but wakeful percipient.

Such ideas bring us to a point where we are able to bring a little more clarity to our statements about animism, adding to our developing definition. In many ways they are self-evident if not tautological, but they mark the point we have reached. The first confirms that we have dispensed with any notion of mind as an elementary substance: *the subject of perception - mind - is composed of the primary stuff of nature.* Secondly, *the mind creates of nature's essential data a world comprehensible within the bounds of its own beliefs and experience,* its phenomenal world.

That it is possible to dissolve any sense of a subject/object divide intimates that such a divide does not exist or persist within nature. The belief that nature is constituted of something other than mind and matter is consequently fundamental to animism. That we naturally experience this sense of integration when the self is not to the fore suggests too that in our everyday interactions, moment by moment, albeit half blindly, we are actually engaging with nature at a fundamental level. Thirdly then, although our conscious self is to varying extents constrained by the subjectivity of the mind, *we are in a perpetual state of interaction with the primary stuff of nature, for it comprises every moment of existence.*

So what is this stuff? I have spoken here of the data of the neutral monist in its various hues, from Mach's elementary sense data, and James' raw data of unprocessed experience, to Sayre's information in the form of abstract mathematical data. Are any of these close? Not quite.

The Flow

Maybe because the basic tenets of neutral monism were from the outset sufficiently broad, it allowed the philosophy to develop in ways that were diverse enough for criticism to become easy. Some blame Bertrand Russell's enthusiastic expansion of those tenets for what was effectively its demise within academic circles, and with the fine exception of Kenneth Sayre very few use the term now; property dualist materialism has become the more popular angle. Through the twentieth and into this century, however, a few other theses developed as views close to the panpsychist and animistic. The most interesting of these is perhaps process philosophy.

In his 1909 text, *A Pluralistic Universe*, William James continued to extend his ontology of nature. Making overt his panpsychism, he suggested that everything must exist 'for itself', having its own mental perspective, its own interior vibrancy, for everything is comprised essentially of nature's pure experience. In fact, so confident and inspired was he by respected contemporaries exploring similar views that James anticipated 'a great empirical movement towards a pluralistic panpsychic view of the universe'. With science making inroads into an increasingly microcosmic world that, even at the smallest levels, revealed a vibrancy of energy and movement, James' optimism was understandable. A few decades earlier, the Victorian sociologist and biologist Herbert Spencer had expressed the excited view of his own era of 'a Universe everywhere alive', at least in appearance.

One of those contemporaries of James at the turn of the twentieth century was the extraordinary intellect Henri Bergson, with whom he was in correspondence. Half English, half Polish, born in Paris, Bergson was to become the brightest star of French philosophy during his lifetime, developing a dynamic vision which, amidst a period of social, political and scientific upheaval, acknowledged nature's continual state of evolving change. In his doctoral thesis in the late 1880s, published in English as *Time and Free Will, An Essay on the Immediate Data of Consciousness*, Bergson challenged Kant's thesis of time and space, asserting the necessity of disentangling the two. On the one hand, he recognised the notion of time as a tool of perception: created by the thinking *I*, time spatialises and separates, and as such is wholly implicated in our perception of matter and space. Operating in the way of a mechanical instrument, it measures nature as a series of distinct and finite instants, one coming after another, giving the impression of an inevitable process of causality.

However, Bergson then distinguished this idea from what he called *duration*, the sensation or experience of time: how we *feel* it deep inside. 'Pure duration', he wrote, 'is the form which our conscious states assume when our ego lets itself *live*, when it refrains from separating its present state from its former states.' In other words, duration is time as a whole, not cut up into pieces by the thinking *I*. It is that temporal interiority that is wholly present yet in some way boundless, where the past is integral to the experience of the present. While the intellect processes perceptive data into subjectively comprehensible chunks which it then reconnects into an illusion of flow, in nature that flow already exists; it is the raw data of nature's inherent continuity. Bergson used the term *pure mobility* to emphasise this uninterrupted fluidity.

Like James, Bergson knew that understanding such a state could be inherently problematic. To begin with, immediately the thinking self is engaged, the process of conceptualisation deconstructs perception, and the experience of duration is lost. He observed how language can further add to the process of deconstruction, shattering duration, and considered how the 'brutal word which stores up what is stable, common, and therefore impersonal in human impressions crushes, or at least covers over, the delicate and fleeting impressions of our individual consciousness', smothering our experience of nature's flow with an illusion of both constancy and inertia. The first line of the *Tao Te Ching*, written in the sixth century BCE, can be interpreted in the same way. The *tao*, generally translated as the *way*, is at the heart of nature. Perceived as an eternal flow, Lao Tzu declares it ungraspable: 'The tao that can be told is not the eternal Tao', or human thinking about nature's essence is inevitably limited by human thinking.

For Bergson, the only means of accessing this duration was through what he called *intuition*, a way of stepping right inside a moment instead of observing it from the outside where filters of belief and analysis would break it apart. However, reading the logical precision of his philosophy as the exacting poetry of theology, his idea is easy to comprehend: for here is the animist's principal desire to achieve the experience of integration, that state where the thinking self has slipped momentarily away, leaving the wakeful attentiveness of purely perceptive being, that alert yet meditative state 'where one passes, by minute gradations, from one state to another: a truly lived continuity'.

Without the limitations of analytical consciousness, that gentle perception embraces a far broader reality, indeed one which Bergson argued is nature's elemental actuality. In our experience of duration, then, we are in fact experiencing nature *in itself*. Again reading his words from the perspective of the polytheistic animist, his duration is a beautifully articulate description of the ancient god that, generically, might be called Father Time. Accordingly, the way in which duration can be not just understood but experienced is simply a case of being awake to the deity's presence. Remembering that the animist is not obsequious before the gods, but ever seeking to perceive (empirical) and understand (rational) these powers of nature, in a world where our human lives are lived at such speed, coming to terms with the nature of time is an important part of finding peace and sustainability. When we are able to feel Time, strolling quietly alongside us, always critically present, there is a divine integrity in every step we take, for Time also holds every moment that has past, and every moment anticipated. As such,

Time is the keeper of memory.

And as it is to the animist, to Bergson memory was crucial. He perceived nature's memory as what enables its continuity, its enduring fluidity and creativity. It is the whisper of what has just happened that connects a moment to the next moment. In 1922, in *Duration and Simultaneity*, he explained how he felt it 'impossible to imagine or conceive a connecting link between the before and after without an element of memory and, consequently, of consciousness'. He knew the word consciousness had anthropomorphic connotations, but his use of it confirms what is effectively his panpsychist view. If we are able to avoid making the mistake of conceiving mind as equating always to human mind, he believed it possible to see how 'duration is essentially a continuation of what no longer exists into what does exist. This is real time,' he wrote, 'perceived and lived'. Being fundamentally integral to nature, duration therefore 'implies consciousness; and we place consciousness at the heart of things for the very reason that we credit them with a time that endures'. In other words, the continuity we perceive in nature is made possible by its capacity for memory: nature is thus universally minded.

In *Portraits from Memory* published in 1956, Bertrand Russell was considering the same strands of thinking, looking at how memory is expressed even in inorganic matter. Using the example of a river, the channel of which is worn into use by the current, he suggested it may be said 'that the river bed *remembers* previous occasions when it experienced cooling streams'. He is aware of the possible response from readers who would conflate memory with human thinking, but 'if thinking consists of certain modifications of behaviour owing to former occurrences, then we shall have to say that the river bed thinks, though its thinking is somewhat rudimentary'. To dismiss the terms used here is to miss the point. That Russell and Bergson employ such words as *consciousness* and *thinking* is not slack on their part: they are pushing the boundaries of philosophy into landscapes where the ground underfoot is very different from that where substance and human consciousness are considered essential and special. In doing so they walked deep into territories native to animism.

Bergson's philosophy has always been infamously hard to categorise metaphysically. His recognition of the intellect's need to conceptualise, and so deconstruct the fabric of nature, spills into his own unwillingness to be labelled. Nonetheless, his thesis of continuity placed him within the field of process philosophy and, certainly, the key proponent of process philosophy, usually agreed as the mathematician Alfred North Whitehead, shared much common ground with him. Interestingly, Whitehead's thesis provokes a crucial question that Bergson's duration more naturally addressed: the issue of coherence. That subject will be dealt with fully in the next chapter, but a few words about Whitehead will take us closer.

In the three volumes of *Principia Mathematica* published just before the First World War, together with Bertrand Russell, Whitehead sought to expound a solid foundation for all mathematics; though far beyond my ability to comprehend, it is lauded as an extraordinary piece of work. Once complete, however, both seriously questioned the metaphysics of its logical premise. Russell moved towards what was an increasingly dynamic neutral monism based upon *events*, perhaps picking up on the ideas of Bergson and James. By the late 1920s he was suggesting that the primary stuff of nature 'should, I maintain, be conceived as a series of occurrences linked together in some important way'. By the same time, Whitehead was lecturing on what would become his key work on process philosophy, *the* key work: *Process and Reality*.

Whitehead is hard to read. At times I wonder if, like Kant, his ideas are not as complex as his ability to express them implies, hampered as they perhaps both were by obsessively meticulous minds, without the fluency of the natural writer. As if aiming to tear off the blinkers of his own hyper-analysis, and truly let go into the exceptional breadth that underlies his insight, he strove to weave together areas of thought - the aesthetic, religious and ethical - that had increasingly been separating under the dominant influence of Victorian science. Like others mentioned in this chapter, he believed the prioritising of the subjective ego was a philosophical mistake: while subjective experience is a critical part of epistemology, when looking at ontology focus on the thinking *I* was an error. Equally, he saw dependence on abstraction as potentially meaningless. Asserting the need to balance the empirical and rational, he added to these two traditional sources of knowledge the value of speculation and its use of imagination, particularly its ability to draw ideas back down to the groundedness of experience. Such an embracing of the rational and creative mind while retaining the importance of tangible empiricism brought his thinking close to animism.

Furthermore, Whitehead's panpsychism came through his rejection of mechanism in favour of a dynamic organism. Were something to have no capacity to perceive he declared it would be 'vacuous'. Nature, however, is constituted not of a substance or even a stuff, but of what he called 'actual occasions' existing in 'a basic field of proto-conscious experience'. Such occasions are similar to the monads proposed by Leibniz two centuries earlier, but most unlike Leibniz's monads these are quanta in a perpetual state of change, instances, moments of perfect immediacy filled with becoming, 'buds or drops of perception' emerging within time and space, perceiving then evanescing. He suggested that each had a physical and a mental pole: momentarily a spatial object, an occasion influences an adjoining occasion which becomes a subject of experience, flaring up with the spatiotemporal energy of self-determination and self-formation, thus itself becoming a causal object, influencing another before disappearing.

I like the word *occasion* and, exploring its etymology, I can understand why Whitehead may have chosen it. With documented use back to the fourteenth century, its Latin antecedent *occasio* means an opportunity, juncture or reason, but deconstructed further, its core base is the verb *cadere*, to fall. The mutated prefix *ob*, like many prepositions, has a dozen translations, the best here being perhaps on account of. An occasion, then, we might say poetically, is the perfect moment in which to fall. It brings to mind the image of deciduous autumnal leaves which, in the stillness of a windless day, find the exact moment to let go. It feels close to the word *moment*, which I use in animism for a similar reason; rooted as it is not just in the Latin *movere*, to move, but also its cousin *momentum*, meaning importance, it imparts a sense of what is the crucial instant of movement. Whitehead's occasions are moments, their movement based upon an intrinsic and essential flow of becoming.

It is an excellent vision, one that seems simpler yet more intangible the more one is able to consider it without slipping into the mistaken default of basing it upon substance. The subject of perception is as momentary as the object of perception, mind being no more than a succession of such occasions, nature flowing through it in a continuous process of becoming and dissolving. From this perspective, the universe can be understood to be a complete organism, self-organising, self-maintaining, ever transforming through its integral and comprehensively contextualised flow of creativity. Each occasion is not an innovating individual; Whitehead makes it clear that there is dull repetition in nature's activity, yet every moment is thoroughly and exquisitely active, interactive, alive.

Such an idea concurs with the animist's sense of nature's wakefulness. Indeed, it holds with every defining statement so far presented here about animism: the essence of nature is minded, manifesting in what we perceive to be mind and matter within a framework of time and space. While I have dismissed the subject/object divide on an ontological level, Whitehead retains both states as integral to nature's essence, but they are intensely fleeting and without substance. It is the process of inter-action and its inherent creativity that are affirmed as central to his thesis, and these, as we shall explore in the coming chapter, are equally key within animism.

When examining nature at such a fundamental level, any thesis can seem abstract compared with our day to day human experience. Yet, as the possibility of drifting off into abstraction increases, questions provoked by any sense of disconnection become even more pertinent.

What we are now considering is a universe comprised of strings of fleeting occasions, moments blinking in and out of existence. Just how human awareness glues these together to create our apparent worlds is the subject of a later chapter. For now the exploration must hold to the paths of ontology and, heading down to the very foundation, address two questions the idea now raises. Why do occasions happen in nature, and how do they come together to create its coherence? The answer is to be found somewhere in that creative process of interaction, and this is the subject of Chapter Six.

Chapter Six

Interaction

Of course, William James' great hopes about a panpsychist future came to nothing. Seriously challenging the long-established premise of substance, the radical theses of neutral monism, panpsychism and process philosophy were all presented through a period when the pace of scientific development was only strengthening the growing trend towards materialist metaphysics. In such a climate, the wealth of industrialisation and imperialism was entirely dependent upon continuing technological advances. With Europe fast sliding towards the Great War, then staggering through the subsequent depression, it would no doubt have felt both reasonable and patriotic to declare that science was on course to solve every puzzle nature could lay before it: what had not yet been found by some probing instrument of measurement surely soon would be. Contributing to the materialist position, CD Broad and others put forward their theories of emergentism, and the anti-metaphysical stance of the logical positivists, determined to exorcise the unprovable from philosophical debate once and for all, only added to the certainty of James' posthumous disappointment.

Materialism, however, has not solved the problems. It is still nowhere close to an explanation of consciousness. For the animist, it simply lacks *integrity*. For in its search for the primary building blocks of the universe, materialism is culpable for nature's comprehensive atomisation. With so much panpsychism in philosophical debate currently based on materialist property dualism, there are serious problems which that too does not resolve. Indeed, even where a thesis discards the substantial foundation in favour of something inherently transient or momentary, as neutral monism and process philosophy do, the question is softened but it remains. If the universe is comprised of all those separate little bits and pieces, how are they glued together?

Combination

Reading *On the Nature of Things* by the old Roman poet Lucretius, it is wonderful to witness how the intensely curious and intelligent mind explores nature. Basing his ideas on the work of Epicurus and Democritus who lived centuries earlier, and without the benefit of modern science, Lucretius suggested that nature's most basic components, its *primordia rerum*, are a great variety of different particles, all perpetually moving through the void at speed. With a little retranslation, two thousand years later, much of his thesis in fact sits pretty well within modern secular physics, not least his idea that nature is created neither by some inherent *telos* nor by an external deity guiding its form, but simply by the random movement of those minute base particles within their immediate context. In a state of eternal transience, continually colliding, deflecting off one another, he declared that now and then these particles must unexpectedly swerve off course; indeed, even this *swerve* is now found by some within the possibilities of quantum dynamics.

His tiny *rerum* were not just the building blocks of matter: with countless properties, their moments of interaction generated every aspect of nature, from sheep and stones to thoughts and souls. Crucially, however, they did not 'cohere inseparably'. Where certain movements temporarily persist, creating regular patterns, these events humming with energy on the micro scale are what we perceive on the human scale as the stable world within which we live. The analogy he gave was of a flock of sheep: viewed on a distant hillside, they appear not as a gathering of individual living creatures but as a single white object. Solidity is no more than an illusion of perception within a wholly random universe.

Likewise acceding to neither a creator God nor an Aristotelian *telos*, many philosophical materialists and physical scientists today are reasonably content that they have an adequate hypothesis for how bits of matter come together to create form. The frontiersmen of quantum physics may admit to an uncertainty, but biologists, chemists and physicists have a catalogue of laws and forces to explain the coherence of cells, atoms and smaller particles. Yet, as David Chalmers writes, we may have 'a good understanding of the principles of physical composition, but no real understanding of the principles of phenomenal composition': the measuring sciences are making progress with their material world, but how does the stuff of *mind* come together to create the *mental* forms that are evident in the breadth of what we know to be human experience and consciousness?

For pure substance dualists and idealists, mind is understood to be so entirely different from matter that there need be no compositional dilemma. Integral to many religious beliefs, such views often present mind as crafted by a greater mind or divine creator, a deity who can provide all necessary assurances that mind has been specifically designed for its immediate purpose, even if that is (perhaps inevitably) beyond our human ability to comprehend: where questions draw rational blanks, God is the given answer. Indeed, even where deity is not acknowledged, if mind functions by way of processes that are wholly specific to a mental stuff or substance, it is still possible to explain the properties of mind simply by building the rational from the empirical, and so composing a cogent definition with whatever may be necessary in order to do so.

However, where the mental is understood to be an aspect or property of the physical, as materialists of all colours enthusiastically assert, material laws must apply, yet its coherence cannot be explained in the same terms. For most panpsychists in the twentieth and twenty first century, the issue is key. Chalmers describes it as 'easily the most serious problem for the type-F monist view'. If the smallest building blocks of matter are minded, if each speck has its own micro-mind capable of perception or experience, how can these merge together to create larger subjects of perception? As David Skrbina asks, 'How can a unified collective consciousness arise from the mental qualities of lower orders of matter, such as atoms or subatomic particles?' In other words, how can the individual units, abstractions so small they are always at the very edge of our ability to study empirically, yield what we would recognise as human consciousness? Young English philosopher Philip Goff expressed the crisis in Strawson's *Consciousness and Its Place in Nature*: 'Assuming that my experiential being is *wholly* constituted by the experiential being of a billion experience-involving ultimates, then what it is like to be me can be nothing other than what it is like to be each of those billion ultimates (somehow experienced all at the same time)'; yet, the 'phenomenal character of my experience is surely very different from the phenomenal character of something that feels as a billion ultimates feel'.

William James called it the 'combination problem', offering a useful analogy to clarify the point: if you give to each of ten men one word that makes up a sentence, however hard they might try none of the ten will grasp the whole sentence unless they speak their word aloud, for each individual is contained within their own mind. In 1890 it seemed to him to be an insurmountable obstacle. In his 2002 paper, Chalmers was still questioning whether the problem could be solved: 'we need a much better understanding of the *compositional* principles of phenomenology: that is, the principles by which phenomenal properties can be composed or constituted from underlying phenomenal properties, or protophenomenal properties'. Whether or how lesser or simpler minds might cohere to create what we feel to be the rich complexity of human experience is beyond most thinkers, and for critics of panpsychism this is the potential deal-breaker: if a solution cannot be found, the thesis must be false.

Connection

Three hundred years ago, Leibniz's dualist version of panpsy-chism offered a solution of sorts. With his inimitable weaving of mathematical precision, radical insight and conventional tradition, the indivisible monads he envisaged as the *primordia rerum* were not all identical specks of nature's finest dust. They were point entities - they had no extension (or size) at all - yet, like modern particle physicists, he insisted these were not abstractions but actualities. Each monad he believed to be a definitively complete concept, uniquely individual yet able to 'mirror' the entire universe, and as such had no need to interact: so did he evade the dualist's enduring problem of how mind and matter might communicate. 'Laden' with its past and 'pregnant' with its future, each monad contained, indeed comprised, its relations to every other monad, and with no 'windows' through which it might influence or be influenced, unaltered by inter-action, each held to its specific role within the fabric of nature. Like perfectly crafted clocks, each existed as an eternally isolated yet self-sufficient whole, moving in unfailing harmony within the universe. Such perfection could only affirm God as the creator, the master craftsman who had set all the clocks ticking in the very beginning.

At a time when the new mechanism was challenging the old scholasticism, in his earlier writings Leibniz overtly supported the Aristotelian conviction that Form is necessary to give nature's Substance its functionality. By the time he wrote *Monadology*, however, his thesis on substantial forms had altered. As wholes that could not be broken down into component parts, monads congregated through the natural flows of movement, and where such gatherings could be seen to be organisms, these functioned by way of the control asserted by a substantial form or dominant monad. So a block of marble or dead body is no more coherent than a pile of stones, a simple aggregation of monads, while a living human being is a compound body directed by its dominant monad, its soul.

Beautifully reasoned as it was, the hypothesis was nonetheless fastened together with theological glue, God filling in the gaps that would otherwise have demanded rational answers. He doesn't explain, for example, how a collection of non-extended monads could cohere to create an extended form, a body with shape and size: the answer is simply in the deity's design. Yet, recourse to God does not now cut the philosophical mustard, and as such Leibniz's solution lacks some validity in today's debate.

Process philosophy once again comes closer. Indeed it is close enough to the animist solution for it to be worth exploring here in some detail. To start with, in its rejection of a primary substance, from the outset it avoids the inevitable problems of considering minded *matter*. However, although it need not find a way to merge countless individual particles or monads, the momentary events or actual occasions of Whitehead's thesis still need to be brought together to create what we might understand as consciousness. If we are starting with those momentary actualities of occasions, the fleeting transience of droplets of experience, there still has to be a bottom-up build. Whitehead does this by distinguishing between what he terms true individuals, compound individuals and aggregate societies, but with a comprehensiveness far greater than that of Leibniz, and here I am indebted to David Ray Griffin for his clarity, for Whitehead's language can be complex, especially where he is pushing at the shifting boundaries of his own understanding.

In the last chapter I mentioned Whitehead's vision of the rolling process of emergence and evanescence: an actual occasion, glowing in its intensely brief moment of presence as a creative subject transforms into a causal object, becoming part of the past that, in turn, inspires the next subject to come into the vitality of momentary being, becoming another actual occasion.

Within this constant flow of becoming, as moment meets moment, in Whitehead's words, an actual occasion is 'a relatum in this scheme of extensive connection': a piece of the ever-changing fabric of nature.

Actual occasions are minded at the very simplest level. Whitehead uses the word *prehension*, the general definition for which describes perception without cognition, but there is a richer strand to it. What Whitehead means is a relational awakeness, an awareness of one's contextual being within the transience of becoming, without the thinking self processing the raw data into abstract knowing, very much in tune with what I have called passive perception. As an actual occasion prehends, in its brief moment as a subject of experience, *feelings* are provoked - a word beautifully used by Whitehead to describe the most fundamental impact of connection. Internally, these feelings give the experiencing subject its concrete actuality, its state of becoming as, incorporating the past, it transforms into an object rich with experience; externally, these feelings are then expressed in its next moment, fuelling and guiding the nature of that moment. Constituted of an instance not a substance then, each subject of experience prehends, feels, grasps the influence of the immediate past in its own fleeting, unfolding moment of perfect presence.

Nature is not a scattering of individual occasions though, but a perpetual bustle of innumerable flows or series of actual occasions, for which Whitehead uses the word *aggregations*. Aggregation: I love the word. Rooted in the Latin *grex*, a flock, with the mutated *ad* prefix the meaning provokes images of a multitude of creatures gathering together, thousands of starlings soaring and diving in unison, shoals of fish or swarms of bees moving as if with one mind. A heap of sand may be thought of as an aggregation, but in process philosophy the term is made broader: an aggregational *society* is where the flow of actual occasions expresses a softly changing continuity, each moment informing the next, which informs the next, with only the tiniest inevitable modifications in the data each time. That flock of starlings, with its shifting patterns moving through the skies, appears as a particularly dynamic society, but a society of occasions can be far more stable. At the micro level is the process that Whitehead suggests creates *enduring* entities, forms that build to the point where we can recognise them on a human scale as coherent. For occasions are neither random nor radical, but entirely held within the context of their becoming, moment to moment.

At its most fundamental level, an enduring entity is a true individual, *true* because it is a subject of experience: in other words, a series of occasions through which a persisting self-determination is a key part of what is inherited. All aggregations are comprised of true individuals. An example given by Whitehead of a true individual is an electron, or a series of 'electron occasions', each moment of its trajectory a prehensive event fractionally changing with its context: although difficult for an orthodox materialist to accept perhaps, the image of an electron *feeling* its way through time and space provokes a vision of exquisite wakefulness at that fundamental level.

Some aggregations of true individuals Whitehead describes as compound individuals. Making the distinction, Griffin explains, is 'an empirical question, to be decided in terms of whether the behaviour suggests a unity of responsive action that involves an element of spontaneity'. For an aggregation to be a compound individual, there must be more than the obvious flow of causation from previous events. 'Rocks, lakes, and computers have a merely aggregational, not a subjective or experiential, unity': they are comprised of true individuals, each with its own capacity for prehension and self-determination, but the form we perceive is not an individual. The rock as a whole is not prehending, feeling and responding, although its component individuals are. What allows a series of occasions to become a unified and enduring entity, a compound individual, are 'dominant experiences', powerfully subjective flows of occasions that create a pattern for the whole. Molecules and atoms are considered to be compound individuals; however, the more subjective experiential information there is in its series of occasions, the more self-determined a compound individual can be. In a mammal, within its structured society of billions of occasions, the nervous system could be said to be the dominating series of events. Whitehead described a human being as 'organised and coordinated by a single dominant occasion (that is, the mind)', its numerous flows of becoming, moment to moment, creating tides of feelings that, occasion by occasion, build to a wakefulness that could be called consciousness.

Distinguishing between individuals and aggregations has serious ethical ramifications. For if subjects of experience are electrons and molecules, brown bears and human beings, but nature fails adequately to coalesce the minded essence of mountains, rivers and trees to allow them any kind of a coherent mentality, or unified prehension, then we have effectively drawn a line. That which is declared an individual requires consideration - it has its own value, for itself, as itself - but the aggregation does not.

As I shall explain in the next section, Whitehead's thesis is indeed very much in tune with the animistic, and his mathematical mindset allows for an explanation that is far more meticulous in its philosophical precision than I have the capacity to present. However, is this distinction between individuals and aggregations another way of affirming a human right to use nature for its own profit and convenience? Is this where the path bifurcates, taking Whitehead in one direction and animism in another?

Wholeness

Let us review where we have come to with respect to animism.

The following has already been established: as a monist metaphysical stance, animism acknowledges there to be a single fundamental essence, and that essence is minded. It is not a substance. Interactions within that essence can generate mind; in other words, the process of interaction utilises nature's capacity for mind. At its simplest, this is passive perception, or prehension, a relational awakeness to the immediate context of being. Taking the raw data of interaction, the mind creates an image of its surroundings as it perceives them to be, enabling it to respond. If using the complexity of human consciousness, the images created by the human mind are of our human world, with all its physical and mental realities.

Going a little further, two more questions can now be answered: what impels this interaction and how do such interactions generate nature as we perceive it? They are not questions that can be solved by empirical exploration, however. We can't just observe nature until the answer is revealed.

Standing at the farthest reaches of what humanity has as yet empirically proven, it is important to consider the options at hand. Religions have taken the collective vision and used meticulously worked rational argument to state their case for God's existence, allowing divine power to explain all that is otherwise beyond comprehension. Deducing from observations, science employs the rational language of mathematics to construct its various hypotheses, proposing the existence of forces that stretch and compress the universe, at the quantum and the cosmic scale. Such results are more descriptive than explanatory at this level, but hope is fuelled by each new discovery, extraordinary minds conceiving unlikely theories within the realms of rational abstraction.

Recognising himself to be so often at the point beyond which there is obviously solid ground, Whitehead wrote of the value of our ability to speculate, letting the imagination craft possible solutions without the immediate limitations of language and knowledge. Taking these possibilities, we can then use reason to test and temper them, to hone their viability as ideas, all the while bringing them closer, until we are able to judge how they integrate within the context of what we do know.

Of course, the rational arguments that back an idea may not be universally agreed, and with our experience of life so diverse, each individual will be viewing the idea from the context of their own position. Furthermore, there is a danger that such ideas may slip into belief, glued together with half hidden assumptions, reason being then employed to determine them to be *fact*.

Articulating the two questions above, I recognise that I now stand looking out beyond the reach of empirical certainty. I must address the questions knowing that there are no provable answers. With the value of stories and poetry well acknowledged within animism, Whitehead's advice is easily taken, and I shall use the imagery of animism, aware that in doing so I may be seen to be wandering out into the imagination. Articulating the answers in this way, I can bring a richness to my words, heading deeper into ideas that have no empirical foundation, that reach beyond reason into the hues and tones of vision. My aim is then to explore through reason and sense.

The animistic *story* might flow like this.

Ancient Greek mythology proffered the idea of the αρχή (*arche*), the original principle or basis of nature. Although later thinkers began to think of this as a substance, such as Thales' idea of water, the oldest writings describe something much deeper, something beneath our ability to understand or explain. In his seventh century BCE *Theogony*, Hesiod speaks of the *arche* as a formless surging immateriality out of which the gods and nature emerged. He called it χάος (*kaos*): Chaos. Although in philosophical or theological debate it is possible to redefine and weave words so tightly that they tangle the mind into knots, it is often the very ordinary words of our daily language that are best used to describe what lies on the border of our ability to verbalise. Even if we have little understanding or knowledge of such ancient myths, it is not hard to imagine that primary state of absolute chaos. It is another very ordinary word that I offer as the *arche* of my own British animism, a word I have raised already in this text, a beautifully rich and misunderstood word that is equally easy to imagine: darkness.

At its most fundamental, nature is darkness. Nature's primary state is darkness. In stillness, formless, in the darkness, nature is whole. Yet, nature is minded: it exists with a wakefulness of its own being. Aware of itself, nature turns within itself in self-reflection. This essential movement of nature is the breath of existence, the sacred wind of being. As movement moves against movement, this motion of self-reflection provokes edges within the unity: there are gusts and storms, gentle breezes and spiralling cyclones, a myriad of *verses* arising within the *uni*versal flow of awareness, each constituted of nature's dynamic and wakeful essence, each one a part of the universal whole.

As verses move with and against verses, merging and changing, energy is exchanged, wakefulness shared. Moment by moment, event by event, patterns emerge, *spirits* fleetingly finding form, shapes shifting and changing, on every scale of being, before dissolving back into the whole. Yet nature's wholeness ensures that each interaction, each pattern created, influences the patterns made by subsequent interactions, verses informing verses, as tiny whispers of being and as storms that sweep across the universe. Now and then interactions become entangled, provoking an iteration that grows sticky, patterns repeating, spirits humming with vibrancy, their glimmering forms persisting, evolving slowly, moment by moment, before the wind of some other verse breaks them apart, allowing a new scattering of patterns to emerge.

Poetry is an invaluable form of our language. Its power is in its ability to blur the defining edges of words, allowing meanings to spill into each other, like watercolours on a palette as the rain begins to fall. It allows the mind to relax and feel, prehensively.

One word, however, I shall catch in order to observe it a little more closely, to turn it over in the light. It is a word I have begun to define in previous chapters: spirit. So clichéd with overuse, so loosely and lazily used, it is almost tempting to avoid it, but to do so would be disingenuous, as if denying a friend. Honing a comprehensive and comprehensible definition of animism, an articulate understanding of spirit is now vital.

With its ancient roots in the PIE base *ane-, to breathe or blow, definitively there is movement in spirit. Perhaps around the same time that Lao Tzu was writing of the dynamic nature of the *Tao* three or four thousand miles to the east, in the sixth century BCE the Milesian philosopher Anaximenes decreed *pneuma* to be nature's primary element: the vitalising breath that holds the soul or consciousness. This sounds like spirit. Not a stuff or substance, I described it earlier as nature's vitalising and empowering force, yet it is not a verse in the language of animistic poetry. It is the raw data of action. Adding to our ongoing definition of animism, I now suggest the following: *entirely formed by the momentary configuration of its context, spirit is the pattern created by the crucial moments of interaction.*

Restating the story above, then, each moment of interaction within the darkness of nature creates a pattern, a *spirit* fleetingly finding form, flashing momentarily into being before dissolving back into the whole - except where interactions repeat, allowing a pattern to persist, the spirit lingering in its ethereal form.

Let us then ground the poetry a little further in order to clarify the answer to the first question: what impels the interaction?

Nature is all there is. That is a metaphysical statement in that it excludes any creator existent outside of it, but otherwise it is semantic: I have defined nature as the complete universe and its entire contents. Nature is everything. Further, I have argued that nature is inherently minded, and mind entails perception; if there is nothing but nature, no Other to perceive, nature's principal expression of mind must be its perception or awareness of self. So is self-reflection inherent within nature.

What provoked nature to utilise its capacity for mind *in the first place* we cannot know. We know there is not darkness because we are aware of ourselves, and not necessarily as thinking beings. In the simplest prehensive state, we are still aware of our contextual environment, our inner and outer experience of being. Because we exist, nature must have been awake to itself.

Holding to the ancient conviction that nothing can be created of nothing, and with no belief in a supernatural creator god who can do otherwise, in animism there can be no beginning. In other words, if nature is everything, nothing can exist before or outside of nature. There was no point before the darkness, nor a point when that darkness awoke and, considering itself, the winds began to blow. There has always been nature, dark and still, and there have always been the winds of mind moving within the darkness, the spirit patterns of nature shifting with each inter-action. Nature has always been minded and nature has always been awake, aware and ever engaged in the currents of its self-perpetuating creativity. There is no brute emergence.

The second question is then pertinent: how do these winds create nature as we perceive it? The question is ontological, for if it is mind that, activated by interaction, takes the data and trans-forms it into the mental and physical of its perceived world, have we not reached an idealist stance? The animist would not cede to the thesis that nature is only mind.

The answer is simple in the poetic language of animism. When patterns become entangled by repeating interactions, increas-ingly spirit takes on what the animist might poetically call the lore of earth: its form settles, slowing sufficiently until it may be perceived in our phenomenal world. However, perpetually shifting and entirely present, when spirit becomes perceivable form it does so fleetingly, for the briefest instant of physical being. When first I read about quantum physics, it felt to me that the poetry of the two may well correlate: subatomic particles seem to emerge and disappear as waves of possibility collapse, fleetingly finding themselves in observable forms, and it is hard not to imagine these micro creatures as spirits momentarily settling. When I read Whitehead's description of the mental and physical poles of an actual occasion, the causal object weighing on the physical pole, I thought too of the settling of spirits. The occasion in its subjective state flares with the energy of its self-determination, burning out, slowing, settling into its objectivity now filled with experience: my words are blended with Whitehead's, exploring the merging of imagery, but crucially there is no sense of an ontological difference between the perceivable and the spiritual, simply a difference in the moment of becoming. In the animist thesis, their essence is the same.

Nature is more than moments of interactive sparkle, though. Whitehead suggested that the effects of each successive occasion are most often intensely minute, reflecting the tiniest changes in contextual data moment to moment, and it is this rate of change that allows for continuity. In animism the same thesis works: interaction to interaction, the shifting in the patterns generated can be gradual. Furthermore, when the affecting exchange of perception and response in an interaction evokes a feedback loop, a reactive and iterative cycle, that sticky tangle, a specific pattern is given the chance to continue and develop, in experience, complexity and stability. That pattern, slowing, settles into what we might perceive as enduring form.

I say it *can* be gradual; equally, feedback loops *can* occur. The greater part of the universe is darkness: modern astrophysicists speak of there being some 95 per cent of the universe that is beyond our ability to perceive, emitting no electromagnetic radiation as light or any other wave we can detect. Within the poetry of animism, this sounds like the formless darkness that is utterly still, but this is also the chaos: the dance of countless fleeting instants, spirit interacting but not acquiring form, moments of potentiality within the quiet of that endless darkness. Nature's entities are infrequent within this swirl of perpetual movement.

For an entity, a form, is not crafted of one interaction. Indeed, equally, no interaction occurs between just two verses. The animistic verse is not a separate thing; so it cannot interact with another separate thing. As a moment within the mind of nature, a verse is an integral part of the flow of universal movement, perpetually engaging with its entire context of verses, tiny and vast, micro- and macrocosmically. If we are to understand how nature creates the world we are perceiving, the focus must be not on the verses, but upon the patterns generated, for each pattern expresses the complete context of a flow of movement.

This brings us at last to that other powerful word explored in previous chapters but not as yet given its place within the definition of animism: the *soul*. Far more than the vibrant dance of each transient pattern that is spirit, the soul emerges where patterns of patterns recur, a form gently building, evolving, interaction to interaction. Yet, crucially expressing the integrity of nature, a soul is not a defined individual: it is the wholeness of a being. As the incorporation of every moment of its experience, every influence of its contextual heritage and environment, a soul is the presence of its complete past.

We might consider the formation of a star with its orbiting bodies, within the movement of its wider galaxy, and in referring to the soul of that sun we are acknowledging every moment, every interaction and relationship, that has brought it into the present. The soul of a human being expresses its genealogical and environmental web in just the same way, as does the soul of a valley, its ecosystem formed by all that has gone before. Here are subjects, perceiving and responding: at the moment of each and every interaction, potent with the shimmering patterns of its experience, the soul engages with its environment, expressing what the animist calls its *song*. However, my definition here is of the soul – I am not yet distinguishing between an individual and an aggregation.

The importance within animism of the notion of *soul* is this encapsulation of the past as critical to the immediate context, which is very much a part of our experience of life as human beings, albeit with limited conscious awareness. Equally, because the definition of soul applies to nature as a whole, it helps to establish the understanding of integration.

As nature's spirit is the pattern of its entire being in any passing moment, with each fleeting pattern part of that integrated whole, the soul of nature is the fullness of its totality. Nature's soul comprises every moment that has been and every relationship it has known, for nature is both itself soul and comprised of every individual soul. As such there is a comprehensive interconnectedness in every moment's interaction. Whitehead called this the Principle of Relativity: each occasion is dependent not just on its neighbour, but upon the entire web of events, informed by what has just happened and influencing what will happen next, the immediate context being connected to the whole. Indeed, each event is only as it is because of the pattern of the entire universe in that moment. So each soul holds a form that has effectively been created by the whole of nature. In this respect, Whitehead's ethics are wholly in tune with animism, for they are founded upon an awareness of nature's absolute interconnectivity, its inherent integration.

Like nature, the soul is neither mental nor physical: it is both. Within its gentle process of perpetual becoming, there is the flow of spirit, the shifting patterns of existence, emerging and evanescing, settling into form and dissolving into darkness. This is nature's interiority and nature's creativity. In the language of Whitehead's philosophy, an actual occasion is a process of creativity, fuelled by its context of prehended feelings and immediate history, the fluidity of unfolding and dissolving events providing constant regeneration at a fundamental level. In animistic poetry, here is the essential wakefulness that shines through every interaction, informed by the emotion and reason of its heritage, held by the threads of its immediate environment, connected to the universe as a whole. As such, creativity can be thought of as a spirit or god of nature, a brilliant pattern of energy formed and driven by its context of relationships, a force that saturates nature, constantly pushing us, affecting us, filling us and tearing us apart, and as such it is profoundly honoured.

Whitehead articulated his own faith as panentheistic. Acknowledging one God, the deity of the panentheist incorporates the universe, interpenetrating it, yet is infinitely greater than it. A distinct being, this God is an intelligent consciousness expressing its creativity through nature; indeed for some panentheists, God is the principle of animation, bringing form and life to nature, not from a separate position as transcendent observer, but as a pervasive yet coherent and directive mind. Whitehead's God was fully involved in the tides and currents of nature and deeply affected by them. Indeed, at times it is hard to see where his God is separate from nature. At the very end of *Process And Reality* he expressed it beautifully:

It is as true to say that God is permanent and the world fluent, as that the World is permanent and God is fluent. It is as true to say that God is one and the World many, as that the World is one and God many. It is as true to say that, in comparison with the World, God is actual eminently, as that, in comparison with God, the World is actual eminently. It is as true to say that the World is immanent in God, as that God is immanent in the World. It is as true to say that God transcends the World, as that the World transcends God. It is as true to say that God creates the World, as that the World creates God.

However, for Whitehead, God was not synonymous with nature. Perceiving creativity to be so central to nature's fundamental becoming, his God was a co-creator of the universe, taking an essential role. Creativity was 'that ultimate notion of the highest generality at the base of actuality': like Aristotle's substance, in other words, it is both absolutely fundamental yet has no intrinsic form. For Whitehead, it was God that provided nature with its necessary guidance. By embedding an aesthetic impulse within each and every occasion, God gave the creative force a desire for order, for value and meaning. Indeed, it was crucial to Whitehead's sense of integration that the 'teleology of the universe is directed to the production of Beauty'. It's a delicious vision.

There are no such benevolent gods in the pantheon of the animist. I have described the numerous gods of the polytheistic animist: they are the most powerful spirits or patterns of nature's configurations of interaction, persistent forms, beyond our human ability to comprehend. I might now add that some gods may also be souls, holding histories, traditions, mythologies through relationships over eons. Stretching way beyond the horizon, kilometres in depth, its internal currents and rivers flowing, maintaining countless ecosystems, its soul holding the memories of millions of years, the ocean is a body we can viscerally experience but it is too much for us grasp its wholeness. Equally, lust is a pattern of nature that we can feel searing through our being, making us ache with a hunger for that particular kind of physical contact, an experience that moves through the cells of our form which we can ride or hold, at times contain, yet its power is far greater than we can fully understand.

One might also consider a goddess like Brighid, whose stories tell of womanhood, community, power, sacrifice and sanctity, stories that are thick with a people's experience of life and landscape: a soul goddess, she is far greater than the memories held by generations of her people. Such are three of the many gods of the polytheistic animist, the first of which we might perceive as more tangibly material, the other two more ethereally mental, but all requiring respect, for in their own differing ways they have the potential to destroy our lives.

The animist, however, is also a pantheist. He has to be. For nature is a continuity, from the briefest moment of interaction to the apparently eternal, from the single celled amoeba to the blue whale, from the spinning electron to the spiralling galaxy. The pattern of the entire universe, the wholeness of everything, is spirit: God. Nature's complete story, held within its soul, its creativity heard in its perpetual song, is that single completeness: God.

Unlike panentheism, pantheism does not regard God as separate from the universe. God is nature, nature is God. In other words, there is nothing outside of nature: the *super*natural is a contradiction, an actual impossibility. Or rather, if there is anything beyond nature it is entirely outside the potential to influence or be influenced by this universe. Amidst the many gods within nature, there are gods with whom the animist forges personal relationships, committing with dedicated devotion to the god of the landscape he calls home, the god of a river he travels on, the god of fertility, regeneration, justice, or whatever may be the focal energies, skills and understandings of his own life and work. It is no less possible to experience the spirit of God viscerally, to hear its soul-song. Here is the breath, the movement, the flow, the very connectedness of nature and every relationship within it.

Pantheism has an ancient history. Almost all the philosophers mentioned in these pages have been described as pantheists, going way back to the pre-Socratic Heraclitus and the Stoics. Unsurprisingly, Christianity made such warmly embracing beliefs wickedly heretical for over a thousand years, but they continued as fundamental in Eastern religious traditions: both the *Tao* and Hindu *Brahman* can be described as that boundless spirit of nature that is life and order, nothing existing beyond it, its energies pervading everything that is. In Europe, Bruno's belief in nature's comprehensive sanctity had him burned at the stake, and later that century Spinoza was condemned as an atheist for his exquisitely rational yet pantheistic perception of God as nature. As the Church lost its authority to the rising power of empirical science, the German idealists, Fichte, Schelling and Hegel, spoke in pantheistic terms, acknowledging nature as God. Horrified by the abuse of the natural world by the Industrial Revolution, fuelled as it was by the new science, many in the European Romantic movement expressed pantheistic religious perspectives, very close to the integrated views of the animist, as did their later American counterparts.

Pantheism is a religious view, though, and while it has been important in previous centuries for thinkers to include an understanding of deity and sanctity within their metaphysics, nowadays philosophy requires religious language to be put to one side. As I suggested with Leibniz above, any inkling that there is a dependence on God for answers invalidates a philosophical perspective. However, I would rather deconstruct the jargon, finding the underlying reasoning and value, than pander to the residual logical positivists and quail before the fundamentalist atheists, neither of whom have answered the core questions of philosophy to any degree of conclusive satisfaction.

Indeed, within the context of these pages the value of the pantheistic position is about to come into its own, for I shall now tidy away the question that many have placed as the central issue of panpsychism: how does it all hang together?

God

The problem for the regular panpsychist, as William James explained, is how countless individual specks of mind-drenched dust might combine to become larger entities with coherent minds. A subject of experience is, after all, an indivisible unit: our own experience of consciousness informs us of that. If each subject is indivisible, a discreet entity within itself, a subject cannot be broken down into smaller subjects, nor can it be melded with others to create a larger subject. There can be no combination.

Even where panpsychism blends into neutral monism or process philosophy, as opposed to the materialist stance of property dualism, the problem remains. Reading Whitehead, Russell and others in whose philosophy the notion of a subject has been redefined and a primary substance completely discarded, there are moments when I find myself pausing, frowning. Whitehead's actual occasions can feel atomistic: they require a thesis to explain just how they might aggregate, combining to create larger subjects of experience. On some level they still feel like individual and distinct units and, as such, can feel substantial, requiring a Lucretian coming together across the substance-less void. If we are presenting nature as fundamentally comprised of numerous tiny bits and pieces, however insubstantial they actually are, unavoidably a bottom-up solution is going to be needed. However, what if we were to consider it differently: not as a bottom-up or even a top-down enquiry, but in terms of the whole and its parts?

Two German philosophers, Ludwig Jaskolla and Alexander Buck, working with the Munich-based *Geiststaub* (mind-dust) group, recently published a paper in which they suggested that the most economical answer to the panpsychist problem is *panexperientialistic holism*. Defining the term, they state simply that 'there is exactly one entity - the Universe itself'. It is such a wonderfully conclusive phrase, one would almost like to reject any additional explanation, other than perhaps a victorious 'full stop'. They do clarify, however, offering a concise description of this single subject as, '(i) an objective matter of fact, (ii) objectively structured, i.e. not completely homogeneous, (iii) a subject of experience and (iv) exemplifying experiential content'. In other words, their Universe is the wholeness of nature as I have outlined it above: a comprehensive expression of nature's inherent mindedness in its full flow of wakeful creativity. Their use of the term panexperiential instead of panpsychist simply affirms that what we are talking about need be no more than an elementary level of perceptual processing; Griffin also uses the term, evading or challenging the lazy critics who assume a human-style consciousness is being attributed to nonhuman aspects of nature.

As the two point out, given this premise the materialists' dependence upon a flawed thesis of emergence is removed. Instead of utilising the usual panpsychist argument about the integrity of nature's continuity, however, they point out that there 'are no *simple* material constituents in the Universe, therefore no brute emergence can be found'. More crucially, however, it is the combination problem that they feel confident they have solved. While others have struggled for millennia to work out how separate minds might be added together, combining, merging, unifying to create larger subjective wholes, they affirm that actually 'there is nothing to sum because there is just this one subject'. In the Germans' words, the 'Universe is a big experiential subject that can be dissected into various experiential parts'. How can one subject be dissected though? If we cannot combine, then we cannot divide. The answer is in their original definition: there is only *one* subject of experience, the entirety of the Universe. The rich diversity that we perceive as so many individual subjects is made up of *parts* of that whole. Indeed, they go on to say that our 'human selves are to be understood as relatively stable experiential patterns within the big experiential subject. These patterns originate, re-produce themselves for some time and finally dissolve'. Not only does this natural transience also concur with the animist thesis, but I am heartened to see the Münchner fellows also using the word *pattern*. From the Latin father, *pater*, through the Old French *patron*, the older meaning of pattern was as an example to be followed, the final *r* transposition not occurring until the eighteenth century; as such, its implications point to parts of an originating whole. The myriad of individuals that comprise nature, shimmering with the wakefulness of mind, are all patterns within that universal whole.

This is pantheism. Indeed, in their paper they suggest the thesis also offers 'the possibility of a intelligible concept of *God*', and I am reminded again of Spinoza, whose *Ethics* is such an exquisite celebration of God, yet who was indicted as an heretical atheist by both Jewish and Christian communities. To restate what I have said before, if one is only able to understand the word as denoting the Abrahamic father god, the notion of God here will be hard to grasp. The *theism* in pantheism will be entirely misconstrued. For the Pagan, however, the living heart of the word still pounds with its pre-Christian Germanic roots, heading all the way back to the PIE base of *gheu-* or *gheu(e)*, meaning to make an invocation or offer a libation. As an animist, this God that is nature hums with the potential and the satisfaction of life, itching with hunger and howling with joy, moving to the rhythms of wingbeats and footsteps. Ever present but never judging, God's power is in our breathing, in the breaking open of seed husks at the point of germination, in the cracking of lightning across the skies, in the smile of an infant and the rattle of the dying, in the claws of the cat and the pain of our bleeding. God is our aching, craving, surging, striving; God is our release into sleep and stillness. In every moment, in every sparkle of movement, with every tap of my fingertips on the keyboard, every photon that touches the papers beside me, every raindrop that hits the window, dancing in every tumbling cloud above, careening with every asteroid around some distant sun, rolling with galaxies and exhaling into dark stillness, instant by instant, God *sings*, every soul-song an expression of perception, of feelings and sensation, of experience absorbed, moments affected by moments, evoking responses that affect moments, and so on and on and on: magnificently and completely awake.

Of course, for many it will seem unnecessary to use the term God. Yet where there is no sense of an unwanted authority, no looming presence that measures our progress and worth, the word is not a threat. It is a celebration. It is not a call to submit, but a reminder of sanctity. In the animist worldview, as individuals, as communities, as a species spreading over the planet, achieving sustainability can be found only through living with respect, acknowledging the lines between need and desire, striving never to cause any unnecessary harm: the word *God* reminds us of that. Equally, the capacity to thrive is found through gratitude; yet, although the animist's prayers may poetically call out his thanks to God, it is not God he is thanking, for God has as little human-style consciousness as a rock or a mountain, a beetle or a stream. He is giving thanks *for* God, God as nature, nature as God, and again the word *God* reminds him to do so.

In his *Confessions*, Augustine expresses this with his customary blend of grace, sensitivity and passion. He was a devoted monotheist in every way, but Augustine's dedicated exploration of introspection reveals such a visceral experience of sanctity that he perceives God in everything, including himself. 'What is it that gleams through me? What strikes my heart without hurt? What makes me shudder and glow, impassioned? This force is so unlike me, so I shudder. But this force is what I was made to be like, so I ignite.' As an animist, I read his words as a reference to the soul of nature, to God, and I breathe in with the pleasure of empathy.

Considering the developing definition then, we can now add to it with the following: *animism is a relational ontology*. Indeed, for some, those last two words capture the definition completely.

The term is broad though. Used within various fields of study, its meaning can be limited to wholly abstract ideas, or refer merely to the effects of interaction between distinct entities. In most philosophical spheres the words are used more comprehensively, so the understanding is closer to the animistic: rejecting the Aristotelian premise that relations are subordinate to entities, relational processes are acknowledged to be nature's essential creativity, without which there would be nothing. In other words, as an example, although our thinking self presents it as such, we aren't talking about the squirrel and the hazelnut coming together to share a moment; ontologically, the shifting patterns that are the sensation and experience create the transient actuality of mind and matter, and the transient reality of the subject and object, within nature. Nature's primary being is not a substance but an instance, an interaction. The animistic interpretation can be further highlighted if we look at what can be seen as the theological roots of the term *relational ontology*, for they add a vital element.

In the early days of Christianity, as it was forging its principal doctrines, debate raged as to how it could be possible to maintain a pure and undiluted monotheism if God were not only the father but also the son and the holy ghost. Retaining the omniscience and omnipotence of the single deity seemed impossible if the other two were distinct and affecting minds. It was three fourth century scholars in what is now Turkey, known as the Cappadocian Fathers, the bishops Basil the Great and his brother Gregory of Nyssa, together with archbishop of Constantinople, Gregory of Nazianzus, who contributed most productively to the debate. The resolving distinction they made was between persona, using the Greek *hypostasis*, meaning property or existence, and *ousia*, essence: the Trinity could thus be seen as three separate personalities while remaining a single essential whole, the Godhead. Their ideas were laid down in the final version of the Nicene Creed, where Jesus is said to be *homooúsios* with God, or of the same essence.

In animism, interaction is the expression of nature's *ousia*, its ubiquitous and fundamental mindedness, present on every level. However, what makes a truly relational ontology is not just interaction, nor how one entity engages with another. As the Cappadocian Fathers knew, the crucial element is the integration: every relationship with and within the whole *is* the whole. In animism, every whisper of mind and matter is a pattern within the soul of nature, within the complete being and becoming of nature. It is that integration that is the whole, and that creates the ongoing viability of the whole.

Inevitably perhaps such a current of thought leads us on to the Gaia theory. Developed in the 1970s by chemist James Lovelock and biologist Lynn Margulis, it describes Earth as a complex system, the tenability of which is dependent upon each interconnected element. At first the two suggested it was the collective biota of organic matter that created the necessary stability for life: within the biosphere of countless ecosystems, each creature's involvement with the cycles of soil, water, and air contributes to maintaining the narrow band of viability in temperature, acidity, salinity and so on. However, with scientists working on the ideas in fields from climate change to geophysiology, the theory has now recognised nature's universal continuity: the system is now comprehensive. Needless to say, it was ridiculed at first by fundamentalist atheists like Richard Dawkins, who projected erroneous assumptions onto the theory, but Lovelock repeatedly affirmed that he had never included a designing creator or inherent teleology in his thesis: nobody was in control, no divine consciousness, yet neither was it random. It simply self-regulates. In animistic poetry, this is nature's song. There is no supernatural force, no über-natural creator, no caring extra-natural father keeping watch over his flock. There is nature as God, God as nature, comprised of every moment of perception and response, from the subatomic to the galactic, every moment, every pattern, contributing to the stability that maintains the whole.

David Abram suggests the word animate simply means the ability to self-organise. Working with Lovelock for a while in the 1980s, his words are richly poetic and pantheistic, vibrant with his passionate love of nature. In *Becoming Animal*, his descriptions seem often to be a celebration of the whole:

> The air is not a random bunch of gases simply drawn to earth by the earth's gravity, but an elixir generated by the soils, the oceans, and the numberless organisms that inhabit this world, each creature exchanging certain ingredients for others as it inhales and exhales, drinking the sunlight with our leaves or filtering the water with our gills, all of us contributing to the composition of this phantasmagoric brew, circulating it steadily between us and nourishing ourselves on its magic, generating ourselves from its substance.

Considering mind, he is keen to dislodge the idea of separateness, emphasising the interconnectedness of being and the fundamental process of relationship. 'What if thought', he asks, 'is not born within the human skull, but is a creativity proper to the body as a whole, arising spontaneously from the slippage between an organism and the folding terrain that it wanders?' In other words, mind emerges as the interaction within a wholly minded nature. Furthermore, it is not simply embodied mind that he is exploring, but the notion that mind, so much more than brain, is also more than the individual, for 'mind is not experienced as an exclusively human property, much less as a private possession that resides within one's head. While there may indeed be an interior quality to the mind, for a deeply oral culture this interiority derives not from a belief that the mind is located within us, but from a felt sense that *we* are located *within it*, carnally immersed in an awareness that is not ours, but is rather the Earth's'. Again he writes, the 'fluid field of experience that we call *mind* is simply the place of this open, improvisational relationship - experienced separately by each individual body, experienced all at once by the animate Earth itself'.

Community

In the sixteenth century, pushing against a thousand years of Christian oppression, Gerolamo Cardano's ontology drew a picture of nature as a whole comprised of countless parts, each of which are both whole entities yet also composed of smaller parts. He saw the *anima*, or soul, present in each coherent entity, as allowing its unity. In the integrated metaphysics of animism, the soul doesn't create the unity. It *is* the unity.

Ontologically, then, if we accept nature to be a pantheistic whole within which patterns emerge, some of which endure and settle into form, there is no need for a theory of aggregation in order to create coherent minds. What we do need, however, is an understanding of why patterns come into being as they do within that whole, like eddies and currents in the ocean, like gusts and swirls in the winds of a storm. The question will be addressed in the next chapter, but I bring this one to a close by introducing another of those words that adds to the structural framework of animism, a word that is integral to the issue of pattern: *community*.

The etymology comes through Old French *comunité* from Latin *communitas* meaning a fellowship of common ground, relations or feelings, the Old English *gemæne* meaning what is common or public, *gemænscipe* being the community and what is in common ownership, all of which are rooted the ancient PIE of **ko-*, together, and **mei-*, exchange, suggesting what is shared by all. It is a powerful and pivotal word in animistic traditions, beliefs and communities, a word that guides understanding and decisions.

In his own engaging style, author of *Animism* and scholar of religions Graham Harvey outlines the ontology of nature using metaphorical turtles to represent mind. Turtles, he explains, '*go all the way down* (one turtle below the next) because each element of the cosmos, each particle of matter, is consciousness or aware *in some sense*'. However, equally important are hedgehogs - 'synecdochal' hedgehogs, for they 'represent themselves (true anarchists!) as well as the living community (all of us) of which they are members' - and hedgehogs '*go all the way round* because the whole cosmos is a community of life'. In many ways his words emphasise the need to push down the boundary fences that segregate humankind from the rest of nature. Having acknowledged mind throughout nature, there is no justification to keep humanity separate. Abram's aim is the same: 'The surrounding world, then, is experienced less as a collection of objects than as a community of active agents, or subjects. Indeed, every human community would seem to be nested within a wider, more-than-human community of beings'.

In some ways we are talking about ecosystems, but only if we understand ecosystems as existent at every level of being from the micro to the macro, shimmering with the wakefulness of mind. Every ecosystem is a community of beings, perceiving, sensing, experiencing, responding and more, each community, the whole community of life, being in a constant flow of interactions. A community, then, is a pattern of relationships; within each pattern there are countless smaller patterns, and each pattern itself is a part of a larger pattern and a part of other different patterns. For, like verses, patterns and communities are not separate things; as Cardano explained, they are wholes that are parts of greater wholes, and at the same time they are wholes made up of countless other wholes.

As an example we perceive as physical, I would proffer an

oak. Comprised of leaves and wood, flowers, sap, nuts, and so on, each of these is comprised of cells, atoms, subatomic particles, while the tree is itself a part of its environment, perhaps a woodland of thousands of trees, upon a broader landscape. At every level of interaction, the patterns hold the stories of moments, of drought and storms, of photons and weevils, of oxygen and war. Within its soul the oak also carries the history of its parental and ancestral trees, stories it has given to oaks it has sired, and the stories of its genus and its species. These are shared patterns which tell of the communities to which it belongs, communities which make up its being.

In the same way, a human being has very many communities: I am part of the integrated whole of the valley and the village that is my home, the coherence of people with whom I live, the soul of my bloodline, the mind of womanhood, and motherhood, as well as those communities with whom I have shared briefer stories. Further, within me there are countless ecosystems, communities of blood and belly, tiny mites and bacteria, subatomic worlds spinning with stories of interaction.

As human beings, with access to our interiority, in thinking of our own communities we perceive a blend of both the physical and mental. Because the animist does not distinguish ontologically between the two, some communities are intangible patterns of interactions that are felt to be entirely within the realms of the mind. For example, words too have communities. In languages and cultures, in meanings and connotations, words are patterns within nature that exist, developing within various communities, communities that themselves grow and break apart. Rich with nature's mindedness, as accumulations of meaning, permeated by stories, words play with words, pushing against the person who speaks them aloud, growing and diminishing, evolving over centuries. Given the animist definition of soul as the wholeness of a being with all its history of interaction, it could be said that words have souls. Beyond the simple demand for discipline in definition, this is one of the reasons that I have given etymological sketches of key words, drawing them out of the notional and the abstract, allowing them to be creatures of nature, patterns of being and becoming, acknowledging their lives and interactions. Words too are parts of wholes, and whole made up of parts, contributing to the integration that is nature as a whole.

In this chapter I have established that it is the process of interaction that utilises nature's capacity for mind. At its simplest, this is a relational awakeness, a basic perception and response, the data of which the mind uses to create the world as we perceive it. Such a focus upon interaction may initially imply that nature is crafted of distinct bits and pieces that need to be combined, but within a fully integrated metaphysics that is not the case.

Affirming that it is nature not matter that is minded, early in the chapter I dismissed the materialist panpsychist's need to combine their very tiny pieces of mind or minded stuff. Having discarded the notion of a primary substance as well, I explored where animism and process philosophy shared common ground, considering how patterns develop, shifting in form, emerging and dissolving, passing data from one moment to the next, both in Whitehead's language and in the poetry of animism.

However, because animism is pantheistic, its relational ontology allows nature to be based on wholes and parts, not bottom-up combination. From such a perspective, animism regards *every pattern as integral to the complete being of the universe*. Having secured this layer of our foundation, in Chapter Seven we shall look more deeply at how subjects, selves and individuals are integral to wholes.

Chapter Seven

The Self

A good deal of what is described as work on the philosophy of mind is epistemology. Content with Descartes' declaration of certainty, the thinking *I* is taken as the starting point, and what are produced are various studies of what consciousness and the self might be, all of which begin with the primacy of the subject and explore from there. Sticking to an epistemological position does evade the need to bridge the ravine now manifested by materialist sciences between neurology and psychology, or indeed the possibility of stumbling into that ravine, blinkered by hidden assumptions. There is no doubt that such an approach is a valid and useful investigation.

However, a purely epistemological exposition can imply that the subject is fundamentally actual, and any such thesis cannot help but provoke the ontological problems raised in earlier chapters: even if we don't much care what it is made of, we cannot ignore the question of how this mental entity - this subject who perceives - engages with the outside world. Starting from such a position, the typical idealist dismisses the issue by making the non-mental illusory; the typical materialist, facing in the opposite direction, asserts the experience of mentality to be a fiction generated by the actions of chemicals or subatomic particles. While the interface problem may be addressed by taking the monist stance in terms of substance, both these theses have further intrinsic problems, problems that the integrated metaphysics of pantheistic animism overcomes, as I have already described.

However, in removing the subject as a starting point, animism is left with another question: so what is the *I*? It is the answer to this that is necessary if we are to move smoothly from ontology to epistemology.

Deep in the stories of our cultural and individual imagination, we can reach for ideas as to why nature is as it is. Painted in the rich colours of myth and legend, some such ideas have always retained their freedom to change, adapting with each new dawn, meandering across rivers and hills, inspiring reflection, thanksgiving and awe. Others have been formulated within rational parameters into religious and scientific convictions that are more brittle, requiring not just the telling of the tale but its justifications and implications.

To the animist, every story is important, and particularly those of his own heritage. When it comes to the ontology of nature, it is simply that some ideas demand a more substantial stretch of the imagination than others: for example, the existence of a God that is greater than the universe, a God with a human-style consciousness whose creativity is expressed through a divine design that is manifested as nature, a God with a special focus upon the little furless mammals that are *Homo sapiens*. I sometimes wonder how comforting it would be to believe in a loving God who, existing outside of nature, watches and cares for each living soul, but concurrently how very confusing nature's merciless violence would seem to be.

With no sense of humanity's pre-eminence, acknowledging nature's complete integration, the animist may feel that the soul or God that is nature's totality does have a plan or purpose. He is unlikely to assert that his own tiny mind has any true understanding of it though: God's consciousness must, after all, be as different from the human mind than that of an electron. However, because of nature's continuity, he knows that a whisper of that purpose must hum within every mind in the universe, and in meditation or reflection he may experience it as a delicious sense of order, as inklings of intention determining a structure within nature's currents and drives, a will that is so very much stronger and broader than his own human soul. Yet, as patterns of interaction come into being, shimmering with intensity, forms emerging out of the mists of potential balanced on the gossamer threads of momentary viability, as quickly connections then change and forms dissolve, breaking apart the coherence that afforded the appearance of order. Communication through interaction, moment to moment, provides a sense of continuity - sometimes - but nature is so beyond our comprehension, it doesn't take much to see how brutally and dismissively chaotic it can also be.

Indeed, while darkness may be the fundamental state of nature, that ancient Greek concept of χάος is always close. Chaos: after a few centuries of the new science and the rigorous arrogance of Victorian structure, it was an American meteorologist who brought chaos back to the table of serious discussion. In the 1960s, Edward Lorenz found that his basic equations describing air currents could actually have entirely unpredictable outcomes: his *butterfly effect* is now familiar in everyday parlance. Any system as vibrant and dynamic as nature is so intensely sensitive in its complexity that the slightest shift in the initial conditions observed can lead to radically different results. Beautifully, as Lorenz discovered, this seemingly random behaviour can be found even in simple mathematical equations, leading scientist Robert May to describe the revelation as 'the end of the Newtonian dream'. Effectively chaos theory declared mechanistic certainly to be indeed an act of faith. Of course, the materialist may attribute the problem solely to immeasurably small changes, allowing him to maintain a hope that one day science will be able to grasp and measure them, regaining control. The animist would concede that science may well reveal more, but that is not really the point.

The ubiquitous mindedness of nature removes the validity of mechanistic logic. Whether as human beings we see order, structure and form, or chaotic dissolution, is dependent purely on the limitations of our own human perception and comprehension. While nature's processes of creativity are not divinely designed, neither are they the mindless inevitabilities of inert matter. On every scale from the micro to the macrocosmic of the universe, what generates the patterns of nature is the same: interactions provoked by and provoking the flow of perception and response.

So what is the *I*?

Subject

Within the apparent chaos of nature, as human beings we appear to manage our world through the framework of the self, the *I* that is the subject, the person looking out at reality.

If we are seeking to understand ontologically, however, it is only once we have released the belief that we are perceiving nature *in itself* that the distorting lenses of that human self can start to fall away: the *I* has a way of perceiving which, epistemologically, is useful for its own survival, but is not necessarily correct in terms of nature's actuality. Having acknowledged the perceptive veil, when we are also able to let go of the primacy of the subject, then do we have the opportunity to consider nature animistically: purely as currents of minded interaction. Each moment, drenched in the data generated by interaction, is utilised by nature's minded essence, roused to perceive and respond. In turn, each response is then a new interaction, creating another vibrant moment rich with perceptive data. Formed by this data, each mind is a subject, an *I*.

Crucial to the thesis is the central pantheistic premise that nature as a whole is also a mind, a subject of its own internal perception: each individual subject is a pattern of being within nature's complete minded being. Furthermore, like nature as a whole, each subject is awake not only to its immediate context within the entirety of the universe, but also to its interiority.

Where the feedback of iterative interaction persists, the subject is allowed a continuity. It grows, building from the percepts given by its context and its inner being, the *I* developing with the experience of repeating patterns and forms.

It is where the configurations of mind allow for self-reflexive consideration that we find that which human beings have long declared the pinnacle of nature's evolution, and what animists tend to view simply as one way of being within the great diversity of the universe: the thinking *I*.

For millennia, philosophers have declared it only possible to know the world through one's own mind. Such a sense of isolation is perhaps inevitable, manifesting in part because every moment exists solely within its own particular context of being, its immediate environment of data, moment after moment. Certainly, we can only hope to give a reliable account of our own view of reality. It can be extremely hard even to imagine the qualia of another mind. With our understanding of another's experience necessarily drawn from our own limited perspective, we repeatedly fail to do so with any real accuracy when dealing with other humans. It is not surprising that we fail so comprehensively when it comes to other animals, let alone plants and rivers, molecules and hurricanes. Yet each of these is equally comprised of the data of interaction, of the exchange of perception and response that is mind.

Furthermore, the mind is not actually imprisoned within its own boundary walls. As I began to describe at the end of the last chapter, the coherence that is the subject exists within countless different and interwoven communities of being. On every scale within nature interactions generate data, subjects of perception responding within their contextual environments - within the belly, within blood cells, within atoms and electrons, indeed *as* the belly, as blood cells, as atoms and electrons, one within another. Looking at larger communities: corals, oceans, planets, solar systems are also subjects created by perceptive data, one existing within the other. Indeed, if we accept the universe to be a subject, the simple logic of its continuity informs us that nature is comprised of selves within selves, subjects within subjects, minds within minds, fractal-like patterns within patterns. Each subject is a part of a larger subject, and each subject is comprised of countless subjects, interacting, generating data, communicating, creating patterns, electrons and galaxies, micro- to macrocosmically. As Newton also expounded, reaching back into the texts of Hermetic mysticism, 'That which is Below corresponds to that which is Above, and that which is Above corresponds to that which is Below, to accomplish the miracles of the One Thing'.

So our question has evolved from asking what the *I* could be, to why or how individual entities emerge within that spectrum of wholes.

Although we can consider nature's interactions one by one, as the meticulous process of moment by moment exchange, instead of imagining two drops of water meeting we are better to think of an apparently boundless ocean: those two drops quickly become indiscernible in that vast surging body with its currents, tides and eddies. Within the mass of data, fleeting interactions are forever scattering information out into the general flow, creating the merest flicker of mind, a subject awaking and dissolving once again. Feedback loops and iteration, however, can create curves that naturally gather up data. Coherences of percepts become circles, cycles, systems which in turn allow for greater self-perception. They may be based upon simple levels of passive perception, of prehension, the pattern's intrinsic introspection creating repetition, or develop through a continuity based upon the strength of those iterating patterns, allowing for self-regulation and viability, perhaps settling into mental or physical form. In the language of animism, it is with these circling patterns of interactions that we find enduring subjects and their communities.

In process philosophy, Whitehead and others were clear about the distinction between an aggregation and an individual; an aggregation is a gathering of individual subjects with no shared interiority. Griffin states that while a dog is an individual, a rock is an aggregation. In animism, the distinction is not so clear cut: indeed, little in animism is. The reason for striving to differentiate is to ascertain which are entities perceiving with a single coherent mind and responding accordingly, and which are gatherings acting through the numerous responses of their component individuals. From an animist stance I might say that a community is an aggregation, a flocking together of percepts in shared loops of communication. It may consist of any number of subjects, one particularly affecting the whole community at one moment, its data influencing those around it, then another subject in another moment. Such communities are softly shifting patterns, with edges blurring and changing. Certainly, although any community will be a part of a larger community, its subjects may not cohere sufficiently for that community to feel itself to be an individual in its own right.

However, Griffin was right to say that it is an intuitive decision as to where the distinction might be made, because it is not black and white. Perceiving the same information, a community's perpetual interactions ensure there are strong common patterns within its form. Self-perception and iteration may be tight enough for there to be a shared sense of self, to the point of self-reflection and self-determination. With dominant moments influencing the whole, guiding interactions and colouring the perceptive data which create the subjects, more distinct edges may be felt, and a sense of subjective being grows. However, we need not leap to the point of declaring this community an individual: its component subjects may remain stronger than the merged coherence of the whole. In animism, this community is a tribe.

Unlike community, *tribe* has always been a very human word.

Its roots are in the Latin *tribus*, being the Ramnes, Tities and Luceres, the original three groupings that made up the ancient state of Rome. The word survives in closely related languages, such as Spanish and Italian, its etymology probably spilling into the Welsh *tref*, meaning a town or inhabited place. Like *person* and *people*, it is a word used within animism as a way of extending to nature more widely the respect normally only accorded to humankind. So the animist will talk about the tribe of his home landscape, and in doing so he will include amongst its members not just the human beings, but the nonhuman animals, the hedgerows and trees, the waterways and mists, even the gods whom he reveres as affecting or protecting that ecosystem. Tribe, then, infers a sense of identity. A tribe is a community with a shared and coherent will to be, a sticky desire for continuity, an instinct to survive. Not every member of that community may have sufficient mental capacity to act for the tribe, but every member feels the protective embrace that is affirmed by those that do.

Together with community and tribe, the third state is that of the coherent individual: this is what the animist will refer to as a *person*. Regardless of whether that individual is human or not, it is a system whose component subjects respond not simply with the whole but as a whole. This is not a category shift. If it feels as if it should be, the premise underlying the animist definition has not been grasped. The spectrum of common ground, of empathies and continuities that allow for any coherence, is as transient as any other aspect of nature. As was stated in Chapter Six, being comprehensively minded, nature's perception of itself is a fundamental axiom; given that integration entails continuity, the self awareness of the whole must mean that self awareness is inherent throughout nature. At its simplest, this may be an inner prehension, but through natural feedback the sensation or sense of self can develop, and reflection upon that sense can create an identification with that self. As the subject becomes self-defined, it asserts a measure of control, adjusting its perception of its external and internal context, honing the coherence of its own part of nature's mind. The inner community of minds develops the capacity to respond as a coherent interiority of mind. It is a development that is happening all the time. For some, it is a process that continues until the perceptive data allows for thought, consideration and consciousness.

My words suggest that such a process is part of a natural evolution. Of course, it can be. However, a decoherence is as likely, an individual no longer capable of feeling itself as a single mind and breaking up into its component subjects. If we recall that to the animist there was no beginning, no seven days of initial creation, and that each individual is part of a larger whole, we can see that increased complexity and coherence is not nature's goal, it is simply one facet of nature's rich diversity of being.

Some examples may help to clarify.

Take a pub, early on a Friday evening in a city square. The chatter of conversation, the scents of whisky and beer, the place is crowded, individuals sharing the air they breathe, half hearing, half thinking, responding to the flow of perceptive data. Here is a community. Moving with each other, people turn towards the noise of a falling glass shattering, their focus then shifting back into the chatter, traffic passing, eddies and swirls, currents of interaction, people leaving, arriving, pausing, merging into the whole, drifting with it, allowing themselves to be moved. It is an entity that emerges at opening time and disappears when the doors are finally closed. There is no permanence about it, nor about the status of its component subjects. Each person may feel themselves an individual in the moments they consider the pump labels and converse with the barmaid ordering their pint, and when they are laying down an opinion with friends at the table, but there are long moments when the thinking self is not active at all, or not considering itself, and the influencing coherence of the community is far stronger. Most would agree, however, that this is no more than a community; there is seldom if ever a coherent sense of the pub as an individual, for there is no coherent self-reflection, its form being too loose. A siren breaks the air outside and the community ignores it. A girl shrieks and the community turn to its dominant percepts, a few individuals emerging to deal with her momentary crisis while the majority slip back into the softly humming embrace of the community.

Now think of the football match, supporters segregated on opposite sides of the stadium, their voices, their muscle tension, their heartbeats synchronising with the chants that rise and fall, feet stamping, fists punching the air, responding as one creature - not a polished and precise machine, but as a natural system, a tribe, acutely aware of itself, protecting itself, expressing itself. Here again, there is no complex shared mental activity; from the outside, it may seem as if this is a single individual, responding through a shared mind, and to some extent it is, it does. A supporter who drifts into his own subjective being will stumble, to be carried by the tribe for a while until he re-finds the pattern, re-forms from its percepts, rejoins the tribe or is left behind and, feeling isolated, removes himself completely. Each person on the stands is an individual subject of perception and experience, but their individual selves are temporarily lost to the shared mind of the tribe. Again, this is no permanent state. While the moments of the match offer a specific array of perceptual data out of which a fellow's subjective *I* is comprised, walking home he stops to consider his day, an individual once more. Pausing in a quiet street to sit on a bench, he looks up at the clouds, and once more his individual self slips away: he is part of the community of that moment, not a conscious thought in his head, the leaves of the plane tree beside him moving in the breeze. Then slowly the subjects within his belly become dominant, growling with hunger.

In animistic poetry, there would be no question that there was a *spirit* of the football club: this is the vibrant and ever-changing pattern that is the momentary flow of its sum of interactions, its immediate state of coherent becoming, expressed as players and fans. Does the club have a *soul*? Those (animists) within the embrace of its tribal community, drenched by its percepts, aware of its heritage and drive for continuity, would say yes. To say so does not imply that the club has the coherence of an individual self. Would it be so ludicrous to suggest that it did? A club surely could not have the ability for self-reflection. Yet, the animist may also concede that, if it did, its mind would be beyond the experiential reach of any of its component individuals.

As human beings, we believe ourselves to be discrete individuals at all times. However, we are not in a constant state of conscious and independent thought. We are subjects of perception, and as such we are also systems, comprised of many subjects, indeed at times dominated by individuals that are parts of our subjective whole, and concurrently we are parts of larger wholes. With my thinking self dominant, I can consciously experience the coherence of my inner being, informed by the scents of autumn where I lie in the meadow, the changing light as the clouds cast shadows of the sun, the wind on my skin, the optimism of my positivity, but a moment later that inner self may be broken apart by a different set of data. Watching a flock of fieldfare move over the meadow, or a skylark rising on the notes of its song, my self dissolves, spiders finding shade beneath the folds of my coat, spinning webs between the long grass and my boots, the mind of the meadow subsuming what had been this sense of *I*. It is a temporary state, but the change can be complete.

More dramatically, a twinge in my head may be perceived by my subjective whole, but if the pain is too acute my self can disappear, its coherence shattering as in one way or another I lose consciousness: again I lose the *I*. Exhaustion, emotional trauma or physiological shock can do the same, the experience dislodging the thinking self, and breaking up the ability to perceive coherently at all.

The key understanding is that, if we are truly to relinquish the primacy of the subject, we must acknowledge that systems retain a constantly shifting state, the coherence of the subject and its individuality being wholly dependent upon the context of each moment and its given percepts.

Taking the thesis further into the scope of animistic understanding, I could explore community, tribe and individuality within antelope, starlings or bees, but such examples are too close to the human. We all have sufficient perceptive ability and empathy to have seen what is clearly collective and individual decision-making in such creatures, even if only on television. It would perhaps be more challenging and more valuable to look at entities that are widely considered insentient from a non-animistic perspective.

Let's take the community of a wood. With the blackthorn seedlings creeping out into the meadow, the rooks flying out at dawn, walkers and thinkers treading its tracks, the deer meandering, its population of birds and rodents falling and rising, the woodsman felling old conifers to replace them with deciduous natives, the edges of this being can feel loose and inconstant. As a community, its members are each individuals striving for their own survival, whether birch sapling or bluebell, bolete or beetle, down to the photons dancing between the leaves. Yet the woodland is also a self-regulating system: it has a coherence that allows it to manage issues that arise internally and externally, each subject adapting according to its informing percepts, prehending and responding within the context of the ecosystem as a whole.

Accepting the premise that all nature is minded, we have established that every part of nature perceives, and not only its external environment but its inner community as well. The woodland is awake, then, each subject within its community adding to that wakeful perceptiveness, but is it making decisions as a whole? In its internal perception, is it feeling its inner being as a community of individual subjects, or as the interiority of a coherent self? Just as for the football club, there is certainly a *spirit* of the wood, a *soul*, but does it have the ability to be an individual self? The same questions could be put with regard to a single tree within that wood. It is also a community, comprised of the countless subjects that are its own molecules, its population of bacteria, fungi and insects, all of whom work together as an interconnected system maintaining its own balances to ensure sustainability. But does it have a sufficient vision of its own community to work for its wellbeing, identifying with that collective enough to feel any threat from intrusion and protect itself accordingly *as a whole*?

While acknowledging the wood and the tree as communities, whether the animist would also use the term tribe or individual would be an intuitive and personal decision. Epistemologically, if he were to perceive the tree as an individual, not only would his own reality change, his world being enriched by the inherent subjectivity and consequent value he has accorded the tree, but ontologically that would change him too, for as a subject himself he is also created by the data he perceives. Within animism, such a rationale is important, affirming an ethical stance and a basis for prioritisation and respect, but would his decision have validity beyond that? The same implications are, of course, true for the football club, and for every community within nature.

From an animistic standpoint, the need to determine absolutely who has the coherent interiority of an individual is not felt that urgently. Its only pertinent relevance is in regard to culpability, where the agency and autonomy of a decision maker must be debated, about which more will be discussed in the following chapter. After all, the defining line between a community of subjects and an individual self may be drawn with some clarity in philosophical exploration, but in nature that distinction is not so clear. A tree as much as a human being is likely to have a transient sense of self, that transience being a reflection of changing perceptive data and mental states, moment to moment, allowing it to be now a single tree, then a part of the wood or of the valley through which the winds move as a whole.

Furthermore, it is worth acknowledging that we cannot know whether a tree has the capacity for a coherent interiority. It is easy to dismiss a tree as lacking autonomy or consciousness because it behaves differently from how most human beings behave, but we have no accurate knowledge of a tree's experience of qualia, a tree's sensation of time or community, of care or ecstasy. To the sensitive observer, some trees *feel* to be sturdy and subjective presences, not just observing but wilfully influencing their surroundings, like family matriarchs overseeing their realm, while other trees feel like puppies tumbling in a pile of limbs and fur and warmth, incapable in that moment of identifying themselves as separate beings, branches and roots intertwined, leaves fluttering in the wind. Walking through ancient woodland, few would disagree that such a place exudes a sense of integration far greater than that of a younger wood. An eight hundred year old oak has a character all of its own. Indeed, recognising that our human intuition can suggest the capacity to be an individual can grow with experience, the next step here is to explore just how that may be. In doing so, another layer of the issue is brought into the light.

Memory

In Chapter One I laid down a preliminary definition of experience. I suggested that, as more than simple perception, an experience notes the *effects* of what we are perceiving. As such, even at its most basic, experience is more than simple prehension. Exploring what that really means requires a detour, however. We must now consider another word, one that I have as yet consciously avoided, but for which an initial definition would here be useful.

Memory: in the 1200s, as the French-born baron Simon de Montfort was demanding of King Henry III that a share of England's wealth and power be given to its noblemen, the Anglo-French *memorie* meant not just a recollection but a mental awareness, a consciousness of something. One can imagine the word being sounded in grave and passionate debate. The Latin root was still strong in its verbal soul: *memor* can be translated as mindful, thoughtful, grateful, and so implies that which must be remembered. The PIE base of **men-* or **mon-* imbues all of its descendant words with the act of thinking.

Scientifically and philosophically, ontologically, however, memory is not easy to deconstruct. In *Dominion of the Dead*, Robert Pogue Harrison writes, 'Nothing is more difficult than to get a firm conceptual grasp of the retentive nature of the human mind, since at any given time we find ourselves inside a retaining framework the boundaries of which we can never fully circumnavigate'. As a mental process, it is simply not possible to step outside of its reach in order to observe it with any objectivity. With an optimistic confidence so typical of his time, in the eighteenth century the materialist and early psychologist David Hartley suggested memories were tiny physical vibrations, 'vibratiuncles' that reflected past sensory experiences. Few modern materialists express such certainty, for purely physical structures have only present states, not an accessible past: we can't turn in the direction of the past and walk on into it. Certainly, traces of the past can be found everywhere in the physical world, but understanding the mental act of remembering by way of a materialist thesis is something else. Thinkers have suggested that we store memories in genes, in 'neural maps', in the zero point field, and handfuls of other conceptual possibilities, but if the methodology used is scientific materialism, the physical structure or framework of memory is as impossible to locate or prove as consciousness. Of course, any metaphysics that allows for the existence of a separate mind stuff relinquishes the problem, but philosophically we can't just smile and shrug as if the question has been answered by God. In truth, unless we are willing to rely on a specific mind stuff or a divine design, we have very little to go on. Once again, rational deduction and imagination must come into play.

In animism, there is an obvious starting point. Because memory is so completely integral to mind, nature's mindedness must surely confer the capacity for memory to every part of nature: *memory is as ubiquitous as mindedness in nature.* In other words, it is not that there is memory only where there is a certain complexity of mind. If perception is to be understood by its subject, memory is an essential foundation, a flow of perceived data being quite meaningless if there is no recognition. Even using the limited instruments of modern scientists, we know that single cell organisms are capable of recognising a toxin on second contact and avoiding it. At the most basic level of prehension, then, memories allow for appropriate reactions, without which forms have no potential for continuity, the data of interaction simply scattering. However, the key is this: memories are not laid down *in order that* we might perceive. As subjects, we have not learned to remember in order to understand our world. Such a thesis places the subject first, and if we are to reject the primacy of the subject this is not a rational standpoint. Instead, animism's integrated metaphysics suggests that subjects are formed by memories just as they are formed by any other data.

So is there a difference between the data of an interaction and memory? There must be a difference because an immediate inter-action provides a sense of presence, while a memory accesses data that is apparently not in the present context. In various arenas I have heard thinkers talk of impressions, grooves or even ruts left by an event or flow of interactions, and aesthetically such an idea appeals to my imagination. Event impressions could provoke and guide future interactions, supporting repetition, promoting continuity of form, allowing for habit and memory to be maintained. Yet such an idea also implies that the minded essence of nature is a substance into which indentations can be made, and the thesis I have presented as animistic suggests this not to be the case. It is necessary, therefore, to think about it in another way.

With no substance within which memories could be stored, there can only be current interactions within nature's minded essence: a perpetual and shifting flow of comprehensive interconnection. Indeed, remembering this to be the animistic premise, and recognising that each interaction communicates data, passing information along, moment influencing moment, we can see how memory is entirely integral to the animist understanding. In actuality, it is only because nature is minded that there can be any continuity: nature's continuity could equally be called memory. As such, memory need not challenge us to find a passage back through mechanical time. Memory is wholly present.

How then can past events persist? In Chapter Six I described how the poetry of animism languaged the difference between nature's essential interaction and the world as we perceive it: spirit slows according to the lore of earth. When the rate of interaction is slowed through the sticky flux of iteration, patterns settle into the percepts of form. Those percepts are not only the physical world of tangible matter, but the mental as well, the emotional and cognitive world of thought, sensation, dream and imagination. The former are simply heavier, slower, than the latter; the latter we feel to be less tangible but are no less perceivable forms. It is here that we find memory, in the patterns of interactions which, settling into iteration, find a relative stability of form, whether mental and physical.

Considering our world, the past is indeed then all around us.

In the lines of the landscape, of woodland edges and hedgerows, of rooftops and lanes, in the curves of the chair beneath me and the empty bowl beside me, in the music of a melody that moves in my fingertips, in the words I have just written, in the stories that make up the inner forms of every community, every tribe, every individual, there are the ongoing iterations of memory. Here is the creativity of our ancestors, the creativity of moments just past. Each whisper of history is simply the soft repeating of interactions, undercurrents of being still in their process of becoming. It is this framework of memories that provides the substance of the manifest world, the structure of our mental being and our becoming.

In the language of animism, such an understanding allows a broader grasp of the soul: whether oak tree, hoverfly or human being, crafted of memories, the soul incorporates every experience of a individual's contextual heritage and environment, and humming with the integration of its location within the universe, it continues, awake, to perceive and to respond.

On that basis, let's take another example to clarify further the notion of subject and self.

Griffin spoke of a stone as being an aggregation and not an individual. Its component electrons and atoms are individuals, and as such they respond for themselves, as themselves. The stone, however, has no collective self: Griffin would say it has no cohering consciousness that allows it to act as a whole. Whether his distinction is one that accords with the animistic view or not is worth exploring. Certainly we can find minded forms within a stone, each of these perceiving, responding, cohering according to their various environments and contextual interactions, but are there any subjects within a stone larger than those existent at this barely perceptible micro level?

Of course, we can have no more knowledge of a calcium

atom's sense of interiority than we can of an electron or a ten ton megalith of limestone. So many of the measures we would use to judge another human's subjective coherence are not valid when considering a stone, just as they weren't when we were looking at the tree or woodland ecosystem. For example, like the tree, a stone comprehensively fails to kick or bite or flee when threatened by a destructive blow. To determine an entity's coherence based on the apparent strength of its capacity for self-protection seems somewhat biased, but is it a good measure? If we defined an individual by its desire to survive, Griffin's atom would also fail. I suggested above that a tree may be considered an individual: it does strive for survival within its own parameters, building immunity from disease, creating symbiotic relationships for mutual benefit, but from an animist perspective these still feel too prescriptive as measures of self. Individual survival instincts vary radically according to contexts, even within human beings and other mammals. There are moments when the right thing to do is to die, when the community or the tribe is stronger than the individual self. That we can experience this within our self-focussed human mentality, armed as we are with wit and adaptability, able in many circumstances to fight or run, we must imagine that such instincts are far more determinative within the subjective being of a stationary individual.

Again working from the limitations of a human perspective, the distinction may be found in natural delineation: the calcium atom, or even the calcium carbonate molecule, can be defined. If it were to sense itself - and the animist thesis suggests that with nature's inherent introspection, even simple prehension provides an awareness of the inner and outer environment - it would feel its own edges. One might say that could be possible too of the calcite crystals or oolitic grains within the limestone, but these may not be quite so precisely determined. As for the rock itself, unless we are talking about the entire formation, we are looking at a chunk that has broken off that whole, from which more bits may crumble, so how might this piece be considered a whole? Without definite edges, one can surely only consider it as a community.

Just as with the tree and the wood, I would suggest that whether or not a stone is felt to be an individual would be a personal and instinctive decision, simply because we cannot know one way or the other with any surety. In *Intelligence in Nature*, interviewing an Amazonian native in Peru, Jeremy Narby asks if each small stone has a soul. The fellow replies that a 'simple little stone does not. But a stone which is 10 square meters, or huge rocks which are 15 square meters, have mothers. Tiny little grains of sand do not. But when you go to the beach, you find that all the sand taken together, as a beach, has a mother, or a soul'. The Shawi Indian's sense of a soul (or 'mother') is an inner coherence. Using the term to include any member of an ecosystem, community or tribe within nature, he declares that all living beings have souls: 'If they did not, they would not have a reason to live'. In other words, with no vision of the vibrant and spinning microcosmic worlds that exist within a tiny grain of sand, the Indian's view was entirely the opposite of Griffin's.

For myself, as an animist with a Western education, I stand on the beach, with thousands of sand grains between my toes, around my feet, countless more in my immediate proximity, and I can sense the collective coherence that is its community. I can absorb the wider environment of sea and sky, where the winds and the tides bring waves sparkling and foaming over those sands, where the warmth of soil and the breath of trees meet the dunes, feeling the perpetually shifting but wholly formative percepts that create the beach and myself in that moment of perception. I can lift a handful of sand, letting most of it slip through my fingers until just a few glistening grains remain, soft golds and white and grey. Tiny as each one is, I am filled with respect. Whether or not this little thing is an individual, or indeed the silica atoms within it, or the beach as a whole, feels to me to be an unnecessary question: at every level of collective being and individuality there is perception and response, and the transience of each moment ensures a shifting dynamic of coherence. Peering at the little cube with its edges polished smooth, almost beyond my middle-aged ability to see, I have a sense of the journey that it has taken, from its original deposition perhaps in some river who knows where, worn away from the riverbed and flushed out to sea, tumbled and rolled and left on this shore. A good part of what I perceive is the data of memory.

Memory: instead of the vivid energy and shifting patterns of spirit, what we perceive is the depth and breadth of soul, and every soul is an integral part of nature as a whole. In animism, determining the separateness of each individual is acknowledged to be fundamentally unhelpful: nature's integrity offers us the peace of interconnectedness. While our thinking self may holler its declaration of independence, the larger part of our being is not so isolationist, bathing instead in the wholeness of nature's mind. As Abram writes:

> Each entity participates in this enveloping awareness from its own angle and orientation, according to the proclivities of its own flesh. We inhale the awakened atmosphere through our skin or our flaring nostrils or the stomata in our leaves, circulating it within ourselves, lending something of our unique chemistry to the collected medium as we exhale, each of us thus animated by the wider intelligence even as we tweak and transform that intelligence.

I sit now on the grass beside a path of old Cotswold stone, turning a piece of its limestone over in my hand, watching the evening light touch the lines of a fossil shell embedded in its golden body, the dust rubbing off on my fingers. Is it an individual? I look up and see a kestrel hovering over the grass, and instinctively I know it to be an individual, watching the rodent trails, measuring the distances, feeling the currents of hunger, hunter and wind in that moment. Above, clouds meander silently passing by, some white, some heavy with rain, and my instinct is to feel them to be people, a crowd, a gathering of stories above me, responding to the higher winds and the fading sunlight, finding their form within their own context of being. The kestrel swoops drawing my gaze back down into the long grass, wondering if he has caught a mouse or vole, and that sense of his individuality is lost in the drive of his predatory nature. I wonder, gazing at the grass: here I can feel the meadow plants stretching across great areas of the field, intertwining with each other, merging, and I have a sense of grass people, but only in their collective, responding to the weight of my form, the bouncing feet of the running hare, the faintest touch of the settling butterfly. I lift the lid of my laptop and, feeling a thousand stories, I tap the words into the keys: spinning letters together, thoughts, memories move around its form. In the plastic keys, in the silver and black frame, in the humming of its battery, its chips and wires, its softly lit screen, I feel a growing sense of community, currents moving together, atoms settling together, but here there is no individuality. I sigh, and look up at the ash tree whose leaves are beginning to fall, littering the grass around around me. A dozen chattering birds take to their wings as a gust of the evening breeze moves the drying leaves, and I feel the tree feeling the birds feeling the movement, awake.

Much as some would object, it is simply not possible to compile a list of what are individuals and what are communities from an animistic perspective. This is not slack philosophy. In theory, the distinction is very clear: an individual has the capacity for a coherent interiority of self which allows for it to respond as a whole, while a community is simply a form within nature comprised of any number of other communities and individuals. While a community may make shared decisions, these are agreed or synchronised, not made by a unified mind. Furthermore, a community's edges tend to be loose and flexible, while an individual has defined edges, albeit only within the moments of its individuality. In reality, however, beneath reason where nature's actuality is in play, such distinctions blur - because nature is fundamentally a series of interactions, not a population of subjects.

Location

As Whitehead suggested, when addressing the hardest questions in philosophy, using only empirical and rational thinking can be quite inadequate: speculation, or imagination, allows for a broader approach, one that is willing to consider ideas not immediately evident through experience or reason, ideas that can be carefully filtered through reasoning later, and so grounded in the real world. Yet what is imagination?

From the ontological stance of our metaphysics so far, I propose that imagination comes through the percepts of memory. In other words, instead of the flood of data that creates an immediate context, imagination is inspired by the settling forms of our mental and physical environment. If we also recognise that an individual is not an isolated mind, it is possible to see how both memories and imagination can spread through communities, individual subjects picking up on ideas, forms and patterns that are within the shared mind of the community, from simple currents of directive emotion to flashes of insight. Furthermore, on the premise that nature has no beginning, and thus no point at which there were no memories, we must suppose that imagination has always been an integral part of nature's soul.

Epistemologically, as individuals seeking to understand our worlds, we use imagination in order to inspire our own comprehension and creativity. Some thinkers transpose our experience of imagination into nature's ontology: it is through the use of imagination that entities find coherence and form, guided by patterns already laid down. For biochemist Rupert Sheldrake, this sense of nature leading from ahead rather than being pushed from behind is key: a 'potential future state is what directs and guides and attracts the development of the system in the present'. Whitehead talks of the 'appetition for completion' that is inherent within nature, fuelled by God's governing aesthetic, and Smuts' theory of holism is based upon what he believed to be a natural desire for cohesion and hence growing complexity.

In my own understanding of animism, however, there is no draw from ahead that inspires an ever increasing intricacy of form, no innate goal of perfection leading us closer to a divine creator or complete knowledge. The world we perceive is poignantly balanced on a knife-edge of viability, with the vast part of nature's universal soul scattering its data, formless, into darkness. Memory, and so imagination, does inspire forms to develop and perpetuate, but simply because each interaction communicates its data, moment by moment, event to event; there are no templates to be filled by what might be considered nature's otherwise aimless creativity. It is the past that informs the future, the soul's bank of experience providing the data for each following moment within the whole. Indeed, if we are able to extend it from the human mind to every part of nature, the definition given by the philosopher and psychonaut Terrence McKenna is a little more animistic: imagination is 'literally a descent of the world soul into all of us. We are atoms of the world soul. We open our channel to it by closing our eyes and obliterating our immediate, personalized, space-time locus'. In other words, letting go of the self, we are able to sink into that state of passive perception which is less bounded by the individual mind, and absorb the precepts of nature's memory which, uncontextualised, feed us as imagination. For those aspects of nature not enclosed within the limitations of a thinking self, being open to nature's soul must be integral to their sense of being: most of nature must then be saturated in nature's imagination.

In Chapter One I described Kant's notion of the synthetic *a priori*. These are the very basics of understanding, without which we could not function. They are cardinal tools of the mind which allow us to comprehend our perceived world, including that crucial ability to grasp a 'space-time locus'. As I stated earlier, however, within an animistic theory of memory, without the primacy of the subject, memories are not laid down in order that we can perceive. Yet Kant's theory has an unshakeable logic. In the interconnected and integrated ontology of mind within animism, this foundational data is found in the hum of nature's memory, and in the imagination that memory allows. Absorbed from the broader minds in which we gestate, into which we are born, from the minds of our mother, our environment, our species or perhaps nature as a whole, these percepts give us the foundations from which a sense of self can then grow, with its capacity for learning and self-reflection.

By including time and space in his list of synthetic *a priori* knowledge, Kant's declaration that they are part of a requisite net of beliefs was an exquisite kick at the pedestal of human certainty. He didn't determine that they were nonexistent beyond our perception, however, simply that it was necessary to remember the gap between (how we understand) what we are perceiving and what is actually there.

As tools of measurement in our phenomenal world, time and space do help to define edges, whether as individuals, tribe or community, and as such they support the process of development from momentary subject into enduring self. As mechanistic utensils, they allow us to locate ourselves and others in relation to us, within the past and the future, within the spatial environment. This sense of self location is a crucial part of what changes simple perception, sensation, experience, into the richer feedback of consciousness: instead of simply feeling one's presence in the world, there is a knowledge that one is in fact present in the world.

Underlying every whisper of the universe is nature's essential darkness, within which there is no time or space. This essence, without substance, is undifferentiated within the dark, and as such it is both still and formless, conferring a fundamental unity to nature's entirety, its complete and indestructible integration. In the poetry of animism, this darkness is 'within us, behind us, beneath us': in other words, it is present even when life is bathed in sunshine and understanding. Within every entity, each neutron and galaxy, each raindrop and ocean, each perception and emotion, there is utter darkness. With no perception, no subject, no self, no separation, that dark stillness is immeasurable, infinite and eternal. On the edge of its dense emptiness, there is perfect presence, but stepping into its breathlessness, there is everything and nothing at all.

In the movement of nature, however, there is time and space: time and space *in itself*. Although Kant questioned whether we could know anything of nature's actuality, in animism it is not considered wholly beyond our perception, for in our simplest prehensive state, without the limiting cognition of consciousness, it is possible to sense the soft breeze that is all we might feel of nature's truth. Here time and space are entirely different from the measurable and measuring forms that the thinking *I* uses to locate itself within its phenomenal world. Very much in tune with Bergson's rich description of *duration*, time flows but it is not linear. In that state of wakeful yet passive receptivity, we can glimpse its circularity: for time stretches out in every direction, a timescape of being, becoming and dissolving, every moment entirely present, the centre of its own extending circle, and at the edge of the horizon more circles ceaselessly unfolding. Indeed, it may be more pertinent to talk in terms of a sphere, with potentiality, actuality and memory expressions of temporal being that are each equally present in any given moment. Nothing is dead and gone, and nothing is entirely new.

It may be easy for some to imagine this timescape of presence. Anyone able to create a moment of absolute inner calm, a moment of perfectly wakeful prehension, can perhaps sense the sphere of time, allowing it to drench the thinking and worrying self with an experience of presence. For many it evokes a visceral feeling of self location far stronger than can be found through the mechanics of the clock and calendar. However, it is hard to imagine time without space. Our images of a timescape are most likely filled with objects, people and places: that is not solely a reflection of the tendency to measure the passing of time by the movement of things that take up space. The temporal and spatial are connected, even beyond our normal perception. For space in itself is complete *integration*.

Our reality is made up of separate physical things, things with edges, things we can measure, each located in a specific place. What we are not perceiving is all that our human mind, the human soul and its long memory, has determined it unhelpful to perceive. I see the path and the grass, the trees of the hedgerow, and between here and there I see the empty space through which I can move unhindered; however, there is no emptiness. Nature *in itself* is thick with being, with countless interactions beyond our ability to perceive, with light and connection, vibration and sound, electromagnetism and other dynamic forces. Here is a landscape united with its timescape, wholly present in every way.

Looking out at the world around us, our instinct to separate and identify what we see is strong. However, the instinct is a good deal weaker when it comes to introspection, especially where the thinking *I* is not engaged: sensing one's inner being, there are no spatial dimensions within, no distinctions between past, present and future, simply the thickness of a flow of moments, percepts of memory and imagination in the twilight of the mind.

Dissolution

If we are to understand the boundaries between what nature actually may be and how we perceive it, the development of the self is central to that study. In this chapter, I have proposed a definition of the *I* deduced from the basic tenets laid down, that there is no primary substance in nature, and that the subject is formed of the data generated by interactions within nature's minded essence, finding continuity of form through the iteration of feedback. However, recognising that nature as a whole is also a subject, a mind, there are two choices: either there is only one subject, nature, as Jaskolla and Buck maintain, or there are countless minds within minds within the mind of nature. The animist chooses the latter, recognising that the isolation of mind is an illusion based upon the experience of the thinking self. While an individual is defined as having the ability to access a coherent interiority, in other words, having a sense of autonomy as a separate being, in nature there are communities of subjects, communities of individuals, the edges of any individual mind being transient, according to the data of its immediate contextual environment. Ontologically then, within this animist vision of nature, just as there is no special status accorded to humanity amidst the rest of nature, there is no special status accorded to the individual.

In the next chapter, we shall consider the experience of the self, and in doing so move fully into the epistemology of being. Before reaching that point, however, it is worth considering the disintegration of the self. Fleetingly I have touched on the issue, but while we are still on the boundaries of ontology it is worth pausing to consider it a little more fully.

Within a human context, disintegration may be equated with madness, disease or death, but before getting to that point it may be useful to consider *life*.

Etymology tells us little but that the core of the word is very old. Coming into English through the Germanic tongues, its roots can be found in the PIE *lip-* meaning to remain, persevere, continue or simply to live. The primary definition in the *OED* is 'the condition that distinguishes animals and plants from inorganic matter', inorganic being defined as 'not arising from natural growth'. Scientifically, life is recognised in the capacity to grow and reproduce, to metabolise internally and adapt to the external environment.

Within animism, now and then the word may be used in the same way that person and tribe are used, specifically breaking convention in order to emphasise the need to extend respect to nature as a whole. However, in the main the word is seldom used but in ways that would concur with the usual definitions. That it is not a key word reveals that it is not *ontologically* important.

Nature is universally minded, but not everything is alive. In other words, within an animist metaphysics, while a rock or a river is acknowledged as minded, perceiving and responding within the context of its being, by the above definition of life neither could be said to be alive. Life is a phenomenon within nature that we are able to perceive and respond to as human beings, a particular iteration of spirit which guides us as to how we might interact or relate appropriately. Equally we might say that a lack of some of the qualities that define life, an absence of life, also informs us. Both the living and the not-living, however, are equally minded.

When the functions that sustain life are failing, we find disease, madness and death. For many who hold a dualist conviction, at the point of physical death the soul or mind may be capable of survival. Crafted of a different primary stuff, its ill-defined connection to the body detaches. In a religious thesis, the soul may leave the material world, withdrawing to a subtler realm. The dualist whose beliefs do not include a transcendent reality may consider the mind to remain within nature, returning to forge another physical link through reincarnation or lingering in what may be called a collective consciousness. Some believe the moment at which such a detachment becomes irrecoverable is the moment of death, at which point the physical body is considered inert. For the materialist, death has the same effect: the phenomenon or illusion of mind disappears once the relevant bodily organs cease, and its vital forces ebb away. The physical matter is left inert.

Inert: the Latin *iners* can be translated not just as inactive but worthless; combined with the prefix *in*, meaning without, the key word is *ars*, meaning skill. Nature, inert, has no inherent value, its worth coming solely from what is done with it. Rationally, such beliefs about both nature and death instruct us that when someone dies that *person* is gone, the body becoming the residue, the rubbish left behind at the end of a life. Certainly a dead body feels radically altered. Instinct guides us to release it, the wet decay posing a threat to our own health and vitality, reason encouraging us to step away. Yet those mourning the death of a member of their community still feel the need to hold that person's physical form, at least for a while.

This is not sentimentality. To the animist, within the wholeness of nature, any creature is a community of subjects. What draws that community into the coherent state of an individual is a continuity of patterns, provoked by and provoking further repetition of interaction, moment to moment, event to event. With madness, old age and disease, those patterns begin to break apart, the dominant percepts changing. Patterns become weaker, the edges less well defined, information scattering instead of working to retain what have been enduring mental and physical forms. As the balance of data changes, new influences become dominant, old memories emerge, new interactions losing the clarity of their defining contexts. Slowly coherence dissolves. For those who have been caring for someone who dies gently, the process of release can feel natural, each pattern losing its form, edges blurring, like dusk on a long, warm summer's day, quietly softening the world with its inherent stillness.

At the moment of death, there is a change, but it is not nature's way to rush. The individual may have lost their individuality: they may no longer be a unified, enduring and coherent subject as they once were. They have lost a certain continuity. However, countless patterns and forms are still evident. The community of the physical body will, if left to nature's soft flow of decay, continue the slow process of change, breaking apart, shedding its edges and its identity, creating new communities of being. Throughout that process, memories, thoughts, emotions, stories of that individual continue, not just within the physicality of that body, but within other settled forms: in the people and places who knew him. In the poetry of animism, it is said that the deceased lives on in the wind and the waters of their landscape, in the poetry and songs of the trees and the birds, in the heart and mind of their community.

When death comes suddenly, coherence is shattered, the dominant percepts of the moment coming like a crashing waves, breaking apart connections and forms. Yet nature adapts, and where grief is allowed its process of reflection and change, the storm of new patterns settles, the old memories often emerging as the more stable and continuous forms. When a person is cremated instead of buried, the incineration introduces another shattering of form, violently breaking apart patterns. To believe this is confined to the physical is to forget that the essence of nature is neither mental nor physical: both are fundamentally patterns formed of interwoven percepts, settling in ways that allow us to discern them as mental and physical. And again, nature settles, adapting to the new configuration.

In order to understand more completely, I offer another example: the death of a tree. Perhaps over centuries, an oak has been growing, created by the percepts of its ecosystem, its community of birds and bugs, bacteria and fungi, water and sunlight, warmth and cold, its green understory and neighbouring trees competing for space. With the falling of its leaves each autumn, the loss of limbs torn down in storms, the shedding of acorns, the drought and frost, it has found its form and crafted its memories, year after year. When at last, leafless, it dies standing, skeletal, its form continues as an integral part of the ecosystem, providing rotting wood and shelter, slowly breaking up, no longer striving to maintain its coherence. Were it to have been taken down by a chainsaw three hundred years earlier, the shattering of its forms would have created a great deal more disturbance, but memories would remain, passing from moment to moment, just the same.

Like so much in animism, the thesis removes the distinctive significance of humanity and drenches the whole of nature in the sanctity of commonality. The particular functions that we perceive as generating and sustaining *life* are not as crucial as the patterns that create any coherence of form. So does the animist approach death and the dead in just the same way whether it be a dried up river bed, an old tree, the bones of a long dead ancestor, or indeed a loved one who has recently died: recognising where an individual or a community is now disintegrating, he may profoundly grieve the loss of a companion, but acknowledges too his own role in the ongoing being and becoming of that soul.

Indeed, understanding nature as wholly minded, the notion of inert matter is unintelligible. At death, there is change, individuals and communities shifting their edges and coherences, but some patterns remain for longer than others: the environment of memory. As such, the physical remains of the dead are as important as the memories that linger in our minds, or in the creativity that soul has left behind. Although the dead may lose their ability to perceive as individuals, the animist does not strip them of their personhood, for a person is not only a person when they are dominant in their vibrancy, independent in their individuality, and wholly conscious of the affect they have on their surroundings. A person is a being whose influence we acknowledge. A person is a soul whose history we remember. As long as memories are still forming a being within a community, that being is a person, and must be accorded an appropriate degree of respect.

In other words, there is no annihilation at death, but neither do some parts of nature have an immortal soul that retains its form and self *ad infinitum*. There is instead a continuity that is wholly natural.

I said above that the dead *may* lose their ability to perceive. In Chapter Eight, the penultimate of this text, the focus will move from what nature may actually be to how it is that we experience what we do. It is only once we have established an understanding how the *I* is formed that we can grasp an opportunity of crafting a thesis of consciousness.

Chapter Eight

Consciousness

It was not my intention to write a book on psychology. However interesting it may be to extend this text, diving deep into the realms of the thinking self and consciousness, my purpose here was instead to head into territory very much less explored: the metaphysics of animism, in particular animism as it is practised within modern Western culture, using the language of that culture and its philosophical heritage. As is often the way with my writing, I set myself the task of writing the book for which I myself had long been searching, the book I had hoped someone else had already written.

Of course, there are now a great number of books that look at how the mind may work which don't touch on metaphysics. While the majority tend to be based upon materialist neuroscience, most are so wholly focused on the experience of being that there is no need to look at what is happening beneath that surface level. However, animism and the metaphysics I have here outlined proffer such a different worldview from the modern secular materialism and Christian dualism that now underlie Western thinking that there are a few issues worth laying out and considering.

Breaking the Surface

In the course of writing this book, the inevitable conversation has often arisen when someone has asked me about the focus of my project. While some enquirers are genuinely interested, there are others who wish simply to pass the time of day and an explanation of metaphysics, however concise, is not easily achieved within the confines of English pleasantries. Over the months I have honed a reply that is sufficiently brief and inconsequential, if somewhat inscrutable, to allow the enquirer to feel they can nod politely and ask no further questions: the book is 'about the experience of the world, but instead of a looking at how we drive the car, it goes under the bonnet'. For the months during which I have been immersed in writing, the analogy has at times felt particularly apt. Covered in grease and dirt, I have found myself on the side of road in the middle of nowhere, squinting at the engine of this battered old car, a filthy spanner in one hand, an oily rag in the other, tightening this and loosening that, now and then firing it up to see how it rolls. For long moments together I retain a good idea of what I'm doing, but then the plugs don't spark and I'm staring again, clueless, all the while knowing that I am wholly dependent on getting the machine back up and running. In the meantime, cars drive on by and I pause, feeling a wave of envy for those who have no need or desire to know how the engine works: stuck on the verge, such mobile lives seem delightfully simple.

However, it has to be said, the car analogy is an expression of a good day. Spending any time, let alone an extended period of time, meticulously deconstructing reality in search of an ontological actuality can leave one feeling more than a little disoriented. It is a submersion. After all, our functional selves rely on the open spaces of our perceived world, within which we can breathe and move, allowing us the edges of self-definition. Beneath the surface of that reality is like being underwater. There is a blur of form rather than the comforting clarity of distinct and separate beings. There is a weight that is the heaviness of unity, the experience of being undivided, as if pulled down by the whole, with all its mental and physical sensations, its vastness of being. The instinct within the self to breathe, to survive, tugs at us relentlessly, desperate to rise up through that densely opaque water, to break the surface once more, emerging into the clear air and sunlight of individuality. Many spiritual traditions teach ways by which we can lose this need, allowing the *I* to surrender into the whole, but few individuals in our population of many billions achieve the task naturally or fully, more than fleetingly.

The self is something we strive to feel and are taught to do so from our early years. As toddlers we push and holler, exploring the exhilarating and terrifying possibilities of being individuals in our own right, a process that continues through adolescence and on, as we experience our own opinions and desires, finding our place in the world. At some point many relax into an acceptance of what life has given them, but others persist in the search through years of dissatisfaction: *what is it that I really want? If only I could find and express my true self!* Using the tools and languages of therapy, philosophy, creativity, spirituality, solitude, religion, going deep in introspection, we are guided to find motivations, drives, memories, people to blame, ideas to temper and qualities to hone. As human beings, perhaps especially in most of Western culture, we are encouraged to find and be true to this notion of a distinct and unique self, protecting it and expressing it, and protecting our rights to its free expression. Individuality is deemed to be that special characteristic which fuels a person's ability to succeed, allowing them to claim their own slice of real happiness and contribute most valuably to the nation as a whole. Our culture recognises and celebrates the driving need to be *me*. Of course, in practice self-expression can be judged dangerous, demented, or simply too *different*, and individuals are not appreciated if they blunder against the perimeter fence of the social contract. However, those whose wit and power has enabled them to be the authors and editors of that contract are praised for expressing their own self-determined individuality, their self-direction, self.

On a superficial level, there are times when we feel that perhaps we have found ourselves. There is a strong sense of self-location when what we have or strive to have achieved in terms of where we are and what we are doing seems to have hit that perfect balance between creativity and effort. We are no longer fighting ourselves. It may be during a period of hard work or a time of retreat and re-evaluation. It may last but a few moments, it may last years. It may come with an acute sense of self-reflection and honesty, or be accompanied by the numbness of drugs and superficiality. Either way, being ourselves feels good. It allows us to feel as if we're in control.

However, in reality, it doesn't take a great deal of introspection and honesty to acknowledge that this self is not a fixed actuality. There are elements of our character that persist throughout our lives, but when seeking who we truly are these are not enough. I can describe my character as passionate and quiet, as I have been all my life, but this is not my self - I can be noisy and cold if the context provokes it. My self is influenced by my genetic heritage, my culture and education, my history, but equally neither is that all that I am. I am in love, I am hungry, I am writing: these describe my present moment, no doubt also indicating something of my personality, but there is more to my self than these immediate actions and feelings. In reality, as the *I am*, the self encapsulates all these qualities and characteristics, and as such it changes, moment by moment. It is this intrinsic transience that makes it almost definitively elusive. When we reach for it, it disappears.

Yet it maintains a continuity. Dipping briefly beneath the surface into metaphysics once more, into the waters of animist ontology, we recall that a subject is created by the perceptual data of interaction; the self is developed from the flow of moments that are a subject's experience. The self is then inherently transient. Faced directly, there is nothing but the perpetually shifting data of the present. Catching glimpses of it in our peripheral vision, what we see are patterns as they settle into memory, creating a shell or crust which feels more like history than the sensation of immediate reality. This is the self, this residue, made of memories which themselves are continuing slowly to change through ongoing interaction and introspection. It is by picking up on these memories that the thinking *I* creates a mental form of itself, allowing us to determine who it is that we think we are.

As such, the notion of self can be strong. When we do *think* about it, our experience is unambiguous. Inevitably the subject becomes central, as it was for Descartes: what we sense is the presence of a thinking someone who, sitting behind the eyes, considers life from somewhere in our brain, hollering from the base of the belly, or heart, or groin, and stretching out for a short while whenever its appetites are satisfied. In this way, in our day to day experience the *thinking* self entirely corroborates any sense of there being a clever little operator within the body machine, taking us right back to the imagery and ideas of traditional dualism.

The thinking self is only one way in which we perceive, though. There are many other aspects of mind that do not provoke the same experience. Indeed, the simpler our prehension, the more fully we tend to sense nature's comprehensive integration of forms, of being and becoming. The simpler our perception, the less the self is evident or indeed perhaps existent at all.

The Seamless Universe

There is no need to ask why we perceive as we do. Nature's patterns continue to create forms for as long as those patterns are viable, dissolving when they are not. Ontologically, we could say that this particular coherence of percepts is what we term humanity, but staying above the water's surface we could also say that it is our human perception which allows us to see what we need to in order that we might survive and thrive. Every other form in nature has evolved in the same way. The question then is not why but *how* does that perception work?

Perception is often divided into three distinct categories:

external things, bodily things and mental things. In other words, firstly, by defining the edges of our physical self, we can sense what is beyond that form and thus outside us. That is evident and straightforward, and particularly if we recognise that we are not delineating the self here but the physical form as we perceive it. Secondly, we have sensations within that bodily form which can be spatially located: when we experience hunger, touch, movement, and so on, we can identify with some degree of accuracy where that sensation is within the body. The third category is often defined as those perceptions which appear to be within the body but are generally felt to have no specific location: thoughts, ideas, dreams.

From the very grounded and sensuous perspective of the animist, the distinction between the latter two categories seems hazy in practice. We might sense that a thought occurs in the head, but perhaps that is provoked by associations with physical sensation. For example, if I close my eyes and think of a dog, as a sighted person it is natural to picture it and, being used to visual input connected with my eyes, the image of the dog seems to be behind or around my eyes. Discarding the visual image, my sense of the dog may then be created out of the noise of his paws on the tiles, the sound of his breathing, or his musty smell close by, again both auditory and olfactory sensations entering through different parts of my head. Removing these, the dog becomes something quite different: I create him with my hands, feeling him around my legs, or even through a nervous antici-pation in my belly. The dog is no longer a thought in my head. Emerging through the whole of my being, experience and memory inform me that this sensation relates to a dog. There is an awareness of dog that is both mental yet awake throughout my form.

Finding a mental act that is not drenched in the imagination, in memory and its sensory data, is a challenge. Even wholly abstract ideas are formed by such patterns, internally portrayed using the symbols of an apposite language. Emotions further blur the distinction between the inner mental and inner physical: our perception of emotion can be patently visceral - it is often easy to indicate where loss, fear and rage are in the body, whether smouldering or ablaze. Other feelings may be harder to pinpoint, but are still not detached from the physicality: even if my head retains a doubt, I may feel trust in my fingers, in my feet, my heart or my belly. Jealousy can make my whole body growl and joy seems to fuel every single cell with sunshine.

Awareness of this integration varies, of course. An individual human being can be profoundly numb to the experience of his body; such a state is not a healthy one to be in, usually having been provoked by trauma, neglect, denial, or simply a poor balance of focus. Within the daily practice of animism a good deal of attention is given to rebalancing perception where focus has tilted away from the experience of body towards overly relying on the abstractions of thought. Such an emphasis highlights a principle of animism that is worth stressing once again: there is no deprecation of physicality. The physical world is not at the dirty bottom of some *scala naturae*, nor is it an illusion to be shrugged off with enlightenment: it is as much what we are as the subtler patterns of mind.

As such, there need be no outright rejection of neurological research within animism. In saying that we sense a thought to be in the head because of the position of the eyes, I am not opposing the idea that the brain is in some way connected to our processing of visual data. Science still has no convincing arguments to explain how that data transforms into conscious vision creating the qualia of seeing, but studies positively show there to be a connection, the neurons in the visual cortex clearly firing with any relevant stimuli. Nor am I dismissing research that indicates other neural correlates of consciousness (NCCs): not just the brain but the whole nervous system sparks and hums with each sensation, moment by moment. The dog that I am thinking about, with its shape and scent, its noise and behaviour, may well be evident in some way to the neurologist scanning my brain: his instruments of measurement cannot reveal the image in my mind but they can map its chemical and electrical activity to the narrative of my experience. Without doubt such maps, revealing which parts of the brain flare or fail in any given situation, bring valuable information to the library of human knowledge. Nor does the ongoing debate about their validity deflect from that value; that NCCs can be inconsistent and are littered with anomalies only adds to the interest of the ongoing investigation. What we see to be the cells of the brain and nervous system are evidently a part of the shifting, settling, shifting, settling patterns of mind.

However, what we are considering here is the world as we perceive it: even if the dog were not imaginary but actually standing before me, neither I nor my neurologist would be seeing nature *in itself*. Accepting this does not invalidate the neurological study, but it does impose limitations on the relevance of its findings. Given the reality of the perceptive veil, the significance of what is physical and what is mental changes.

Returning to the three categories of perception outlined above, I showed a blur between the latter two, the perception of bodily and mental things. Crucially, this blur applies to the first category as well: external things. Looking at the dog instead of just imagining him, animism's integrated metaphysics doesn't isolate the creature as a physical form separate from the mental form created by the perceiver. To do so would not only firmly secure the yawning gap traditionally found between ontology and epistemology, but also leave us with the dualist's dilemma of finding a way in which mind and matter interacts. In *Understanding Consciousness*, philosopher of psychology Max Velmans underlines this dualism implicit in perception. As many have done before him, he recognises that any philosophy of mind lacks integrity if it does not or cannot address this key problem. 'Nor does', he writes, 'splitting the universe into two incommensurable (material and mental) substances help us to understand the *intimate relationship* of consciousness to matter.' His language is not that of animism, nor even an overt if materialist panpsychism, but his approach is similar. He suggests the solution lies in the recognition of 'a seamless universe, of which we are an integral part, which can be known in two fundamentally different ways. At the interface of consciousness and brain, it can be known in terms of how it appears (from the outside) and in terms of what it is like to be that universe (from the inside)'.

Velmans describes his perspective as an ontological monism combined with epistemological dualism. They are words that I have turned over and over in my mind, in the end reaching the conclusion that they could *almost* work for animism. Given the source and basis of the universe is nature's minded essence, animism's ontological monism is definitive. With its integration rooted in the oneness of that minded essence, interaction, generated within that essence, is *in itself* therefore neither of mind nor matter. But what of the epistemological dualism? Epistemology is about how we understand the world around us. For epistemological dualism to sit happily within an animist metaphysics, while nature's actuality would remain the same unchanged single essence, what we would perceive would be a world that appeared to be formed of two different kinds of stuff: mind and matter. So does nature's essence stay the same?

Bridging the gap with an integrated metaphysics, perception is always at that ever-changing point of presence. Within the thickly woven fabric of each contextualised moment, what we are perceiving is what is creating our form. In other words, whatever the dog is as an external form *in itself*, and however it may be sensed by every other percipient within the context of its community, combined with inner associations and comprehensions of memory it is not only that I perceive a dog before me but that my perception of the dog is actually also contributing to my own form. It is external to me, yet it adds to me.

In Velmans' epistemology, my perception of the dog and what the dog is are two facets of the same actuality. The distinction is only in the phenomena of our reality, in other words, in how we see and understand the world. What it feels like to be the dog is the dog's mental form, while the paw the dog licks is his physical form. My experience of my self is an experience of mind, while my perception of my body and its environment is of a material world. From this stance, it is feasible to acknowledge the tree, stone or river, the molecule or photon, to have its own inner mental state, a natural self awareness that allows a sense of *what it's like to be me*, while what the *me* perceives beyond itself is nature as a physical reality.

I like the idea. It feels tidy and simple, and a good number of thinkers have been convinced by the argument. From an animist perspective, I too would concur that nature is always *essentially* the same. However, I would add a little more in terms of ontological clarity: when iterating patterns settle into form, creating what we perceive as memory and matter, there is a change. The essence has not altered to become a different kind of stuff, but the form has taken on a different state. It is this change of state that evokes an epistemological dualism, for it allows for the shifting patterns and percepts which in turn form the subjects and individuals who perceive them.

Communication

That we cannot know with any surety what nature is beyond our own perception of course leaves the question open and effectively unresolvable. We might debate the details of an epistemological dualism, but as the arguments move around in my mind, I find no need to secure a certainty, even by rational means. What remains crucial in terms of what forms the animist's perspective, and thus not only his attitude but also his self, is fundamentally the understanding of nature's integration. Crucially here, consti-

tutive to that integration is nature's continuity, and if that continuity is durable it must entail a consistency in terms of how the
mind works. While the grey matter of the brain may reflect the
subtler patterns of mind, there is no point in only searching
neural networks for answers. To do so would be to abandon
another fundamental premise of animism, that there is the
capacity for perception in every part of nature, the greater part of
which has no such physical apparatus. However, if we are to
dismiss the focus on such physical systems, where do we look for
the mind?

To some extent the question is a reflection of a materialist
perspective: the need for tangible and measurable evidence that
can substantiate existence. Animism doesn't always provide
satisfaction in this respect, yet neither is it satisfied with answers
that point to an incorporeal mind wholly distinct from matter.
There is validity in questioning whether it is possible to understand how another individual might process information,
especially a nonhuman subject, just as it is impossible to feel
another's qualia. However, at the heart of the animist position
there are clues.

Every creature, every tree and beetle, every lake and
mountain, every atom and galaxy, is its own pattern of being,
integrated within the community of its evolving environment.
Furthermore, every being is composed of or interconnected with
numerous other individual beings, each of these also existent
within its own web of communities, while at the same time firmly
held within the fabric of nature's universal soul. The animist key
is yet again that this fabric of nature is made of interactions -
internal and external. In the poetry of animism, we might
describe how every community is comprised of the relationships
within it, those relationships making up the inner structure of
every ecosystem - and, vibrant with energy, those relationships
are perpetually humming with *communication*.

In the terminology of modern physics, every electromagnetic

and auditory wave expresses a moment of interaction. Conveying the fundamental forces of nature, these and many other waves, known and not yet known to science, reveal nature's essential connections. Integral to its mindedness, each one communicates something, adding to the patterns that make up the whole, forming the relationships that constitute each fleeting contextual moment. Human perceptive capacity tends to limit the notion of communication to those bandwidths of sound and light that are easily accessible with our senses, but such anthropocentricity deafens us to the myriad languages of nature. Here are the waves of nature's movement, the music and dance of the universal soul. Here are the vibrations and colours of nature's fabric which saturate us, moment by moment, its currents and tides, the eddies and flows of percepts that make us.

Using the natural gift of prehension, not allowing the thinking *I* to push its ego forward, it is easy enough to fill our senses with an awareness of nature's conversations. Within the range of our simple senses we hear the wind moving through the trees' canopy above, the sunlight flickering between the leaves, the shifting pools of shade on the forest floor, the chatter of birds and the shifting hues and shapes of clouds, the sound of hooves on the dry earth of the track, the bark of a dog, the call of a child careering down the lane on his bicycle, the fluster of hens at the farm gate: everywhere there is communication. Even the rumble of traffic in the city beneath the hum of conversations, the music drifting out of open shop doorways and cafés, the whir of sirens, the flight of starlings, the weight of our feet as we walk, the falling leaves, all are expressions of communication. Nothing can be said to be just noise and light and force.

Is this language? Coming from the Latin *lingua* meaning tongue, the word is another with very human connotations, and one which, like person or tribe, is used by animists as an active way of extending respect to nature beyond humankind. Employing the word communication, however, is not unreasonable, for what we are referring to is certainly what is held *in common*.

Remembering the subject is not primary but is formed of percepts, these waves of communication are then fundamental to how the mind works - whether we are considering an individual with a brain or without. Every subject, every individual, with its own inner net or network of relationships, is awake to the murmur of communication that makes up its environment. Just what it picks up, how sensitive its net may be, and in what way it responds, is a part of that being's interiority, its qualia, its own mental form, about which we can never know. Yet, this is the qualia of which the mind is comprised.

Regarding communication in this very animistic way may feel too broad. Some determine the notion to be so definitively purposive that it can only be achieved through a language made up of identifiable audio or visual characters. Indeed, as a complex interplay of symbols and sounds, language can be accorded a tremendous importance, some consequently believing that only human beings are capable of articulate communication. As a result, a good number of materialist and behaviourist thinkers, such as Daniel Dennett, have declared that a sophisticated language is only available where there is consciousness.

His use of the word *consciousness* confirms, however, that the relevance of his focus is limited to human nature. Certainly, when considering the issue with the thinking *I*, our thoughts find clarity in language, emerging consciously as they do so: it is not then surprising that thinking, language and consciousness grow entangled and feel indispensable. However, such standpoints not only express the primacy of the subject, but also tend to dismiss nature as inert, without the need or capacity for communication at all: particles mindlessly touch and react. Nor do such ideas address communication on the pervasive levels of prehension and experience, or communication outside humankind.

Just as animism does not claim there to be human-style consciousness throughout nature, neither is there a complex and abstract language that is likely to be recognisable as such to the human mind. In his *Philosophical Investigations*, exploring language and its meaning, Ludwig Wittgenstein noted that even if a lion were able to speak, it would not be possible for a human to understand him, for his world is so entirely different. From the animist stance, the problem is further that the lion's mind is comprised of such entirely different percepts that anything he might wish to communicate is likely to refer to a reality that is beyond our comprehension.

Animistically, the verbal element of human language can be understood as a flow of interactions with deeply rooted yet evolving word forms, and as such it is not a creation of the human intellect but another series of relationships which go to create the mind, the subject and the self. It could be proposed that other individuals within nature have relationships with pockets of meaning in just the same way.

However, with verbal language such a very small part of any communication, it is also not such a prominent focus. Acknowledging that mind and communication are ubiquitous, striving to understand the community of his environment the animist listens, watches, sensing, learning about the world within which he lives, its forms and needs, its calm and agitations, its joys and hunger, its growth, intentions and release into decay, just as every other entity within nature. It is not consciousness that is predominant here, but the simple wakefulness of prehension, of sensation and experience: nature wakeful, and in perpetual communication. The ability to be aware of one's environment on this level, and so to listen to this communication, is considered at least as important to human understanding as that mental capacity which seems to be so thoroughly yet often clumsily honed in *Homo sapiens*: consciousness.

Consciousness

Though casually used in everyday speech, it is a word that holds a significant punch. Consciousness: a weighty word in the philosophy of nature and mind, when it comes to the more practical business of health and social welfare, of law and indeed any arena where decisions are made with regard to autonomy, agency and the capacity of mind, the word demands precision, both in its understanding and the application of that understanding. Indeed, when I was conceiving this book, sketching out its progression, I anticipated coming to it a good few chapters earlier. In the event, it is only now that I feel a sufficient foundation has been laid to explore its meaning, and the implications of that meaning.

In general conversation the word tends to be used with a comparatively modern interpretation: the sense of being conscious as active and awake is documented from the 1830s. This definition may have value in contexts such as medicine, but it is too slack for philosophical thinking and any practical action based on that thinking. In animism, certainly, both defining words describe states inherent to nature as a whole, and not only those that I would call conscious. My use of the word here, then, reaches back to its older and more firmly established definition.

In Chapter One I proposed that an obvious Latin root of the word is *conscire*, which can be broadly translated as to be aware. It is a word that readily breaks up etymologically, giving *scire*, the verb to know, and its prefix, mutated from *cum*, meaning with or together, suggesting a situation where knowledge is held in common. However, that my 1957 *Collins* pocket Latin-English dictionary gives *conscire* as 'to be conscious of guilt' infers that some sense of self-reflection may have been intrinsic to the word from the beginning. Evolving out of the same roots is another Latin word, *conscientia*. Coming into the English language through the Old French in the thirteenth century, conscience spoke not only of being privy to another's personal thoughts or feelings, yielding a shared knowing with another soul, but also of an inner awareness, the act of quietly listening within, allowing one to hear the calm voice of virtue, perhaps to find divine reason or insight, to *know with* God, and so then to express oneself with a moral conviction.

The word conscious had a different journey, but its relatedness to conscience remains clear. In the sixteenth century it came to English straight from the Latin poets as *conscius*, more directly reflecting *cum-scire*, its meaning being simply to know something in common with another. Over the course of the next century or so that meaning changed, however. A Latin phrase known to scholars was *conscius sibi*, a literal translation of which would be 'knowing with oneself', in other words, knowing that one knows, or being aware of one's own knowing. As the reflexive *sibi* fell away, *conscius* retained the intention of the phrase. It was upon that foundation that in 1690 John Locke described consciousness as 'the perception of what passes in a man's own mind', a meaning that was taken on board by thinkers through the centuries that followed.

More than simply wakefulness or activity, I would say that consciousness is also more than perception. It is tempting to use the word *awareness*, consciousness being an awareness that relates both to the external and internal environment. The OED defines the adjective conscious as the state of being 'aware of and responding to one's surroundings', the noun as 'one's awareness or perception of something'. However, looking at that word more carefully, awareness comes through the Old English *wær*, meaning cautious, alert or wary; its PIE base *wer-*, to cover, gives it a foundation quite different from what is now needed. Within animism, awareness - as an alertness or wakefulness - is also a quality inherent within nature, affirming nature's wakeful capacity for perception, memory and response. Consciousness is more than awareness, as it is more than wakefulness and perception: 'he is conscious of the oak tree' comprises not just an awareness of the tree, but an awareness of that awareness as it takes place.

In Chapter One, making it clear that I felt the word needed careful handling, I offered an initial definition based on the *scire* in its soul, a definition that focused upon the aspect of mind that *knows*. Although I have avoided using it other than where necessary, and I have pointed out where I feel others have employed it too loosely, that initial if meagre definition has just about carried the word through to this point. To find more clarity now, we must consider what it is to know.

In England, our ancestors used two words to express knowing: the Old English verbs *witan* and *cnawan*. The former grew out of the PIE root **wid-*, to see, implying a cognition that comes from insight, an ability to imagine, to conceive and plan. The second derives from **gno-*, found in the Latin *noscere*, the Greek, γνώση (*gnósi*), the meaning of which is a simpler knowing, a recognition, the learning that comes from observing and allowing the world to be as it is. That modern English now more heavily depends on the descendants of *cnawan* than of *witan* is perhaps expressed in the tendency towards empiricism, focusing more vigorously on the acquisition of knowledge, as our culture does, rather than wit, wisdom and insight.

As very old members of our language, neither belongs to the community of *scire*, however. Beneath *scire* is the PIE base **skei-*, meaning to split, cut or divide. With such a history, we can see how science is by definition knowledge gained not from simply observing what we can perceive of nature, but from a study that cleaves and cuts, dividing the world up into separate bits and pieces. This is a very different path to knowing. If we allow the *cum* in consciousness to infer a shared awareness or an awareness of itself, the **skei-* of its middle syllable can provoke a definition to emerge: consciousness is the knowing we derive from an awareness of our own mind. However, we must recall that this is not simple perception, not a **gno-* action. It is more than the processing of perceptual data. Consciousness is about prioritising and making decisions based upon those priorities. To do so requires the ability to access and review experience, taking apart and separating ideas. By cutting up memories into consecutive moments, lifting experiences out of their contexts, it is possible to craft some notion of cause and effect, deducing what we believe to be the logical consequences of an action. Growing out of its *cum-scire* roots, consciousness is not just about knowing, then, it is the process of gaining knowledge by cutting up our reality, by deconstructing nature's integrated mind.

Consciousness is often declared to be that special characteristic which distinguishes human beings from the rest of nature. Whether it was God, the Fates or evolutionary chance that was responsible, some believe the gift to have been accorded to humanity alone, a gift that can be found nowhere else within the entirety of nature. Indeed, although some long for the human race to make contact with an intelligent and technologically-advanced species somewhere out there in space with whom we could confer, others are horrified by the idea, assuming they would be as violent as mankind, citing films that explore the apocalyptic results of computers reaching a level of consciousness sufficient to challenge our own: the excitement kicks in immediately it becomes evident that the machine is no longer following a program but has started to think for itself, and within half an hour the screenwriters are implying it believes itself to be an individual *I*.

Honed in the human mind, such qualities are a key part of our human identity. Perhaps that is in part why it is hard for many to imagine any other species has them. The dog waits as the woman finishes her tea, staring at her with apparently fixed concentration, and the moment the mug heads for the table he's on his feet: does he know it is time for a walk and if so, what is that knowing? Is it purely the repeating of patterns, is it instinct, or is the dog imagining, anticipating, remembering, thinking? The loving owner may accord the dog with almost human consciousness, but she is less likely to do so when considering animals she chooses to eat, the sow in the crate too tight for her to turn around, giving birth to yet another litter of piglets for pork. Pigs are widely understood to have as much mental capacity as dogs, so is the pig conscious of herself, albeit through a mind addled by the horrors of abuse? When a sheepdog pauses, aware of a rabbit hopping through the grass, and the farmer hollers a command for him to continue rounding up the flock, on what basis is he making a decision between hunting, playing and working? Can his process be called conscious? What of the squirrel scampering across the woodland floor, stopping here and there to find or bury acorns, or the ash tree when its black buds burst open into soft green leaflets, or the stream flowing around stones, carrying leaves, swirling in eddies, or the snow on the mountain as it breaks into an avalanche?

Beneath all these questions there appears to lie a single question: does the entity have the capacity to make a decision, or are its actions an inevitable tumble from one moment into the next. A little further on I will talk about free will and if there is *actually* ever a choice to be made, but for the time being, still focusing on consciousness, let us look a little more at the experience of thinking.

The Dark and The Lit

Consciousness is often equated with our ability to think. To understand the animist view, it helps to find distinctions between these words.

With the PIE base *tong-, inferring the idea of both thinking and feeling, its descendants in the Old English are interesting. Although the word þencan meant to conceive, to consider or intend (its initial letter þ, thorn, pronounced *th*), its close relative þyncan meant to seem or appear, implying a more visual act than thinking does in today's language. Yet, when an individual thinks, what he is doing is gathering up all the information provided by way of perception, sensation and memory, in order to review (to see again) and consider the data prior to action. Thinking, then, is a mental process that happens when we are consciously aware.

Consideration is another pertinent word here. I love the word, with its pentasyllabic rhythm. Coming from the Latin, *considerare*, into the Old French, the word found its way into English in the late 1300s. The meaning remained similar throughout, but the emphasis of the Latin was more an external examination than an inner debate. Breaking it up, the mutated *cum* joins with *sidus*, a star or constellation: to consider was an astrological-astronomical endeavour, to wonder at the celestial bodies above, allowing their patterns to inspire an understanding of what was happening on earth below. As such, its verbal soul imparts a sense that sits comfortably within the animistic view, quietly acknowledging the integrated and interconnected wholeness of each moment. When we consider, we are reviewing the situation, contemplating changes within the broader context. Consideration, then, is also a mental process that entails a conscious awareness. To consider employs the thinking *I*.

However, consciousness need not entail thinking. Indeed, the thinking self is an extremely fleeting state of being. In the process of thinking, we *think* of ourselves as thinking beings, and on that basis we are liable to define ourselves by that ability, but a very small proportion of our mental processing can be described as actually thinking. In fact, very little time is spent with enough conscious awareness for thinking to be possible at all.

For example, as we read, unless we come to an unfamiliar word or pause to consider the meaning of a sentence, there is no immediate conscious awareness of processing the text into comprehension. Listening to music, the sounds often drift into the background of our awareness, altering the atmosphere of a moment but allowing our mind to be elsewhere, or indeed nowhere. It is quite possible for an experienced driver to journey from one place to another and have barely any conscious awareness of the process of driving, or even the journey itself. Touch typing now, I am not considering where to place my fingers, which scamper around the keys as my thinking self focuses on the ideas in my mind. I pause to take a telephone call, letting the person's voice flow into my hearing, responding without stopping to think which words to use: there are brief moments when I consider what is needed, but the interaction is neither complex nor unfamiliar, and I act barely thinking. Needing to get up to find a file, however, while most would do so with ease, I must pause and with a conscious awareness find my numb limbs, reminding them how to move, thinking about the need for balance. Sitting down again, my conscious mind empties but for the relevant name, and flicking through papers I find the file, opening it on the desk, and only then do I start to think again, considering what is needed. The task completed, I turn again to this text, and for a few minutes feel the cogs of my conscious awareness turning as I consider the words already written, seeking out the flow again, a part of me watching the thinking *I* as it struggles to concentrate, to find patterns and then soften its focus as I am again able to let the intuition of language carry the ideas onto the page. I am fully aware throughout the process but the moments of true conscious awareness are actually very brief.

Awareness, wakefulness, alertness, perception, memory, responsiveness: in animism, all these are inherent within nature. The critical point here is that consciousness is too. Being innately introspective, the ability to reflect internally must be available throughout nature. Consciousness is more than simple introspection though, and as such not everything in nature is conscious: consciousness allows an individual to use its own mental content as a resource not just of information but knowledge that backs subsequent action, and as such requires the iteration of an enduring individual. However, as an awareness of the mind, a self-reflection that deconstructs patterns, this process continues even when the individual is not consciously aware of it. Indeed, as I have already stated, for the most part, as human beings, we are not consciously aware of much at all.

Combining *conscious* and *awareness* proffers a phrase commonly used and generally understood. That neither word individually is here used to mean conscious awareness should not be a problem, but common language is not as specific or consistent in its definitions. In his *Anthropology* of 1798, Kant's words were pertinent: 'That only a few spots on the great chart of our minds are illuminated may well fill us with amazement in contemplating this nature of ours'. His words inspire a term that sits more comfortably within the poetry of animism, a term that cannot mislead. The self which is wide awake to the experience of the moment, consciously aware of the sensation of being, thinking about and considering the data of its world, this is the lit conscious, the lit mind.

Exploring the subject, I have come across such a broad range of data that I cannot quote any statistic with confidence. One comes from the Danish popular scientist Tor Nørretranders who states in *The User Illusion* that for every one million bits of information processed in the mind as a whole, just one is touched by conscious awareness. Whether such numbers have validity outside their context of measurement may well be questioned, but the general sense affirms just how comprehensively the lit mind has been over emphasised, perhaps most particularly since Descartes' celebration of the thinking *I*. Proportionately, the unilluminated mind is almost all there is. That can be hard to take on board.

Tracing the history of the dark mind as an idea is not easy. Like a giant *piñata*, we need not go back far before it breaks up under scrutiny and out of it come tumbling demons and dragons, sticky melodies, whispers of scent and cloying dreams. Along with gods and ancestors and spirits of the land, no doubt since stories were first told, such dark forces had been cited as influencing health and wellbeing. When the first inklings of non-scholastic knowledge were creeping into mediaeval Europe, and the existence of demons was first beginning to be questioned, such accounts were gathered up into folktales and nightmares, and the source of sickness and negativity began instead to be sought within the mysteries of the body and mind. The physician Paracelsus was an early proponent: in *About Illnesses* in 1567 he explained how individuals could be influenced or become ill based 'not on thinking but on perceiving'. Along with much of his extraordinary and visionary work, the theory was broadly ridiculed, but the evidence that something powerful yet ungraspable was always present could not be dismissed.

In the language of eighteenth century German philosophical Romanticism, Schelling described *das Unbewußte*, the unconscious, as the first stage in the development of nature or God from untamed primal drives to perfect self-consciousness. It was ideas such as these that inspired Coleridge, the poet and drug addict, in his exploration of the 'insensible' and 'involuntary' parts of the self. By the time the Frenchman Pierre Janet was writing in the late nineteenth century, the Church too, no longer hunting out the influence of wicked demons, was ceding to the new hypotheses of medicine and psychoanalysis. Studying the effects of traumatic memory, Janet coined the term *subconscious*. His Austrian contemporary, Sigmund Freud, preferred the older *unconscious*, and within its darkness Freud declared there could be found all the drives and desires that undermine sanity and decency within a civilised society.

Looking back over the centuries, the process of exploration

and clarification seems to have crafted an elaborate illusion of human nature. The mind, as the thinking self, became a spacious and well-lit Victorian residence, kept clean and tidy by a body of servants, allowing its inhabitants to welcome good company in polite society. The unconscious, on the other hand, became a small room at the top of the house, where dark secrets were kept, locked away like mad Bertha Rochester. Not only is the balance entirely wrong, but the illusion suggests a polarity: a black and white, good and bad, a rational conscious self and a mindlessly destructive unconscious. In animism, indeed in nature, polarities simply don't work.

The point is important. In a naturally minded universe, around the flickering and momentary brilliance of lit consciousness, the wide landscape is one of shadow reaching into the darkness. This is the mind. Throughout this text, this is how I have employed the word, as the wholeness of its capacity, almost all of which is unlit. Not a squalid den of demons and indecency at the back of a beautiful great house, the mind is a vast and ancient wood, the density of its canopy allowing sunlight only now and then to reach through and touch the spiders and mushrooms in the leaf mould of the forest floor. This is who we are.

Less interested in psychology than ontology, the physicist Eddington examined the issue with his usual exquisite sensitivity. Consciousness, he said, 'is not sharply defined, but fades into sub-consciousness; and beyond that we must postulate something indefinite but yet continuous with our mental nature'. He called this 'the world-stuff'; I would call it the minded soul of nature. From the fleeting moments of the lit mind where conscious awareness allows the thinking self to consider its context of being, a moment's light softly fades into the shadows. Yet even as those shadows thicken with a growing darkness, this is still the mind. Accordingly, in humanity and throughout nature, the greater part of knowing is acquired in these shadows, and re-accessed within the shadows, never coming to the light of conscious awareness at all. Whether interacting with a twilit consciousness or a simpler prehensive awareness, the mind need not pause to assess a situation, continuing instead to absorb the environment without the inevitable delay or censorship of considered interpretation.

Unfettered by the thinking consideration of lit consciousness, the darker mind may well be perceiving a world closer to nature's actuality. Without the abstraction of thought, the lack of light blurs edges, making contexts flexible. Boundaries become unclear or disappear as spatial distinctions lose their precision. Standing in the shadows, we forget where we are. Memories relocate. Time is no longer a linear procession: chronology feels more spherical, the distant past being potentially as present as the immediate environment. In *The Wayward Mind*, cognitive scientist Guy Claxton wrote, 'we do not know our own minds, and we do not (always) own them either. They are as much unconscious as conscious; as much physical as mental; as much communal as individual'. The final phrase is cogent: the unconscious doesn't distinguish between the self and others. Having not yet learned to use the lit mind, the child or child-like adult is naturally selfish: in the shadows the world is an extension of himself. Yet equally within the twilight there is a capacity for empathy, allowing individuals to sense or share the experience of others, an intuited connection that is not based on consideration.

Undisturbed by the thinking *I*, the mind is rich with memory and experience, with the connectedness and integrated knowing of nature's wholeness. To the animist this is not just well worth exploring, but its exploration is an essential part of his sacred journey of understanding. While the thinking self may lose itself immediately it steps from the light, it is still possible with a simpler awareness to meander into the shadows, and here to find ancient stories and images that provide insight and wisdom.

Decisions

If we are taking in data and learning from experience without pausing to consider the content, it could be that some of what is learned is likely to be fallacious. Such a view has been used to declare the thinking self to be the only guarantee of rational behaviour, a declaration usually fuelled by a belief in human (even male Caucasian) supremacy. Of course, that heinous acts of violence have been committed by rational, intelligent, thinking human beings somewhat undermines the aim of the declaration. The ability to think, to consider, to have a sense of self, is not a safeguard which guarantees against brutality, assuring co-operation and care.

Learning based on fear, trauma and misunderstanding may well be absorbed by the ever-perceiving unlit mind and, held in the shadows, generate harmful reactions. The floods and tides and breaking waves of emotion, together with other deep and entirely natural drives such as lust and fear, can equally overwhelm us, limiting our ability to pause and consider before we act. Whether lit or not, the landscapes of the mind are not always calm. In his beautiful *Confessions*, Augustine's intro-spection led him to the conviction that we are never innocent, our souls filled with unknown and forgotten memories, a great many of which we are not proud of. On the same tack, psychology has all too often presented the unconscious as a place of danger, of uncontrollable psychosis, the old tales of dragons and demons merely reinterpreted for a modern audience. Distinguishing between the rational *I* and the unpredictable darkness of the unconscious, Freud called the dark mind *das Id*, the it, the other-than-me.

Yet, within humanity, as within all of nature, predominantly unlit though it is, the mind is full of knowing that is crucial to the comfort and peace of the individual. As the American psychia-trist Milton H Erickson wrote in the latter part of the twentieth century, the unlit mind is 'the reservoir of learning' that allows us to function. Keen to emphasise the uselessness of disassociating from the mind, with his irrepressible positivity he stated that undesirable or abnormal behaviour is not to be disowned; it is simply that which doesn't have a fruitful or meaningful purpose for that individual in a particular context. The darker mind can certainly make mistakes with regard to appropriateness, but the thinking self can be equally misguided - and justify itself with rational arguments to boot.

Children are said to meander with more ease through the shadows of the mind. As we grow, taking on information and experience, the darker paths become harder to navigate. We learn more slowly, becoming more rigid in our thinking and beliefs, more reliant upon verbal language, more likely to miss the kinaesthetic, sensory and symbolic language of the darker mind in our process of consideration. As our ability to make rational decisions improves, we are less likely to trust the emotional and instinctive feelings that emanate from the shadows, and as such misinterpret or suppress them until, like a surging spring tide, they drench us, propelling us upon their course. Once again, the animist recognises the need to explore the shadows of the mind, becoming familiar with all that makes him what he is.

Recognising nature's continuity and how much is shared within the greater mind, what he learns about the unlit mind within his own being also guides him in his responses to others of his community. Every individual is the sum of their experiences and beliefs, their memories and ancestors, all of which are held within the shadows of the mind, influencing behaviour moment by moment in ways that may never be considered by the lit mind. On top of that, the greater part of communication is happening without conscious awareness. If we are to interact with consideration and with care, we must accept the shadows of the mind.

Above I asked if a dog were capable of making a decision. In many ways I conflated the question with whether or not the dog were consciously aware or able to think about the circumstances of a moment. The same questions were put with regard to a squirrel and sow, a stream and an ash tree breaking into leaf in the spring sunshine: are they making decisions, and if so, are those decisions made with lit consciousness? In fact, having argued that mind is ubiquitous and consistent, could the significant variations in nature, the interesting contrasts and distinctions, be found here, in how much an individual's experience is available to the lit mind?

The secondary question is easy to answer. Conscious awareness allows an individual to think about a situation, assessing what has happened, what could happen next, and so to weigh up the benefits and disadvantages of an action, considering what the ethical course of action would be. However, when I am thinking, my mental state is an aggregation of all that it is like to be me right here, right now: this is all about qualia, and it is not possible to know what qualia another entity is experiencing. My friend gazes pensively into the fire and, curious, I ask him what he is thinking; absolutely nothing, he explains. In fact, in a state of tired relaxation, he has managed to cut wood, make a fire and brew a pot of tea, pausing only once to consider what herbs to put into the pot, his mind otherwise remaining entirely blank. With not a flicker of light breaking the shadows, he is able quietly to function. The dog, in the meantime, gazes at the fire: unable to ask him the same question, I must concede that I can have no idea of the qualia in his canine mind. Furthermore, there is no sharp line dividing the lit from the dark: as Eddington said, conscious awareness fades. To ask if the dog is consciously aware or not is too black and white. It is likely that he does have a clear sense of what it is like to be himself within the context of the moment, he may have an awareness of images that move through his mind, memories and perhaps imagined events rooted in those memories, experienced with what may be a non-linear mind; he may even be thinking, considering options in an inner language that is wholly outside my human grasp. I simply cannot know.

The question is unanswerable, but it is serious, nonetheless. Only if an individual were able to assess a situation sufficiently to know if a particular action were likely to be harmful could he be held morally accountable for his decision to act. Given a rational and honest human being with whom we shared a common language, we could ask questions in order to gauge whether or not he were able to distinguish what would be considered right or wrong in a situation. With no common language between myself and the dog, it might seem reasonable to test the dog's ability to think by presenting him with options and encouraging him to make a decision. However, as conversations tend to be when only half a dozen words or gestures are mutually intelligible, with or without a species divide, the topics under discussion would be so basic any answers would likely be driven by instinct anyway. A dog cannot relate why he chooses the path by the river instead of that down the field, even if he were able to consider the option and were not simply led by the first scent in the air.

However, and more crucially, decisions are not made in the lit mind.

Scientific studies made over the past forty years, from the groundbreaking work of Benjamin Libet, have shown that neural activity initiating an action happens in advance of any conscious awareness of the intention. Though some still debate the process, the figures are now widely known: the signal from a touch on the arm may reach the brain in one hundredth of a second, but it takes half a second to reach the conscious awareness. Equally, the relevant neurons can be seen firing in the motor cortex a third of a second before the individual is aware of the desire to move. As Libet states, 'cerebral initiation of a spontaneous voluntary act begins unconsciously': actions are initiated in the shadows of the mind.

Such findings challenge the notion of free will. That we are not conscious of the delay is explained by some in terms of a 'backward referral' system, where the lit mind covers up the gap, allowing the retention of a sense of conscious autonomy. Many materialist thinkers, convinced by the deterministic thesis that free will is illusory, welcomed Libet's data; although questioning the research, Dennett affirmed that it did appear to rule out any 'executive role' for the 'conscious self'. Others have explored ways that are not so dismissive. With it taking another two hundredth of a second on average for a movement to be initiated after it reaches conscious awareness, while there may be an acquiescence that allows the unconscious build up of initiative, the decision to inhibit or stop it is still available - even if there is no initiating free will within the lit mind, there is *free won't*.

While such investigations are fascinating, they seem too to determine the distinction between an experiencing consciousness and an inaccessible unconsciousness. Introspective and mystical paths of spirituality and philosophy have long talked of decisions being made in the shadows of the mind. In animism, accepting how fleeting are the moments of lit consciousness, the actuality is obvious. In a slower world, enriched with the self-awareness of spiritual practice, where the shadows of the self are not unknown nor disowned, it is wholly accepted that decisions are made in the shadows. After all, not everything can be consciously considered by the mind.

Claxton uses the very twenty first century metaphor of email. Data is taken in by the unlit mind which deletes the spam, forwards some messages for others to respond, deals with some using simple one word replies, and then sends those that need consideration out to the conscious awareness. Of course, the system is not fool-proof. What is usefully discarded is infor-mation that is safe, familiar, where habitual responses are adequate, but blind spots and denial can also trash messages unhelpfully. Information about immediate needs and interests can provoke the lit consciousness, but an overly stressed system can demand conscious consideration of more than a soul can manage, overwhelming the mind's strength or sanity. Similarly, radically new data can be deemed incredible and trashed as easily as it might be offered into the light.

Does our ability to think and to consider entail better action then? We may rightly be searching for accountability, for culpability, but if decisions are made in the unlit mind, and if the mind learns, absorbing the data of each moment, with little or no conscious awareness, and if we are filtering information for its possible value without conscious consideration as well, that search is not going to be simple. As the 'storehouse' of knowing, Erickson writes of the unconscious as being on the whole 'much smarter, wiser and quicker' than the lit mind. With every decision we face, the 'conscious mind understands the logic of it, and the unconscious understands the reality'.

That includes the consequences.

Hume is the thinker most often credited with shattering ideas of cause and effect. As I outlined in Chapter One, he asserted that although some objects appear 'conjoined', giving the impression of one causing the other, we 'cannot penetrate into the reason of the conjunction'. In *An Enquiry Concerning Human Understanding* in the mid 1700s, he wrote, 'After a repetition of similar instances the mind is carried by habit, upon the appearance of one event, to expect its usual attendant and to believe that it will exist'. Almost two centuries later, in *An Outline of Philosophy*, Russell continued the sceptical line, affirming that we cannot know that A will follow B just because it always has done. Neither thinker is dismissing that there are consequences to an action, simply that it is not possible to know with any certainty what those may be. What we perceive to be the effects cannot logically, absolutely, be proven to have come about because of another particular action. Instead, Russell stated that the idea of 'compulsion' or 'necessity' are 'purely anthropomorphic': natural law is no more than a regularity and habit, created by probabilities and chance.

From an animistic view, causality is very much a notion of the thinking self. The consideration of time and space as linear and measurable means it is possible to judge when and where something occurred, to assess the circumstances and review the events that immediately followed, finding possible links that to some extent accord with both the rational and empirical data. However, allowing that the mind is predominantly unlit, the extent of what is at any point influencing a situation must be accepted as beyond our human ability to comprehend. Furthermore, taking the view of nature from the shadows to be potentially more accurate, to the animist an understanding of time and space considered by the thinking self could be misleading. In other words, causality is not simple, and as a result neither is the notion of predictable consequences.

Freedom

Fate is a fascinating aspect of religious, spiritual and superstitious tradition. In Classical Greek mythology, the three Moirae, Clotho, Lachesis and Atropos, were the manifestation of fate. Spinning, drawing out, measuring and cutting the threads of life, their role was to give each individual his allotted number of days, of wealth and poverty, of love and joy, of suffering and despair. In Ancient Greek the meaning of the word μοῖρα (*moira*) was closer to the modern *méros* or *merída* denoting a part or portion; it now simply translates as fate. In the Roman tradition, the work was done by the Parcae, Nona, Decima and Morta, *pars* also being a portion.

The word fate came to English from the Latin *fata*, a predication, an oracle or what has been spoken by the gods or Fates, deriving from the verb *fari*, to speak. In Classical traditions, fate was seen to be a necessity, its inflexible structure that maintained nature in the state of order that allows it its tenability. Without fate, there would be chaos. Indeed, in the old mythologies whenever an individual refuses to accept what the Fates have determined, not only does he fail to change the course of his life, but his fated path is inevitably one of great suffering and chaos.

In Germanic and Nordic tradition, the corresponding characters are often considered to be the Norns, but the correlation is not exact. For many Pagans who follow northern European spiritual traditions, including the Anglo-Saxon paths in Britain, these female giants are formative elements within their worldview. In the mythic tales, the Norns draw water from the Well of Urðr in order to nourish the tree of life, Yggdrasil, clearing mud from around its base to ensure its great branches don't rot away. As such they can be seen as powers who maintain the structure of nature, but not in the same way as the Fates. Of the many Norns, the three honoured as the most important are Urðr, Verðandi and Skuld, the first, pronounced *wyrd*, giving her name to the Weird Sisters found in Shakespeare's Scottish play. Etymologically, the root of the name can be found in the Old English *weorðan* meaning to become, and in *weorþ* meaning worth or esteem, the shared PIE base being *wert-*, to turn or wind. Urðr, then, is that which has become or has turned to be what it will be, Verðandi is that which is in the process of becoming, and Skuld is that which should be or what is owed.

In this way, the Norns don't equate to the weavers, spinning, measuring and cutting the threads of life as do the Moirae and Parcae. Expressing a more fundamentally embodied state, the Norns are the cloth itself, the weave of nature, of life and existence. Although some translate wyrd as fate, this fate is not imposed from entities existent outside of nature's fabric. Wyrd speaks of the cycles of being and becoming, of the changes that are entirely informed by the context of memory and history, slipping through the present towards a future that is always integral to the whole. Here is fate within the circularity of time. It is not actually a deterministic belief.

Determinism is a thesis which states that for every occurrence there were conditions in place that meant nothing else could have happened but what did. Most materialists considering the philosophy of mind are deterministic, asserting that matter operates within physical laws in ways that are inevitable, and consequently, there is no free will. In opposition are the metaphysical libertarians, such as Descartes who in *Passions of the Soul* wrote that 'the will is by its nature so free that it can never be constrained'. More recently Robert Kane stated that if there are alternative possibilities the responsibility for choice can never be evaded. Facing the crisis of another polarity, many thinkers have walked the centre ground of *compatibilism*: describing the issue to be the most contentious in metaphysics, Hume took this stance, as did Hobbes and Schopenhauer. Defining free will in such a way as not to contradict determinism, the view suggests that we are free to act as we wish, but within the natural confines of a context. In other words, if a person is not chained or drugged or in some other way forced, they must be said to be free to act, even if the natural drives are too powerful to resist, effectively governing their actions. William James declared this 'soft determinism' to be 'a quagmire of evasion' and a misuse of the term freedom. In *The Critique of Practical Reason* Kant called it 'a petty word-jugglery' that failed to address the need to understand moral responsibility.

The issue is about control: how much are we able to control ourselves and to modify our behaviour? How much are we or can we be consciously aware of what forms our decisions, fuelling our actions?

We behave as we do because of who we are, but consequently we can only be truly responsible for the way we behave if we are truly responsible for who we are, and that is not the case. So much forms who we are, each moment occurring within the fabric of its communities, and within the wholeness of nature's soul. It is not possible to delineate the boundaries of influence. No individual is isolated, holding the entire burden of responsibility for his behaviour. The drives and beliefs that guide our decision-making from deep in the shadows of the mind can be beyond our control.

It was the Scottish reformer Lord Kames, one of whose protégés was David Hume, who in 1751 first noted the influence of the unconscious in terms of legal culpability. As Claxton writes, 'We *act as if* responsibility could be assigned because the fiction enables us to punish certain kinds of acts, and, most importantly, to broadcast and dramatise the humiliation and privation of the punished, *pour encourager les autres*'. The hope is not just that such punitive responses will make a potential criminal think more carefully about this actions, but that such penalties affect the unlit mind, usefully influencing decisions *before* the thinking self gets involved. Aware how little thought goes into most of our actions, Erikson noted that it 'really doesn't matter what your conscious mind does because your unconscious automatically will do just what it needs to', and those needs are based on the needs and desires in that moment.

What then is the animist perspective?

Actions provoke reactions. At the level of nature's essence, each interaction is an event that creates a new event, the immediate and minute changes in context, moment by moment, allowing the natural flow of information, communication and generation that is nature's being and becoming. Each enduring subject is the sum of every previous event, each soul comprising the wholeness of its history and heritage. The way we arrive in the present is thus fully determined by the past.

In our experience of every moment, it is possible to make no decisions at all. In the shadows of the mind, our thinking limited to commentary about the environment of which we have a vaguely conscious awareness, our ability to consider confined to the iteration of memory, affirming habit, we can live without free will. All that we have been directs and guides us, allowing us to retain a continuity. If we are healthy and happy in what we are, as long as our environment remains equally slow in its evolution, such a state of stability may be sustainable. Where it is not, however, or where we are miserable, such habituated and thoughtless inertia can only lead to a gradual disintegration, provoking damage along the way.

However, our ability to consider does offer an inkling of freedom. We may be comprised of the past, but in the presence of the moment the future remains free. Fleeting though it is, the thinking self is able to assess the need for change. However, given that so little of the mind is lit, if that self relies only on the data of which he is consciously aware, he is likely to make poor decisions, decisions based purely on the needs and desires of the individual *I*. Recognising the value of simpler perception, knowing that the unlit mind sees more clearly the actuality of nature and the integrated communities, by softly prehending the context of a his being, the animist seeks out the current that has brought him to the moment, listening within the shadows, watching, sensing his world, reaching to feel nature beyond. Ideas emerge for consideration, images are processed into languaged thinking, where each possibility can be judged and reviewed, before the light again fades, allowing the mind to work as it does, weaving memory and instinct, wisdom and environment, to create decisions that are rooted in firm ground.

When ideas come to light that are unhelpful, it is our ability to contemplate the self within its community and its environment that allows us to review what is in the mind. It is a slow process and takes meticulous care and compassionate caring, for we may begin with no motivation to change at all. Comfortable in our blinkers, numb with pain, cluttered with fear, we may be not have the courage or capacity to self-reflect with the lit mind, preferring instead to abdicate responsibility for our lack of success or satisfaction by believing that we are not in control. The dominant beliefs held in the shadows continue to form our decisions and guide our actions. Only if we are aware of those beliefs, if we are able to act other than by their direction, and indeed to alter them, can we be said to be acting with free will.

Within animism, together with increasing our conscious awareness in order better to understand our world, grasping our free will is a sacred obligation. We are never *fully* responsible for our actions, for our lit mind is too limited, but we are fully *culpable* if we do not seize the opportunities we have to enhance our contribution to the world within which we live.

Such a definition might imply that free will is only accessible to those entities within nature that are enduring subjects, that are individuals with a coherent interiority, and with a lit mind of conscious awareness that allows consideration. From a human perspective, it seems to be the latter that makes the difference. However, my explanation of free will above is relevant only with regard to humanity, for the processes are based on human consciousness.

It may be possible to extend the idea to some mammals, and perhaps other creatures whose intelligence seems similar enough to that of a human being for a comparison to be made. Of course, if we were to do so, none are deemed to have as much lit consciousness: the dog, the sow, perhaps even the squirrel may be thought to have moments, but questions must immediately be posed as to whether there is enough.

To do so is to make a simple mistake of projection though, in the same way as if we were basing the mind on the size or complexity of the brain and other neural networks. The reality is that we cannot know if the dog, or the stream or the ash tree has free will any more than we can know if these entities have a coherent mind, a sense of self or an ability to consider. Nature's continuity suggests that the way the mind works must be consistent, but we can say little more than that. In the metaphysics I have laid out here I have proposed that there are fundamental processes of interaction that allow for perception, sensation, experience and even memory through nature's flows of communication, all of which are part of nature's creativity and form. I have also suggested that, while nature is inherently self-reflective, the human mind is predominantly unlit, the moments of thinking awareness being brief, with decision-making and the initiation of action coming from within the shadows. Unable to know the qualia of another creature, we just cannot know if this is true for other aspects of nature as well. I suspect that it is.

In the final chapter, we shall consider whether that is important. Indeed, in crafting a summary of this thesis, the chapter will deliberate on the value of having so consciously deconstructed our assumptions about nature and the world in which we live, returning to that fundamental question: what's the point?

Chapter Nine

The Point

It is often possible when observing a child to anticipate a measure of their adult character from which interrogative words they most frequently use. As a child I was assiduously concerned with the why: my adolescent self ached to understand *why* we are here, but the question was set to one side for most of my adult life, countered by my asking *why* we need to know. When there is suffering, so many people, so many species, struggling to survive through the hunger and horror of conflict, crises provoked by human overpopulation and habitat destruction, the injustices and inequalities only amplified by the gathering storm of climate change, can we really afford to ponder the essence of nature? Both questions have stayed with me, fuelling the writing of this book.

Yet, in many ways the dichotomy is another expression of the apparent gap that is fundamentally the distinction between mind and matter, between our experience of being and the actuality of nature. Yet ethics and metaphysics cannot be separated: they are thoroughly entangled. Even if an individual gives no thought to the nature of mind and matter, his behaviour reveals the beliefs he holds. Taught by parents, his schooling and society more broadly, he maintains a set of assumptions about what is of value, what is inert and what suffers, what deserves consideration and what can be used. Furthermore, those beliefs guide his experience, forming what he perceives and what he does not perceive, affirming his attitude to life, even if all this is done in the shadows of the mind.

Amongst the minority who do consider the issues with a lit consciousness, some look into the metaphysics with such a determined unwillingness to change their behaviour that their ethics severely limit the breadth of their exploration. On the other hand, there are others who are willing to discuss ethics but not their metaphysical assumptions, either because of undebatable religious or atheist convictions, or a simple belief that they are irrelevant. However, although experience, observation and study are unequivocally important, the Kantian veil reminds us that what we are perceiving is our reality, not nature *in itself*. Metaphysics takes us a step further, reaching for what the world might truly be, beyond our perception. Exploring these fundamental questions is crucial, then, if we are to find a sure foundation on which to base the cognition that will not only inform our decisions and guide our behaviour, but craft the filters of our perceptions as well.

In *Parerga and Paralipomena*, Schopenhauer wrote that any belief expressing that 'the world has only a physical and not a moral significance is a fundamental error, one that is the greatest and most pernicious, the real perversity of the mind'. American philosopher Charles Hartshorne, in his 1977 essay *Physics and Psychics*, affirmed the value of the panpsychist stance as allowing us 'to arrive at a view of life and nature in which the results of science are given their significance along with the values with which art, ethics, and religion are concerned'. The words of both thinkers sit comfortably within animism. The animist's sacred obligation to understand nature exists in order to ensure that he knows how to live within an environment with the least unnecessary harm. His integrated metaphysics explains why.

Animism

It would be easy to describe animism within its own poetic terminology. I might say that the song of nature is expressed in a glorious profusion of songs, melodies within melodies, each note vibrant with harmonics that tell the stories of all time. I might say that every whisper of wind, every ray of sunlight, every breath of life, is an expression of spirit within the soul of nature, or that nothing in the universe is but brimming with nature's knowing. However compelling the poetry may be, though, any real comprehension of the words would be limited to those readers who had already a good understanding of animism. Furthermore, all the key words so often used so loosely would retain their reputation as spiritual *fluff* to any humanist reader, and suffer an assortment of interpretations from those of other faiths. Consequently, in the process of putting together a definition through the course of this book, rather than using animistic poetry I have instead primarily used the language of Western philosophy, hoping that by doing so I have explicated not just the spiritual jargon but animism as a whole.

All too frequently those wishing to present a belief with ancient roots tend to seek out some notional origin or Golden Era of wisdom, and dismiss the intervening years. To do so with animism would suggest that the modern animist seeks to return to his Iron Age roots, which is sentimental nonsense. Moreover, it would also be blatantly inconsistent to ignore the influence of centuries, for nature's creativity works as moment touches moment, breath leads into breath. The debate over mind and matter has been discussed within our heritage for over two and a half thousand years; before that there was animism, and animism now returns to Western culture, but the journey through those millennia was day by day, each moment flowing into the next. To recognise the history of animism is to accept each one of those days, and honour each thinker whose life and words have contributed to the animism that is re-appearing in the West today.

Of course, pockets can be found where animism is still expressed as a dualist and superstitious conviction, with spirits of trees and rivers that behave like ghosts in a child's storybook: most philosophies, both religious and secular, can be dumbed down to the point of fallacy with explanations drawn in crayon. The animism I have defined here is a belief system the roots of which can be found deep in human prehistory, yet which also acknowledges its survival through periods of repudiation, and its slow re-emergence over the past five hundred years. It is an animism based upon an integrated metaphysics that makes rational sense within the twenty first century

Let us review that definition.

As a metaphysical monism, animism is based upon the idea that nature's essence is minded. We have no way to language just what that essence is, but - and indeed *because* - fundamentally it is all that there is. Moment by moment, interaction within that essence generates data that utilises nature's capacity for mind, rousing it to perceive and respond. So does each subject emerge, formed of the perceptual data of its context, each response being a new interaction creating another momentary event rich with data. As each moment dissolves, giving way to the next, some subjects find a flow, a continuity of form created by an iteration of interaction. Such an enduring entity may remain as a community of numerous subjects, or it may achieve a level of synchronisation sufficient to become an individual with a coherent interiority, albeit in a state of perpetual change, formed by the percepts of its inner and outer environment.

Mind and matter are not, nor do they ever become, separate substances: they are merely different states of nature's essence, the material being a slower state of interaction than the mental which our human perception then distinguishes and describes as physical. The mind, crafted of percepts, creates of the data a world that is comprehensible within the bounds of its own limitations. This is the mind's reality, distinct from nature, nature being the universal whole, the complete actuality of all there is *in itself*.

Having presented the definition thus far, it is reasonable to review those jargon words so readily used without the responsibility of clarification. Firstly, spirit or spirits are the patterns created by the crucial moments of interaction, ephemeral configurations of a context, the vibrancy of which we may not distinctly perceive but which is nonetheless fundamental to our being and becoming. The soul, on the other hand, is the wholeness of an enduring entity, every moment of its experience, its contextual heritage and its environment, integrated and humming in its ongoing state of change.

So, in his practice of learning and reverence, the animist will acknowledge the spirits of a place, the spirits of a river, of fire and storm, the spirits of a tribe, of motherhood, of the dead, the spirits of a gathering, of an event in time, and so on. In doing so he is reaching to perceive those fleeting patterns that, so filled with energy and potentiality, are the essential moments flowing into moments, the raw creativity that manifests each form, saturating each experience. Awake to that perception, he is aspiring to play an active and respectful part in the creative process of life, even if only though gratitude, awe and devotion. In his practice, the animist will also acknowledge the soul, reaching here to catch a glimpse of what is the summation of all that has been. In the soul of his grandfather, the soul of the land underfoot, the soul of the tribe, the soul of the apple he holds in his hand, he is recognising that in the mental and physical form he perceives there is memory and perseverance, there is wisdom, pain and freedom, there are stories of moments flowing into moments, stretching out to the horizons of space and time *in itself* - and in that recognition, he is acknowledging too the part he himself has played and continues to play. In addition to the spirit and soul, in the tradition of Druidry and the ancient bardic craft of Britain through which I learned so much, the animist will also speak of the song. I used the word a little earlier, conveying how full it is with meaning: the song is the expression of the moment as it unfolds, our soul riding the current of the spirits whose perpetual motion is our becoming. The songs of being are the music of presence. The song is what we express and celebrate in every moment of our living.

Without the previous chapters, the above two paragraphs would be as meaningless in their jargon as the common definition that animists believe everything has its own spirit or soul. The words needed deconstructing. Let us recall the *Oxford English Dictionary* entry: animism is 'the belief that plants and inanimate objects have souls'. Referencing the *OED's* primary definition of the soul as 'the spiritual element of a person, regarded as immortal', the animist is clearly a fool. With an animistic understanding of soul, however, the definition is not so erroneous as simplistic.

The other definition heavy with assumption, that the animist believes all nature to be conscious, I have explained as yet more jargon badly used. In the last chapter, I spoke of how consciousness requires a continuity in terms of coherent interiority. Subjects are as fleeting as the percepts that form them, perceiving and evanescing, moment to moment, and although some do find an enduring form through slowly shifting data, not all communities of being are individuals, and not all individuals have the capacity for consciousness. When the animist talks of nature as minded, then, he is not saying that mind equates to consciousness. The fundamental process of mind is simple prehension, perception that is no more than the passive if wakeful reception of data. The processes of experience, of sensation and response, must be explored before we can reach the active deconstruction of consciousness. Beyond that is the conscious awareness of the lit mind, the brief moments of light that allow for thinking and consideration within what are otherwise the shadows and darkness of the mind.

Finally, but crucial to our summary definition, because nature is itself a subject, a mind, a being, introspection must be fundamental within the universe. Introspection, self-awareness, must therefore be inherent to every mind that comprises the wholeness of nature. If it weren't, there would be nothing but darkness.

Harmony

To précis: everything in nature is awake, both perceiving its environment and with a sense of its own being. As Hartshorne said, everything contains 'inner aspects of feeling, memory, and expectation'. However, I am not proposing that everything is capable of making considered decisions, nor that everything could then be said to be accountable for its actions as if it were self-determining.

In his process philosophy, Whitehead described self-determination as integral to the mental pole of each occasion: so does the asserting subject, in becoming itself, initiate the next occasion before dissolving away. Whitehead's vision embraced the active input of a panentheistic creative force which at first he called God, in time preferring the term 'Eros of the Universe' or 'the Universe as One': as the instinct for creativity within each event, for beauty and perfection, he saw this Eros to be comprised of all potentiality. With every part of nature touched by this potential, each occasion faces a spread of possibilities, just one of which must be chosen. So did Whitehead declare free will to be inherent to nature.

He was not, however, confusing this process with what the human thinking self might experience as free will. He was not implying that a *human* notion of accountability could be justified at the fundamental level of nature. Nonetheless, if we are to discard the conclusion that nature is entirely deterministic, trudging down a path of mindless and rigid inevitability, there must be choice, and accepting that minded nature must have consistency at all levels, choice must indeed be inherent throughout. Without Whitehead's immanent and transcendent creative force though, the animistic view differs, if just slightly. Where there is not the consciousness to consider, interaction is guided by a broader mind: not a supernatural God but nature itself. A subject responds, informed by the community or communities that make up its context, which in turn are held by the mind of nature as a whole. Importantly, in doing so, it cannot help but act in tune with its environment.

What strives to determine its own path must have an inner coherence and consciousness sufficient to desire change within its ecosystem: as such, it pushes itself forward, influencing the spirits of the moment, affecting the patterns of becoming. Such a drive is fuelled by an innate desire to find ease without effort, to alleviate craving and be comfortable in passivity. In other words, the capacity for true self-determination allows an individual to affect and alter its environment, so creating what it needs or wants, instead of merely responding to it as part of a community. When an individual is not at ease but fails to assert itself, there is either the ongoing turbulence of discomfort or a resigned acquiescence that lacks tenability; only when it has achieved the change it desires, and found harmony within its environment, can the individual rest, exhaling into the real peace of acceptance. Such work takes consciousness, although not necessarily the light of conscious awareness. Of course, whether fuelled by a lit mind or initiated entirely within the shadows, self-determination thus enables the individual to push against its environment, provoking disharmony that can influence the system as a whole.

Harmony: it is another key word in animism. The oldest documented use of the term in English is in the context of music in the twelfth century, the word expressing the influence of the Greek goddess of concord and agreement, *Harmonia*. The PIE base *ar- means to fit together, and given a metaphysics based on interaction and integration, harmony is of course pertinent. On a metaphysical level, within nature *in itself*, harmony is what allows the universe its enduring continuity, and as such it is what we perceive as beauty, what we sense as sustainability. With the song of the soul and its relationships the principal focus, so is harmony crucial to animistic ethics.

In that period before animism was negated by monotheistic

authorities, as old animism was being re-languaged by a new way of thinking, Aristotle spoke of the state of *eudaimonia* (εὐδαιμονία), a word often simplistically translated as happiness. Its full meaning is more nuanced: *eudaimonia* expresses how an entity thrives when it is living within the laws of its own nature and the nature of its environment. In other words, when we are not endeavouring to be other than what we are, nor grasping more than the fates have allotted as our share, we have a chance to thrive. Of course, in a culture obsessed with growth and wealth, the notion of thriving implies a material richness, and to some extent Aristotle didn't disagree. The Stoics thought otherwise: they asserted that *arete* (ἀρετή) was all that was needed in order to find the truly creative peace of *eudaimonia*. The word is translated as virtue, but that can now imply an austerity not meant at the time: the Stoic *arete* was the resolve to live in tune with nature. Emphatically this was not the following of every brute lust and hunger but the seeking to understand nature's fundamental reason. Guiding their adherents to be aware of the 'passions', the drives and desires that lead to excess, to inequality and suffering, the Stoics' goal was to live within the patterns of nature that allow for peace and sustainability: harmony.

It is such a beautifully animistic attitude, for those patterns of nature are not abstract algorithms, they are the beauty of nature's mind in all its expressions of form. Each form, each individual and each community, shimmering with the wholeness of nature's soul and with its own, is awake to itself and the moment by moment configurations of its relationships. Harmony allows those relationships the *eudaimonia* that each individual craves, the peace of sustainable creativity.

Such a perspective must recognise that everything exists for itself. The conviction that everything has its place within the greater soul of nature, that everything is in wakeful relationship with every other member of its community or communities, confers to everything an inherent value. Within the language of animism, the summary shorthand of this is unequivocal: everything is sacred. It is another jargon word. Usually referring to an object with particular religious significance, what is sacred in most religions is set aside for special reverence, even veneration, and care. Yet, if we believe *all* of nature to be sacred, how can we live, let alone in harmony? In order to sustain ourselves, at a very minimum we must find food and shelter, and in doing so we cannot help but have an impact, compromising the extent to which we can live with respect for others' form and purpose.

If nature were neatly divided into conscious beings and inert matter, the former could (and indeed do) feel free to use the latter for their own benefit, but the animist has no such comfortable, self-serving perspective. His ethics are not so easily delivered. The decisions he makes about how he lives within the context of his world must be based on his cognition of that world. If he is to have a chance of living in a manner that is truly appropriate, respectful and sustainable, he must study that world, working to understand what influence his living has on others, and so what his mantra of *least unnecessary harm* means in practice. Harmony is found then, not by setting aside the sacred for special consideration and using the rest with less care, but by relating to everything equally, with a recognition that everything is awake, formed of its percepts, its soul being a vibrant and integral part of the soul of nature. The animist then knows well that his self-determination is powerful and valuable, yet potentially a very dangerous aspect of his human consciousness, for it has the capacity to derail the natural harmony.

When describing this book to one of my former students, she listened for a while to my rambling explanation, then laughed and shrugged, reciting back to me the phrase that I have so often used to encapsulate animism and the native tradition of Druidry: 'relationship is everything'. In *Living With Honour*, as above, my thesis outlined how relationship is pivotal to animist ethics. In this book, with its aim of laying down a metaphysical foundation for that thesis, I have affirmed that relationship is also at the heart of animist ontology. In other words, the importance of relationship isn't just in those we make as conscious individuals wanting to live with care within the world we perceive. The very basis of nature's creativity is its ongoing flow of interactions and, with each moment emerging and evanescing, where form finds continuity, gaining sustainability, it is where relationships achieve the exquisite ease of harmony.

The Fabric

That the self is not a fixed actuality in nature further contributes to the animist's ethics of harmony. The boundaries of each mind meander according to the environment, according to the percepts that form it, allowing a response that draws on the experience and wisdom of whatever is appropriate.

Amidst bluebells and stitchwort beneath the April canopy of hazel and birch, in a state of meditative release I merge into the community of the woodland, my thinking *I* dissolving into its greater soul, and sense through the soft prehension of its mind the movement of the deer, the breeze in the leaves, the intertwining roots and quiet of the birds, perceiving more clearly the ancient pathways trodden by humans and other mammals. And when, a while later, I emerge back into the meadow, the experience still fills me with a sense of wealth, of life's beauty and value, a sense of my own belonging. Such animistic practice is more than communion: it is integration. If I were to have walked the woodland tracks holding onto my human individuality, I would have perceived comparatively little and been nurtured only by the fact of having been briefly in a different environment. In the same way, in the dark and noise of the nightclub the music shatters my edges, and again the *I* disappears as my soul melds with the vibrations of sound and light, joining the collective movement of each soul who has done the same, voluntarily overwhelmed and subsumed into the tribal mind - until some rigid *I*, dancing without this shared synchronicity, bumps into me! And again, as my infant son cries, although my lack of experience of motherhood affords me no rational answers, immediately I let my self melt away, the wisdom of my grand-mothers emerges in my hands and voice, the experience of generation after generation flowing with confidence, and my responses at last come intuitively with a peaceful efficacy. Held by such a community of mothers, the little fellow calms.

This loose sense of self, this utilitarian view of the *I*, this willingness to release into a collective soul, is a strong part of the animist's understanding of harmony. Just as memory is under-stood in animism to extend beyond the individual, having been laid down in the lines of hedgerows and buildings, the course of lanes and contours of fields, in the stories of a community, in ideas and paintings, in the curve of a smile and the shape of a limb, so is knowing not confined to the individual mind. Subject within subject, soul within soul, the interconnectedness of mind allows information to be shared. Experience, understanding, knowing, intelligence, build patterns that are held within patterns, creating selves that are part of broader selves which, as part of the wider communities of the landscape and tribe, extend to become beliefs, knowledge and lore, traditions and wisdoms.

Despite the filters that allow us not to be flooded with data, to retain some sanity and comprehension, the mind is continuously absorbing information, all of which adds to how decisions are made in the shadows of the mind. As human beings, there may be the potential to access that knowing with a conscious awareness, to review it in the light, to affirm or discard it, to reconfigure beliefs, altering the way in which we might prioritise and respond. Yet, even where there is apparently not the capacity to consider, it is this sharing of consciousness that brings coherence to a community, to a tribe, to a moment in time and space, allowing a (eco)system to function as a beautifully coordinated being within nature. Empathies are felt, the language of communication understood, necessary skills coming out of nowhere. We find dreams and inspiration, the sudden *click* of real understanding, the deep sense of intuition that feels so full of conviction. It is through this shared knowing that we experience recognition, a feeling of intimate familiarity though we are encountering a stranger or a new land. Here too we can understand the vivid presence of a person who has died, music or voices in the head, telepathy and other instances that have no material explanation.

Some animists, as many other Pagans, Hindus and Buddhists, will believe in the transmigration of souls, but my sense of reincarnation can also be understood by this shared mind of nature. Often experienced by young children not yet educated to be separate beings, or adults first reflecting on and doubting their sense of self, and those whose spiritual practice allows for periods of selfless awareness, memories emerge from what feel like previous lives: within the shared mind there is every life, every memory, patterns of being attracting similar patterns of being.

This is the fabric of nature. We might say that the fabric has been or is being woven by the Fates, each thread spun by those ethereal souls who bear the knowledge of all that will be, but such stories teeter along the edge of superstition and the supernatural. I would suggest instead that the threads of the fabric are crafted of interaction, of every relationship and memory. This is the web of *wyrd*, holding together the universe on every level in every way. This is what we are made of, what we breathe and drink, the sound of our voices and the spinning of galaxies, the dancing of electro-magnetic waves and the compulsions of love, the falling of neutrinos and the bark of the dog: percepts, relationships, interaction. This is nature's soul.

Wakefulness

In 1966, the American historian Lynn White Jr. gave a talk entitled *The Historical Roots of Our Ecologic Crisis*. Published in the journal *Science* the following year, White proposed that mediaeval Christian attitudes were the root cause of the impending disaster. The Church's declaration that mankind had a divine right of dominion over nature both predated and underlay the mechanism and materialism that went on to inspire the social and environmental upheaval of the Industrial Revolution. White reflected on the way in which earlier populations had engaged with the land, individuals experiencing themselves as fully part of nature, striving to understand its wiles and cycles in order to find a way of surviving and thriving, but as technology had developed the need for knowledge had critically altered: rather than striving to understand nature, the need was to understand the next piece of technology. As soon as nature could be exploited, the old animistic assumptions were dismissed as outdated, as sentimental and childish, for the brute technological muscle of a new generation was striding forward. Indeed, it was this separation from nature that allowed for a thesis of evolution and emergence to be put be forward in the nineteenth century: given Christian ideas of separation and technological change, a Darwinian model of consciousness emerging from increasingly complex matter became feasible.

In his paper, White made a radical suggestion: only when the notion of a rock being the subject of ethical consideration was no longer ridiculous to the general consensus would the population be ready to address the environmental crisis.

Forty five years later the situation is worse. We are living in an era and culture of untenable decadence, of widespread and worsening social injustice, on the brink of potential global economic collapse, where climate change is being ignored in favour of short-term financial goals that will benefit a very tiny minority. The predicament is increasingly undeniable. That nature is still deemed to be mindless, a resource claimed by the rich and sold to the poor, is equally undeniable. Considering the urgency of the situation, in his introduction to *Nature in Question*, JJ Clarke wrote that a 'sustainable society, it is argued, can only be achieved by a sustainable relationship with the natural world, and hence only if the political, economic, and even philosophical assumptions on which Western Society has been based for the past few centuries are revised'.

Although characteristically contradictory, Colin McGinn expresses the dilemma as well: if, he writes, the premise of panpsychism weren't intrinsically 'false', it would not only be a sweet solution to the mind-body query but it would threaten the entire basis of modern thinking. Such a metaphysics would - and indeed does - demand a *wholly* different attitude. The moral justification to use and consume, to see nature as a resource at our disposal, to have limited or no consideration for others, would be swept away. In *Becoming Animal*, Abram writes, 'If we speak of things as inert or inanimate objects, we deny their ability to actively engage and interact with us - we foreclose their capacity to reciprocate our attentions, to draw us into silent dialogue, to inform and instruct us'. Effectively, we determine ourselves to be deaf and blind to nature. What would happen if that were to change?

The question is entangled with another. So far I have answered my own *why*, offering a reason to explore the metaphysics that underlie ethics. I have yet to answer the question, *why* are we here?

From Christianity to New Age spiritualities, theologies can be found which proffer the comforting affirmation that our lives are innately meaningful. God, in some form, provides life for a reason and preachers and teachers then direct us to understand that reason, most commonly, as the altruistic care of others, or the recognition of one's own failings, suffering and subsequent need for redemption. With careful introspection, we may at some point grasp the specifics, but the immortality of the soul and its transfer to some form of paradise or hell at death is usually involved. Like materialism, animism has no such comfort to give.

As no more than a flow of percepts, of changing contextual data, the self *actually* has no purpose, no meaning at all. The quality of transience is not altered ontologically when a subject finds the continuity of an enduring form, for that entity is still comprised of moments perpetually emerging and evanescing. In animism there is a recognition that the enduring self naturally becomes attached to itself - beneath the surface, iteration builds memories that inspire continuity - and as such the self will fight for its own survival, but that doesn't remove its fundamental unimportance. The self is merely an idea of the mind, and because the mind is not enclosed and isolated within each individual self, where the individual is able to experience its self as integrated within its environment, thriving within the harmony of an ongoing community, any sense of survival is refocused, becoming about the sustainability of that community, not its own individual identity.

Why then are we here? Or, indeed, why should we bother to stick around?

In animism, relationship is ontologically fundamental. We exist because we are in relationship. The point of being here is to be in relationship. Relationship is everything. It is our relationships that form us. How we engage in those relationships informs us, creating the filters through which we then perceive and experience the world. At a basic level, our purpose is no more than to be what we are, within the greater purpose of nature's soul.

I entitled this book *The Wakeful World*, in part succumbing to the temptation of the alliteration for my focus in the main has been the metaphysical ontology, the inherent wakefulness of and within nature. However, if we are to accept the ontology, our purpose is enhanced when we perceive the world as wakeful.

Our purpose, our mission, should we choose to accept it, is then to employ what qualities of mind we can access and hone in order to do so. For when we perceive that our world is awake, the experience of relationship becomes even more profoundly affecting. When the actuality of every glint of nature's mind becomes evident - in the rain and in the air we breathe, in the wet leaves and the photons, in the planet - our values change. When every rustle of perception, every murmur of response, becomes tangible, visceral, it inspires and vitalises the substance of our reality. When we know the world around us to be crafted of memory, it compels us to refine our response-ability, to become more actively involved in nature's ongoing creativity.

Wakeful: in the Old English the verb *wacan* meant to become wake, but its PIE root is **weg-*, a base note which confers to its many descendent words the sense of being strong and lively. That strength and vitality is an inspirational quality offered by the word and its long soul history, and felt by its numerous verbal cousins, among them vigorous and watchful. Wakefulness is a strength that is both the presence of being, and the release that carries us into the moment's becoming. It is the mind, in other words, in all its brilliant action.

We are not important. As McGinn says, together with countless others, 'Too much meaning in life can be a burden; insignificance can lighten the heart'. The words are valuable and true. As human beings, however, we have a power to influence, not only ourselves but the environment as a whole. If we abandon hope, as many youngsters are now doing in the face of the environmental and economic crises, we abandon the need to use our lit consciousness, to consider, to think, and in doing so we surrender ourselves into the tides of nature, and in our thoughtlessness potentially adding to the future suffering of our species and those whose existence we have impacted. Equally, if we cower or scream in fear, pushing against each other in our selfish desperation to survive, using what brute force and resources we may still have, we are equally submitting to nature's flooding currents and crashing waves. The thinking *I*, this conscious awareness, is a huge responsibility. In offering us the potential for self-determination, it also gives us the power of self-separation, of selfish destruction, kicking in a reality that has forgotten nature's integration.

It can be painful for natural wakefulness to become conscious awareness. For the majority, life is hard, filled with pain, struggle and confusion. Staying numb, barely using the lit mind but to perpetuate passivity, is a common choice. Not thinking is not the answer though. We must think. Our human nature has evolved by considering options, reviewing priorities, balancing needs. But equally we must strive to feel, to listen and see, allowing the simplicity of perception, of natural prehension, to give us access to the shadows of the mind and the wisdom held in that twilight.

For the animist, seeking to understand nature, the meditative calm of prehension affords the possibility of slipping the chains of mechanical time and measured space, to bathe in nature's wakeful simplicity, learning there about the purpose of being. The experience of integration which underlies that state allows us to feel too the strength that is the community of humanity. Cutting bread, chopping wood, gazing into the hearth fire, shedding tears of love and loss, walking by the riverside, laughing in a crowd, pausing to find words, in all the small actions of a simple life we become aware of how much we share with our ancestors: over millennia, little has changed in our nature. Feeling that connection with our heritage, within the soul of humankind, accessing its experience, its memory and wisdom, there is more wakefulness, more strength, more ability to live with respect, in peace.

Of course, recognising the self to be a mental construct, allowing it to be no longer as focally important, we are simply putting the thinking *I* into a more accurate and fruitful perspective, accepting it to be the flows of crucial but fleeting moments within the wholeness of our being. Letting it go can provoke grief and disarray. Accepting that we are actually no more than percepts and interactions can feel almost self-negating. But held by the memories and stories of our ancestors, it is possible to feel more located, more settled and complete. Included with nature's inherent and comprehensive integration, we are able to experience profoundly how we sit within the community of our ecosystem, connected to all that makes up our environment. Our focus moves naturally from the *I* to the moment of relationship, the vibrant point of interaction that hums with potential and with creativity, with the music of communication in its myriad languages, with the percepts that fill and form every ecosystem. Abstractions dissolve or blossom into soulfulness, shimmering with memory. Life slows to an experience of presence, in a reality beyond separation, integration allowing for the shared sustainability and peace of harmony.

Far from sentimental, animism accepts nature is not all sweetness: existent for itself, *in itself*, nature is as brutal as it is beautiful. Within a metaphysics of minded integration, however, nature's tenability is based in an ontology whereby every moment is essential to the whole. The attendant obligation that is accepted by the practising animist is then to ensure that, not only does he perceive and respond to the wakefulness of his environment, but that he contributes to its harmony, helping to create a sustainable and peaceful world.

I would end with another's words. In *The Tables Turned*, Wordsworth expresses so much of what in these pages I have sought to describe. The poem reminds us of what is truly meaningful, questioning the deconstructive hunger of consciousness, and encouraging the simplicity of sweet prehension. And in conclusion, its final lines are a perfect weave of both the ethics and the ontology of what I understand to be animism.

Up! up! my Friend, and quit your books;
Or surely you'll grow double:
Up! up! my Friend, and clear your looks;
Why all this toil and trouble?

The sun above the mountain's head,
A freshening lustre mellow
Through all the long green fields has spread,
His first sweet evening yellow.

Books! 'tis a dull and endless strife:
Come, hear the woodland linnet,
How sweet his music! on my life,
There's more of wisdom in it.

And hark! how blithe the throstle sings!
He, too, is no mean preacher:
Come forth into the light of things,
Let Nature be your teacher.

She has a world of ready wealth,
Our minds and hearts to bless–
Spontaneous wisdom breathed by health,
Truth breathed by cheerfulness.

One impulse from a vernal wood
May teach you more of man,
Of moral evil and of good,
Than all the sages can.

Sweet is the lore which Nature brings;
Our meddling intellect
Mis-shapes the beauteous forms of things:–
We murder to dissect.

Enough of Science and of Art;
Close up those barren leaves;
Come forth, and bring with you a heart
That watches and receives.

Bibliography

Where I have given no recent publisher and publication date for a text over a century old, it is either because I have a number of copies, or access the original text on the internet, or have used editions in public and private libraries and not noted the publisher or date of the reprint. They are texts that can be widely found, texts well worth reading in any number of versions. Where there are more than one text by an author, I have listed the texts in order of publication.

Abram, David : *Becoming Animal* (Pantheon Books, 2010)

Abram, David : *The Spell of the Sensuous, Perception and Language in a More-than-Human World* (Vintage, 2007)

Abraham, Ralph, McKenna, Terence and Sheldrake, Rupert : *Trialogues at the Edge of the West: Chaos, Creativity and the Resacralization of the World* (Bear & Company, 1992)

Ackroyd, Peter : *Albion - The Origins of the English Imagination* (Chatto & Windus, 2002)

Agar, Wilfred Eade : *A Contribution to the Theory of the Living Organism* (Melbourne University Press, 1951; first published 1943)

Apuleius : *The Golden Ass* (translation by Robert Graves, Penguin Classics, 1950; written in second century CE)

Aquinas, Thomas : *Summa Contra Gentiles* (http://www2.nd.edu/Departments/Maritain/etext/gc.htm; written 1258 – 1264)

Aristotle : *De Anima*

Aristotle : *Metaphysics*
Aristotle : *Nichomanchean Ethics*
Aristotle : *History of Animals*
(http://classics.mit.edu/Browse/browse-Aristotle.html; written c. 350 BCE)

Augustine of Hippo : *Confessions* (Baker Book House, 2005; written 397 – 398 CE)

Bergson, Henri : *Key Writings* (Continuum, 2002) including *Time and Free Will, An Essay on the Immediate Data of Consciousness* (1889), *Matter and Memory* (1896), *Creative Evolution* (1907), *Duration and Simultaneity* (1922)

Berkeley, George : *Principles of Human Knowledge* (1710) and *Three Dialogues between Hylas and Philonous* (1713) (Penguin Classics, 2005)

Blackmore, Susan : *Consciousness: A Very Short Introduction* (Oxford University Press, 2005)
Blackmore, Susan : *Conversations on Consciousness* (Oxford University Press, 2006)

Boswell, James : *The Life of Samuel Johnson* (Penguin Classics, 2008; first published 1791)

Bowie, Andrew : *Schelling and Modern European Philosophy, An Introduction* (Routledge, 1993)

Bruno, Giordano : *Cause, Principle and Unity* (http://www.esotericarchives.com/bruno/home.htm; first published 1584)

Chalmers, David : *The Conscious Mind, In Search of a Fundamental Theory* (Oxford University Press, 1996)

Chalmers, David : *Philosophy of Mind: Classical and Contemporary Readings* (Oxford University Press, 2002) includes his paper *Consciousness and its Place in Nature*

de Chardin, Pierre Teilhard : *The Phenomenon of Man* with an introduction by Julian Huxley (Harper Perennial, 2008; first published 1958)

Clarke, Desmond : *Descartes's Theory of Mind* (Oxford University Press, 2005)

Clarke, Desmond : *Descartes A Biography* (Cambridge University Press, 2006)

Clarke, DS : *Panpsychism, Past and Recent Selected Readings* (State University of New York Press, 2004)

Clarke, JJ : *Nature in Question* (Earthscan Publications, 2004)

Claxton, Guy : *The Wayward Mind, An Intimate History of the Unconscious* (Little Brown, 2005)

Clifford, William Kingdon : *Lectures and Essays by the Late William Kingdon Clifford* (BiblioBazaar, 2010; first published 1879)

Conway, Viscount Anne : *The Principles of the Most Ancient and Modern Philosophy* (http://www.earlymoderntexts.com/f_conway.html; first published 1690)

Copernicus, Nicolaus : *On the Revolutions of the Celestial Spheres* (http://ads.harvard.edu/books/1543droc.book; first published 1543)

Dennett, Daniel : *Breaking the Spell, Religion as a Natural Phenomenon* (Penguin, 2006)

Dennett, Daniel : *Consciousness Explained* (Back Bay Books, 1992)
Dennett, Daniel : *Sweet Dreams: Philosophical Obstacles to a Science of Consciousness* (MIT, 2005)

Descartes, René : *Discourse on Method* (1637)
Descartes, René : *Meditations on First Philosophy* (1641)
Descartes, René : *The Passions of the Soul* (1649)
(http://www.earlymoderntexts .com/f_descarte.html)

Diderot, Denis : *On the Interpretation of Nature* (first published 1751) and *Conversations between D'Alembert and Diderot* and *D'Alembert's Dream* (written 1769), both in *Diderot, Interpreter of Nature*, translated by Jean Stewart and Jonathon Kemp (NY International, 1938)

Easlea, Brian : *Witch Hunting, Magic and the New Philosophy, An Introduction to Debates of the Scientific Revolution 1450 – 1750* (Harvester Press, 1981)

Eddington, Arthur : *Time, Space and Gravitation, An Outline of the General Relativity Theory* (Cambridge University Press, 1987; first published 1920)
Eddington, Arthur : *The Nature of the Physical World* (Cambridge University Press, 1929)

Fechner, Gustav : *Über Die Seelefrage* (first published 1861)
Fechner, Gustav : *Nanna, The Soul Life of Plants* (first published 1848)

Gatti, Hilary : *Essays on Giordano Bruno* (Princeton, 2010)

Gilbert, William : *De Magnete* (Dover, 1958; first published 1600)

Goswami, Amit : *Physics of the Soul: The Quantum Book of Living,*

Dying, Reincarnation and Immortality (Hampton Roads Publishing, 2001)

Griffin, David Ray : *Unsnarling the World Knot, Consciousness, Freedom, and the Mind-Body Problem* (Wipf & Stock, 2008)

Guerlac, Suzanne : *Thinking in Time: An Introduction to Henri Bergson* (Cornell University Press, 2006)

Haeckel, Ernst : *Monism as Connecting Religion and Science, The Confession of Faith of a Man of Science* (translated by J Gilchrist, BiblioBazaar, 2009; first published1895)

Harrison, Robert Pogue : *The Dominion of the Dead* (University of Chicago Press, 2005)

Harvey, Graham : *Animism, Respecting the Living World* (C Hurst & Co, 2005)

Hartshorne, Charles : *Physics and Psychics, the Place of the Mind in Nature* in Cobb, John B and Griffin, David Ray Griffin (eds.) : *Mind in Nature* (University Press of America, 1977)

Havens, Ronald : *The Wisdom of Milton H Erickson* (Crown House, 2005)

Hegel, Georg : *Phenomenology of Spirit* (Oxford University Press, 1979; first published 1807)

Heisenberg, Werner : *Physics and Philosophy, The Revolution in Modern Science* (Harper Perennial Modern Classics, 2007; first published 1958)

Hobbes, Thomas : *Leviathan* (http://www.earlymoderntexts

.com/f_hobbes.html; first published 1651)

Homer : *The Illiad* (http://classics.mit.edu/Homer/iliad.html; originating in the ninth century BCE)
Homer : *The Odyssey* (http://classics.mit.edu/Homer/odyssey .html; originating in the ninth century BCE)

Hume, David : *A Treatise of Human Nature, Being an Attempt to Introduce the Experimental Method of Reasoning into Moral Subjects* (http://www.earlymoderntexts.com/f_hume.html; first published 1739 - 40)
Hume, David : *An Enquiry Concerning Human Understanding* (Oxford University Press, 1927; first published 1748)

Humphrey, Nicholas : *Seeing Red, A Study in Consciousness* (Harvard University Press, 2008)
Humphrey, Nicholas : *Soul Dust, The Magic of Consciousness* (Quercus, 2011)

James, William : *Principles of Psychology* (1890)
James, William : *The Varieties of Religious Experience* (1902)
James, William : *A Pluralistic Universe* (1909)
(http://ebooks.adelaide.edu.au/j/james/ william/)

Jaskolla, Ludwig and Buck, Alexander : *Does panexperientialistic holism solve the combination problem?* (The Journal for Consciousness Studies, 2012)

Johnson, Samuel : *Dictionary* (*Selections* edited by Jack Lynch, Levenger Press, 2004; first published 1755)

Kant, Immanuel : *Critique of Pure Reason* (Bell & Sons, 1913; first published 1781, second edition 1787)
Kant, Immanuel : *Anthropology from a Pragmatic Point of View*

(Cambridge University Press, 2006; first published 1798)

Lao Tzu : *Tao Te Ching* (http://www.chinapage.com/gnl.html; originating in the sixth century BCE)

Leibniz, Gottfried : *Monadology* (http://www.earlymoderntexts .com/f_leibniz.html; first published 1714)

Locke, John : *An Essay Concerning Human Understanding* (http://www.earlymoderntexts.com/f_locke.html: first published 1689)

Locke, John : *Some Thoughts Concerning Education* (http:// www.bartleby.com/37/1/; first published 1693)

Lucretius : *On the Nature of Things* (http://classics.mit.edu/ Carus/nature_things.html; written c. 58 BCE)

Mach, Ernst : *The Analysis of Sensations and the Relation of Physical to the Psychical* (Dover, 1959, first published 1886)

Magee, Bryan : *The Philosophy of Schopenhauer* (Oxford University Press, 1997)

Magee, Bryan : *Confessions of a Philosopher, A Journey Through Western Philosophy* (Random House, 1998)

Marshall, Peter : *Demanding the Impossible* (Harper Perennial, 2007)

Merchant, Carolyn : *The Vitalism of Anne Conway, Its impact on Leibniz's Concept of the Monad* (http://philpapers.org /rec/MERTVO, 1979)

Milton, John : *Paradise Lost* (http://www.paradiselost.org; first published 1667) de Montaigne, Michel : *Essays* and *Apology for Raymond Sebond* (1580) from *Complete Works* (Everyman, 2003)

Naess, Arne : *Life's Philosophy, Reason and Feeling in a Deeper World* (University of Georgia Press, 2002; first published 1998)

Nagel, Thomas : *The View From Nowhere* (Oxford University Press, 1989)
Nagel, Thomas : *Mortal Questions* (Cambridge University Press, 1979)

Narby, Jeremy : *Intelligence in Nature* (Tarcher, 2006)

Nørretranders, Tor : *The User Illusion, Cutting Consciousness Down to Size* (Penguin, 1998)

Ouspensky, PD : *Tertium Organum* (http://www.sacred-texts. com/eso/to/index.htm; first published 1922)

Penrose, Roger : *The Emperor's New Mind, Concerning Computers, Minds and the Laws of Physics* (Oxford University Press, 1989)

Plato : *Phaedo*
Plato : *Phaedrus*
Plato : *Republic*
Plato : *Timaeus*
(http://plato-dialogues.org/links.htm, written in the fourth century BCE)

Porter, Roy : *Flesh in the Age of Reason* (Penguin, 2005)

Quintilian : *Institutio Oratoria* (Loeb Classical Library, 1920; first published 95 CE)

Rey, Georges : *Contemporary Philosophy of Mind: a Contentiously Classical Approach* (1997)

Russell, Bertrand : *A History of Western Philosophy* (Simon and Schuster, 1945)
Russell, Bertrand : *The Analysis of Mind* (George Allen & Unwin, 1921)
Russell, Bertrand : *The Analysis of Matter* (Kegan Paul, Trench, Trubner, 1927)
Russell, Bertrand : *An Outline of Philosophy* (George Allen & Unwin, 1927)
Russell, Bertrand : *Portraits from Memory and Other Essays* (George Allen & Unwin, 1956)

Sayre, Kenneth : *Cybernetics and the Philosophy of Mind* (Routledge & Kegan Paul & Henley, 1976)

Schelling, Friedrich : *Ideas for a Philosophy of Nature* (Cambridge University Press, 1988; first published 1797)

Schopenhauer, Arthur : *The World as Will and Representation* (Dover, 1966, first published 1818, expanded edition 1844)
Schopenhauer, Arthur : *Parerga and Paralipomena, Short Philosophical Essays* (Clarendon Press, 1974, first published 1851)

Searle, John : *Minds, Brains and Science* (The Reith Lectures, 1984)

Shakespeare, William : *A Midsummer Night's Dream* (1590)
Shakespeare, William : *As You Like It* (1599)
Shakespeare, William : *The Tempest* (1610)
(http://shakespeare.mit.edu/)

Skrbina, David : *Panpsychism in the West* (MIT, 2005)

Smuts, Jan : *Holism and Evolution, The Original Source of the Holistic Approach to Life* (Sierra Sunrise, 1999; first published 1926)

Sorabji, Richard : *Self: Ancient and Modern Insights about Individuality, Life and Death* (University of Chicago Press, 2008)

Spinoza, Baruch : *Ethics* (Penguin Classics, 2005; first published 1677)

Strawson, Galen : *Consciousness and Its Place in Nature: Does Physicalism Entail Panpsychism?* (Imprint Academic, 2006)
Strawson, Galen : *Mental Reality, Representation and Mind* (MIT, 1995)
Strawson, Galen : *Real Materialism and Other Essays* (Oxford University Press, 2008)

Velmans, Max : *Understanding Consciousness* (Routledge, 2000)

White, Lynn Townsend Jr : *The Historical Roots of Our Ecologic Crisis* (*Science*, Vol 155, 1967)

Whitehead, Alfred North : *Science in the Modern World* (Simon and Schuster, 1997; first published 1925)
Whitehead, Alfred North : *Process and Reality* (Free Press, 1978; the Gifford Lectures 1927 – 1928)
Whitehead, Alfred North : *Adventures of Ideas* (Free Press, 1961; first published 1933)

Wittgenstein, Ludwig : *Philosophical Investigations* (Wiley-Blackwell, 2001; first published 1953)

Wordsworth, William : *The Tables Turned* from *Lyrical Ballads* (http://www.poetryfoundation.org/poem/174826; first published 1798)

Etymological sources:

The Oxford English Dictionary (Oxford University Press, Fifth Edition 2002)

The Online Etymological Dictionary (http://www.etymonline .com)

Index

MOON

BOOKS

Moon Books invites you to begin or deepen your encounter with Paganism, in all its rich, creative, flourishing forms.